# Conversations with Edwidge Danticat

Literary Conversations Series
*Monika Gehlawat*
*General Editor*

# Conversations with Edwidge Danticat

Edited by Maxine Lavon Montgomery

University Press of Mississippi / *Jackson*

www.upress.state.ms.us

The University Press of Mississippi is a member of
the Association of American University Presses.

First printing 2017

∞

Library of Congress Cataloging-in-Publication Data

Names: Danticat, Edwidge, 1969– author. | Montgomery, Maxine Lavon, 1959–
   editor.
Title: Conversations with Edwidge Danticat / edited by Maxine Lavon
   Montgomery.
Description: Jackson : University Press of Mississippi, 2017. | Series:
   Literary conversations series | Includes bibliographical references and
   index. |
Identifiers: LCCN 2017006309 (print) | LCCN 2017025177 (ebook) | ISBN
   9781496812568 (epub single) | ISBN 9781496812575 (epub institutional) |
   ISBN 9781496812582 ( pdf single) | ISBN 9781496812599 (pdf institutional)
   | ISBN 9781496812551 (hardback)
Subjects: LCSH: Danticat, Edwidge, 1969-—Interviews. | Authors,
   American—20th century—Interviews. | Haitian American
   authors—Interviews. | BISAC: BIOGRAPHY & AUTOBIOGRAPHY / Literary. |
   LITERARY CRITICISM / Caribbean & Latin American. | LITERARY CRITICISM /
   American / African American. | SOCIAL SCIENCE / Black Studies (Global).
Classification: LCC PS3554.A5815 (ebook) | LCC PS3554.A5815 Z46 2017 (print)
   | DDC 813/.54 [B] —dc23
LC record available at https://lccn.loc.gov/2017006309

British Library Cataloging-in-Publication Data available

# Works by Edwidge Danticat

## Novels

"My Turn in the Fire: An Abridged Novel." MFA thesis, Brown University, 1993.
*Breath, Eyes, Memory*. New York: Soho Press, 1994; New York: Vintage
    Books, 1995; New York: Soho Press, 2015.
*The Farming of Bones*. New York: Soho Press, 1998; Penguin, 1999.
*The Dew Breaker*. New York: Knopf, 2004.
*Claire of the Sea Light*. New York: Knopf, 2013.

## Short Story Collection

*Krik? Krak!* New York: Soho Press, 1995; New York: Vintage Books, 1996.

## Memoir

*Brother, I'm Dying*. New York: Knopf, 2007.

## Young Adult Literature

*Behind the Mountains: The Diary of Celiane Espérance*. New York: Orchard Books, 2002.
*Anacaona, Golden Flower*. New York: Scholastic, 2005.
*Célimène, Fairytale for the Daughter of Immigrants*. Trans. Stanley Péan. Montréal: Mémoire
    d'encrier, 2009.
*Eight Days*. London: Orchard, 2010.
*The Last Mapou*. Brooklyn: One Moore Book, 2015.
*Mama's Nightingale: A Story of Immigration and Separation*. New York: Dial Books, 2015.
*Untwine*. New York: Scholastic, 2015.

## Translation

*In the Flicker of an Eyelid*. Trans., *L'espace d'un cillement* by Jacques Stéphen Alexis. Trans.
    with Carrol F. Coates. Charlottesville: University of Virginia Press, 2002.

## Nonfiction

*Women: A Celebration of Strength*. Ed. with Louise A. Gikow, Kathy Rodgers, Lynn Hecht
    Scghafran, and Anna Quindlen. New York: Legal Momentum, 2007.
*Create Dangerously: The Immigrant Artist at Work*. Princeton: Princeton University Press, 2010.

# Contents

# Introduction

Edwidge Danticat appeared on the literary scene when she was only twenty-five years old with *Breath, Eyes, Memory* (1994), a semi-autobiographical novel that has its genesis in a newspaper article about a young Haitian girl who leaves the Caribbean and comes to America in order to be reunited with her parents. That article became the essence of a short story that Danticat later expanded into novelistic form, a genre that has served the author well during her decades-long writing career. Four years after the publication of her debut work of fiction, the novel's inclusion as an Oprah Winfrey Book-of-the-Month Club selection not only guaranteed the commercial success of that work, it also helped to lay the groundwork for what would become a stellar literary vocation.

At the outset of that career, it was evident that Danticat was indeed poised on the brink of a bright, promising future—one that would catapult her into the global spotlight as a clarion voice for the twentieth- and twenty-first-century creative artist and intellectual. Danticat remarks enthusiastically in an interview regarding Winfrey's selection of the author's first novel that "everything changed."[1] Indeed, Danticat's "writerly" world shifted in significant ways following the publication of her first novel and the work's widespread critical acclaim. She began to garner the attention of a broad reader audience, and since that time, her readership has expanded significantly to include an international gathering of scholars, teachers, critics, and interested citizens who look to her for insight into the complex Haitian American experience in all of its beauty as well as its unrelenting pain. Danticat has received numerous awards for her work, including the designation as "One of the Twenty Best Writers under Forty" from *Granta* (1996), the National Book Critics Circle Award for *Brother, I'm Dying* (1997), the American Book Award from the Before Columbus Foundation for *The Farming of Bones* (1999), and, of course, the prestigious MacArthur Fellowship (2009), which allowed her freedom to travel and continuing writing about a range of issues pertaining to Haiti, Afro-Caribbean culture, and the expatriate life. Although she grew up in Port-au-Prince speaking

Haitian Creole, she chooses to write in English, a language that accentuates the trilingual nature of her compound identity as the daughter of Haitian migrants to the United States. Her novels and short stories have been translated widely into Japanese, Korean, German, Italian, Spanish, Swedish, as well as French.

The interviews assembled in this collection coincide with Danticat's evolving artistic vision, steady book production, and expanding role as fiction writer, essayist, memoirist, documentarian, young adult book author, editor, song writer, cultural critic, and political commentator over the course of a long and auspicious career that shows no sign of decline. With each endeavor, she is mindful of the need to "tell a nuanced story, her version of the truth."[2] The reality that she is most interested in telling is interwoven with the immigrant story, a life she knows intimately as a result of her move to America at the age of twelve. Danticat's journey from her Caribbean homeland to Brooklyn, New York is, in many respects, a paradigmatic moment rife with symbolic significance in terms of its implications for understanding the fluid identity on the part of the border subject. Few authors have recaptured the challenges and triumphs, the difficulties and successes associated with living with "one's feet in both worlds" as brilliantly as Danticat.[3] One thinks of Jhumpa Lahiri, Azar Nafisi, Vladimir Nabokov, Christina Garcia, Chinua Achebe, Gabriel García Márquez, Jamaica Kincaid, Paule Marshall, and the Dominican-born Junot Díaz. What sets Danticat apart from this distinguished assembly of writers is her penetrating acquaintance with the Haitian-immigrant record and the uneasy truce between that life and the history, politics, and culture of the West. She lends her uniquely individual voice to the telling and retelling of a recognizable story at the center of diasporic culture and literature, a narrative involving the migrant's often thorny encounter with issues of longing and belonging, migration and displacement, diasporic and national self-identification, exile and the perpetual quest for home.

The many interviews that Danticat has granted attest to not only her productivity, but also her accessibility to scholars, teachers, creative writers, and journalists eager for knowledge about her life, art, and political vision. Whether those interviews assume the form of a structured face-to-face exchange, an email interview, or a vigorous informal conversation between two creative writers, they underscore her responsibility as both literary craftsperson and political commentator on a range of issues confronting the twentieth- and twenty-first-century world. Included in this volume are interviews covering the publication of her debut work of fiction, to a personal interview that I conducted with the author in 2016. In my conversation with Danticat, which appears for the first time as part of this collection, I was especially interested in accessing little-known details regarding her work, recent political events, as well as her next project. Because the interviewers frequently pose the same questions, some level of repetition and overlap inevitably ensues. Throughout the course of the interviews assembled in this volume, however, Danticat expands upon her answers rather than contradicting earlier remarks. But the development of the author's views manifests itself in her willingness to take up a broader range of issues and amplify previous comments in ways that reflect her careful rethinking of predominant concerns, especially her beliefs regarding the younger generation's role in perpetuating cultural traditions of the past and ushering in a better future. Therefore, the evolution from *Breath, Eyes, Memory* to *Untwine* is one of maturation and clarification rather than revolution.

At times humorous and lighthearted, always engaging and profoundly astute, especially when discussing the devastating effects of the 2010 Haitian earthquake, Danticat displays an unabashed honesty to self that allows an extraordinary glimpse into the public and private life of a somewhat reserved, precocious daughter of Haitian immigrants who once aspired to be a nurse, but later turned to creative writing as a profession. Consistently, however, she is ever mindful of her privileged position as a celebrated author, a self-proclaimed "accident of literacy," as she puts it when discussing the place of education among the Haitian population.[4] She is also someone who is frequently sought after as a spokesperson for Haiti, although she is as quick to dismiss the notion that she speaks for *all* Haitian Americans as she is in denouncing the suggestion that Haitians are passive victims of the many social, economic, political, and natural calamities that have befallen that country. The talented author sees Haitians not as fatalities, but tough survivors, proud bearers of a rich history and culture that constitute a vital aspect of Caribbean life; and she envisions herself as a storyteller or cultural historian, a twenty-first-century refiguration of the ancient African griot or truth-teller whose mission involves chronicling a multi-layered past, even if that role involves personal risk, the threat of censure, or, possibly, death. She is, in every sense, an immigrant artist whose avowed purpose, as she aptly puts it, involves the need to "[create] as a revolt against silence, creating when both the creation and the reception, the writing and the reading, are dangerous undertakings, disobedience to a directive."[5] In fulfilling that purpose, Danticat has therefore been about the business of challenging colonial inscriptions of Afro-Caribbean life and culture in ways that undermine established notions concerning the Haitian immigrant experience. Her works are, in many respects, potent acts of artistic insurgency directed toward a history that is bent on imposing tragic contours on the lives of those in the Afro-Caribbean world.

## II.

It is interesting to note the ways in which history in its myriad figurations—diasporic, national, regional, familial, and personal—serves as a leitmotif linking the interviews collected here in a seamless fashion. Danticat's personal story involving migration, familial separation, and cultural hybridity is inextricably interwoven with the account of the Haitian immigrant population and that group's struggle to maintain an emotional connection with a Caribbean home in the face of displacement and the urge toward assimilation. Frequently, the author mentions the important role that storytelling plays in the development of her artistic consciousness. For her, as well as countless others across a transatlantic Diaspora, storytelling and cultural memory are not just imaginative devices used in shaping fictional works; they assume the role of politically charged gestures of resistance that negate the psychologically fragmenting effects of colonization. Danticat tends to mention her authorial reliance upon symbolic acts of religion, speech, and music as central aspects of her fiction. The re-inscription of the vernacular forms that have played a vital part in the evolution of Afro-Caribbean life becomes a way to maintain cultural continuity with the past while reshaping familiar legends and lore in order to suit the demands of an ever-changing contemporary, increasingly global geopolitical landscape. In other words, storytelling allows her an opportunity to acknowledge the persistence of a diasporic past, even in a New World setting, while laying the foundation for a radically transformed future—one existing outside the established boundaries of nation-state as well as conventional constructions of time, space, and identity.

Clearly, then, Danticat embodies the anxieties of belonging characterizing the existence of the immigrant who must navigate the condition that Edward Said famously describes as being at once both at home and eternally in exile.[6] Much like Sophie Cacou in *Breath, Eyes, Memory*, or Amabelle Desir in *The Farming of Bones*, the author possesses the fluid self-identity of the border subject who is poised between cultures, nations, and worlds. Along these lines, the mother-daughter relationship, which figures prominently in Danticat's writing as well as in her interviews, serves as a symbolic representation of the immigrant's conflicted relationship with genealogical origins, whether that past is diasporic in nature, linked with romanticized notions of Africa, or nationalist, in terms of a connection with Haiti. Similar to other Afro-Caribbean women writers, such as Paule Marshall, Jamaica Kincaid, Merle Hodge, and Michelle Cliff, Danticat ties gender with the gendered motif of Africa as the Mother Country in ways that direct attention to the difficulties associated with the migrant's literal or figurative recovery of a disjointed cultural heritage. Danticat's narrative representation of a gendered Haitian experience is thus resonant with Carol Boyce Davies's assertions regarding the ways in which the woman as Afro-Caribbean writer in the United States "doubly disrupts the seamless narrative of home and of nation."[7] For the gifted author, home is a fraught, contested site that reflects the socialized ambivalence on the part of the border subject attempting to reconcile his or her present locale with vestiges of an ancestral past that is lost to the postcolonial migratory subject, but is still very much a part of that individual's memorial structures.

The twenty-two interviews included in this volume therefore shed a much-needed light on Danticat's singular ability to offer an assessment of an assortment of timely issues from the position of what postcolonial and Diaspora studies scholars such as Homi Bhabha, Paul Gilroy, Gayatri Spivak, Gloria Anzaldua, and others theorize as the borderlands, an uncharted in-between space located outside fixed geographic, cultural, and ideological bounds. Prevalent throughout many of the pieces is Danticat's expressed determination to not only reinscribe the hybrid Haitian immigrant experience, but make that nuanced culture and its vibrant traditions accessible to a wide reader-audience. In accomplishing that lofty aim, she mentions her indebtedness to an assortment of precursor literary figures, including Jacques Romaine, Albert Camus, Jean Toomer, Alice Walker, and, of course, Nobel and Pulitzer Prize winner Toni Morrison, whose works reveal a conversational relationship with Danticat's writing. *Sula*, for instance, is the model for each novel Danticat has written, and the award-winning book *Create Dangerously: The Immigrant Artist at Work* evolves out of a lecture Danticat delivered as part of the Toni Morrison Lecture Series at Princeton University.

## III.

A survey of the many interviews that Danticat has granted over the course of her career—those collected in this volume as well as others—indicates the ways in which those pieces tend to coalesce around key events on a national or personal level. A number of interviews focus on moments such as the author's reflections upon winning the MacArthur Fellowship, the 2010 Haitian earthquake, the publication of *Create Dangerously*, and the appearance of *Claire of the Sea Light*, the first novel Danticat wrote after becoming a mother. It is evident as well that recurring themes in the interviews mirror predominant concerns in Danticat's fiction and nonfiction writing: the ambivalent mother-daughter dyad; the uses and limitations of folklore; gendered sexual trauma; border crossing and the immigrant experience; America's immigration policy; the role of the immigrant artist and intellectual; the place of the mass media; Haiti's checkered political history; ecological matters and the environment; and the importance of ancestry. Discernible throughout the interviews is a trajectory involving a move toward an optimistic assessment of the future and the role that the next generation can play in bringing about a more democratic, equitable, humane, and environmentally sound era free of conflict owing to race, class, and gender.

Aside from the inclusion of her debut work of fiction as part of Oprah's Book Club, if there is a singular event that has thrust Danticat onto an international stage, it is her trenchant commentary on the circumstances surrounding the death of her uncle and the role she subsequently assumes as an articulate critic of the many human rights abuses affecting Haitian immigrants. The 7.0 magnitude earthquake that struck Haiti in 2010 was a catastrophic event with far-reaching economic, social, political, and ecological consequences, and it, too, serves as a watershed moment in the author's life and career. Although the interviews with Kam Williams, Rose Marie Berger, Jennifer Ludden, and Paul Holdengräber take place during the year that the earthquake occurred, with each conversation, Danticat sheds a slightly different light on the calamity and the need for a rebuilding of the nation's infrastructure. Significantly, in the interview with Holdengräber, Danticat reflects on the impact that the earthquake had on her in terms of her writing and the creative process, a subject she returns to in the *Guernica* interview with Nathalie Handal, where Danticat takes up issues relevant to the place of art and the artist as a harbinger of change—core concerns in the powerful, award-winning book *Create Dangerously*.

By the time Danticat enters her forties she displays a more self-assured persona. No longer is she the shy, reticent, self-conscious young girl who once felt out of place in a Brooklyn junior high school. Perhaps the widespread validation from the literary establishment prompted her to see herself as a strong, confident creative artist whose opinions others were eager to hear. Maybe a succession of life-changing familial events, including the birth of her second daughter, served as a catalyst for the author's willingness to embrace the wisdom that comes from lived experience. At any rate, the passing of time bears witness to the author's expanded artistic and political vision. The range of topics taken up in later interviews therefore includes a renewed focus on the mother-daughter relationship—both in terms of the author's bond with her mother, Rose, and Danticat's role as mother to two daughters; progress toward the rebuilding of Haiti's infrastructure following the 2010 earthquake; environmental issues; and the responsibility on the part of youths in perpetuating a transgenerational legacy.

Danticat's 2013 conversation with Dwyer Murphy is one of many taking place upon the publication of *Claire of the Sea Light*, the first adult novel she wrote after the earthquake and after she became a mother. In that interview, she talks about her aversion to what she refers to as the microcategorization of women authors, and she comments on the treatment of female writers and writers of color. She discusses her novel at length, mentioning its biographical elements involving her relationship with an ambivalent home linked with her mother's birthplace along with issues of migration, separation, and loss. Danticat also points out the important sociopolitical function of radio as a medium for the telling of the stories on the part of the community, as well as the ecological and environmental matters that figure prominently in her fiction. In the interview with Kima Jones, Danticat offers a glimpse into the magic of the short story and its influence on the novelistic structure of *Claire* along with her indebtedness to authors such as Alice Walker, Jean Toomer, and Morrison.

The final interview, published for the first time in this volume, is one that I conducted in 2016 after having met the author at a university book reading. I sought to pursue a line of questioning that would move beyond topics covered in previous exchanges, including issues surrounding the inspiration behind her two most recent novels. In that interview, Danticat sheds important light on *Mama's Nightingale: A Story of Immigration and Separation* and *Untwine*, works of fiction that underscore her hopefulness, despite the passage of time and a succession of personal and international crises as she turns attention to the younger generation and that group's role in ushering in a more democratic society. Her comments in the closing interview also reveal her perspective on a host of issues pertaining to US immigration policy under the Obama administration and her predictions for the future in terms of US–Haitian relations.

These interviews are arranged chronologically according to the date the interview was conducted, not the date the piece was published. For those interviews published previously, both the date and place of publication are noted. Transcripts have been edited for readability, and typos in published pieces have been silently corrected. Otherwise, these interviews are reproduced in their entirety.

I would be remiss if I did not acknowledge those individuals who played an important part in bringing this project to fruition. First of all, I owe an immense debt of gratitude to Edwidge Danticat who consented enthusiastically to the publication of this work and granted permission for my personal interview. The many dialogues she has granted over the course of her career have been as informative as her literary works. My very capable research assistant, Jodi Price—one of my department's finest doctoral students and an accomplished young scholar—offered invaluable assistance with the completion of this volume. I am thankful to Jodi for her meticulous attention to detail in carrying out essential work toward the completion of this collection and her insights about the tradition of black women's fiction. Additionally, I wish to thank the graduate students at Florida State enrolled in my contemporary Black Women Writers course for sharing my enthusiasm for Danticat's writing. I am fortunate to have taught some wonderfully engaging students, and I learn from them just as they glean insights from me. Last but not least, I extend tremendous appreciation to my family for their love, encouragement, and unwavering support during the completion of this project: my husband, Nathaniel, and our daughter, Samantha Natalya. You are my inspiration.

**MLM**

## Notes

1. Dwyer Murphy, "The Art of Not Belonging," *Guernica Magazine* (September 2013).

2. Murphy, "The Art of Not Belonging."

3. Opal Adisa Palmer, "Up Close and Personal: Edwidge Danticat on Haitian Identity and the Writer's Life," *African-American Review* 43, no. 2 (Summer/Fall 2009): 348.

4. Kima Jones, *The Rumpus*, January 1, 2014.

5. Danticat, *Create Dangerously: The Immigrant Artist at Work* (New York: Random House, 2010), 11.

6. Edward Said, *Reflections on Exile* (Cambridge: Harvard, 2000).

7. Carol Boyce Davies, *Black Women, Writing and Identity: Migrations of the Subject* (London and New York: Routledge, 1994), 113.

# Chronology

1969    On January 19 Edwidge Danticat is born in Port-au-Prince, Haiti, to Andre Miracin Danticat (cab driver) and Rose Souvenance Danticat (textile worker).

1971    Danticat's father, Andre, migrates to Brooklyn, New York.

1973    Danticat's mother, Rose, migrates to Brooklyn, New York, leaving Danticat in the care of an aunt and uncle.

1981    Immigrates to Brooklyn in order to be reunited with her parents.

1983    Publishes "A Haitian-American Christmas: Cremace and Creole Theatre" in *New Youth Connections*.

1987    Publishes "A New World Full of Strangers" in *New Youth Connections*.

1990    Receives BA in French literature from Barnard College.

1991    Publishes "Dream of the Butterflies" and "Graduation" in *Caribbean Writer* 5.

1992    The play *The Creation of Adam* is produced in Providence, Rhode Island. Publishes "Lost Shadows and Stick Figures" in *Caribbean Writer* 6.

1993    Receives MFA from Brown University in creative writing; her creative thesis is titled "My Turn in the Fire: An Abridged Novel." The play *Dreams Like Me* is produced at Brown University's New Play Festival. Publishes "Between the Pool and the Gardenias" in *Caribbean Writer* 7.

1993–94 Becomes the production and research assistant at Clinica Estetico.

1994    *Breath, Eyes, Memory* is published; publishes "The Missing Peace" in *Caribbean Writer* 8; publishes "A Rain of Daffodils" in *Seventeen* 53.4.

1995    Wins Women of Achievement Award at Barnard College. Wins Pushcart short story prize for "Between the Pool and the Gardenias." Her short story collection, *Krik? Krak!*, is published and becomes a finalist for the National Book Award.

1996    Named one of the twenty "Best of American Novelists" by *Granta* for *Breath, Eyes, Memory*. Awarded Lila Wallace *Reader's Digest* Grant. Publishes "We Are Ugly, But We Are Here" in *The Caribbean Writer*. Publishes "The Revenant" in *Granta*.

1996–97 Teaches Creative Writing at New York University.

1997    The play *Children of the Sea* is produced at Roxbury Community College. Writes the foreword for *Starting with "I": Personal Essays by Teenagers*. Editor to *Island on Fire: Passionate Visions of Haiti from the Collection of Jonathan Demme*. Writes the foreword for *The Magic Orange Tree and Other Haitian Folktales*.

1998    *The Farming of Bones* is published. Wins the International Flaiano Prize for Literature and the Super Flaiano Prize for *The Farming of Bones*. *Breath, Eyes, Memory* is the main selection of Oprah Winfrey's Book-of-the-Month Club.

1999    Wins the American Book Award for *The Farming of Bones*. "The Book of the Dead" is published in the *New Yorker* June 14 issue. Coauthors the art book *Odilon Pierre, Artist of Haiti* with Jonathan Demme. Wins the Prix Carbet de la Caraïbe for *The Farming of Bones*.

2000    Teaches creative writing as visiting professor at the University of Miami, Florida. Editor of *The Beacon Best of 2000: Great Writing by Women and Men of All Colors and Cultures*. Short story "Water Child" is published in the *New Yorker* September 4 issue.

2001    Edits the anthology *The Butterfly's Way: Voices from the Haitian Dyaspora in the United States*. Writes the foreword to Beverly Bell's *Walking on Fire: Haitian Women's Stories of Survival and Resistance*. Short story "Seven" published in the *New Yorker* September 24 issue. Short story "Nineteen Thirty Seven" published in *The Oxford Book of Caribbean Short Stories*.

2002    Marries Faidherbe "Fedo" Boyer. Publishes *Behind the Mountains: The Diary of Celiane Espérance* as a part of the First Person Fiction Series. Publishes *After the Dance: A Walk through Carnival in Jacmel, Haiti*. Translator and author of the afterword with Carrol F. Coates for Jacques Stephen Alexis's *In the Flicker of an Eyelid*. Publishes "The Dew Breaker" in *Gumbo: A Celebration of African American Writers*. Awarded the Prix Gouverneur de la Rosée du Livre et de la Littérature, représentant de la diaspora, Ministère de la Culture, Haïti.

2003    Collaborates with Jonathan Demme for the documentary film project *The Agronomist*. Writes the introduction for the 2003 edition of Patricia Powell's *Me Dying Trial*.

2004    Publishes *The Dew Breaker*. Wins Fiction Awards from *Essence*, *Caribbean Writer*, and *Seventeen*. Wins Lannan Foundation Fellowship. Publishes the short story "The Indigo Girl" in *Sojourners*.

2005    Mira, daughter of Edwidge and Fedo, is born. Wins Anisfield Book Award and finalist for the PEN/Faulkner Award for *The Dew Breaker*. Publishes *Anacaona: Golden Flower, Haiti, 1490* as part of the Royal Diaries Series. Writes the introduction for Paulette Poujol Oriol's *Vale of Tears: A Novel from Haiti*. Writes the foreword to *We Are All Suspects Now: Untold Stories from Immigrant Communities after 9/11*. Short story "Reading Lessons" featured in the *New Yorker* January 10 issue. Publishes "Freda" in *Brown Sugar 4: Secret Desires: A Collection of Erotic Black Fiction*.

2006    Writes the introduction for Alejo Carpentier's novel *The Kingdom of This World*. Pens features in the documentary *Writing and the Immigrant Experience*. Writes the foreword to the reprint of Paule Marshall's *Brown Girl, Brownstones*. Writes the foreword to the collection *Homelands: Women's Journeys across Race, Place, and Time*.

2007    Publishes family memoir *Brother, I'm Dying*. Winner of National Book Critics Circle Award. Contributor to women's history collection *Women: A Celebration of Strength*. Featured in cover story for *Poets and Writers Magazine*. Short story "Celia" featured in *A Memory, a Monologue, a Rant, and a Prayer: Writings to Stop Violence against Women and Girls*.

2008    Wins the Dayton Literary Peace Prize for *Brother, I'm Dying*. Writes the preface for René Philoctète's novel *Massacre River*. Writes the introduction to Ann Petry's *Miss Muriel and Other Stories*. Publishes "Ghosts" in the *New Yorker* November 17 issue.

2009    Leila, second daughter of Edwidge and Fedo, is born. Wins MacArthur Fellows Program Genius Grant. Narrates the film *Poto Mitan: Haitian Women, Pillars of the Global Economy*. Awarded the Best of Brooklyn Award at the Brooklyn Book Festival.

2010    Publishes children's book *Eight Days: A Story of Haiti*. Edits anthology *Haiti Noir*. Publishes the short story "Claire of the Sea Light" in *Haiti Noir*. Publishes the essay collection *Create*

*Dangerously: The Immigrant Artist at Work*. Selected as the *New York Times Book Review* Editors' Choice for 2010, *Mosaic Magazine*'s Best Books for 2010, and the *Miami Herald, Between the Covers* blog's Best Books for 2010; finalist for the 2010 Book of the Year Award in Biography and Autobiography. Writes the introduction for Marie Vieux-Chauvet's novel *Love, Anger, Madness: A Haitian Triptych*. Writes the foreword to Yanick Lahens's *Aunt Résia and the Spirits and Other Stories*. Contributor to the anthology *Haiti: A Slave Revolution 200 Years after 1804*. Contributes poems to Bruce Weber's exhibition *Haiti / Little Haiti* at the Museum of Contemporary Art, North Miami. Contributing editor to *The Caribbean Writer, Volume 24*.

2011     Essay contributor for *Tent Life: Haiti* by Wyatt Gallery. Edits *The Best American Essays, 2011*. Honored with the 2011 Langston Hughes Medal, City College of New York. Winner of the 2011 Bocas Lit Fest OCM Bocas Prize for Caribbean Literature in Nonfiction. Publishes the short story "Hot Air Balloons" in *The F Word*.

2012     Awarded honorary degree by Smith College. Publishes short story, "In the Old Days," in *Callaloo*. Contributes to the anthology *So Spoke the Earth: The Haiti I Knew, the Haiti I Know, the Haiti I Want to Know*.

2013     Publishes children's book, *The Last Mapou*. Writer and contributor for the film *Girl Rising*. Awarded Yale University honorary degree. Wins Association of Caribbean Writers Grand Prize for Literature for *Create Dangerously*. Publishes *Claire of the Sea Light*. Selected for the *Washington Post*'s notable fiction. Writes the introduction for Beverly Bell's *Fault Lines: Views across Haiti's Divide*. Writes the foreword for Évelyne Trouillot's *The Infamous Rosalie*.

2014     Edits anthology *Haiti Noir 2: The Classics*. *Claire of the Sea Light* is short-listed for the Andrew Carnegie Medals for Excellence in Fiction. Publishes "Quality Control" in the *Washington Post*. Writes the introduction for *Haiti Uncovered: A Regional Adventure into the Art of Haitian Cuisine*. Writes the foreword to Louis-Philippe Dalembert's *The Other Side of the Sea*. Contributor to *Caribbean-ness as Global Phenomenon*.

2015     Publishes children's book *Mama's Nightingale: A Story of Immigration and Separation*. Publishes young adult novel *Untwine*. Publishes twentieth-anniversary edition of *Breath, Eyes, Memory* with a new author introduction, essays, interviews, and discussion questions. Writes the foreword to the collection *Poetry of Haitian Independence*. Contributor to *The Good Book: Writers Reflect on Favorite Bible Passages*.

2016    Writes the introduction for the fiftieth anniversary of Jean Rhys's *Wide Sargasso Sea*. Writes the introduction to James Baldwin's *Go Tell It on the Mountain*.

# Conversations with Edwidge Danticat

# Edwidge Danticat

## Alexander Laurence / 2000

From alcoholreviews.com, November 2000. Reprinted with permission by
Alexander Laurence.

**Alexander Laurence:** Maybe we should talk about Haiti. Are you still in contact with people there?

**Edwidge Danticat:** I still have a lot of family there. I still keep in touch with friends and family there. I keep in contact with Haiti. Last December there was an election. At the end of February there was an inauguration of a new president, René Préval. It was the first time in Haitian history that a president had been elected democratically, where one president turned power over to another. It was a big deal. So the new president is trying to move things forward. René Préval's biggest obstacle is that the country is bankrupt because of all the stuff that happened before, since 1986. Our problem is that we are very dependent on outside aid. The monetary fund wants the president to privatize.

**AL:** The relationship between Haiti and the United States has been good?

**Edwidge:** It's been okay. But there are always those moments when it turns a little bit. The last thing the Clinton administration did was establish relations with Cuba. That didn't go over so well with Haiti.

**AL:** What sort of politics are there in Haiti?

**Edwidge:** They have had elections since the dictatorship ended in 1986. The military has stepped in a few times. My uncle, who lives there, is a minister.

**AL:** How did you get involved in writing?

**Edwidge:** I think it started from reading so much. My uncle worked in a school and he gave me books. I started reading when I was very young.

From reading I developed a love for writing. It wasn't because there was a writer in my family.

**AL:** Does your family think that it's odd that you wanted to be a writer?
**Edwidge:** There's so much involved with immigration. So much is sacrificed in my parents coming here. They leave their lives behind. They expect you to do something stable and grounded. My parents wanted me to be a doctor. They got over it. But I was also the oldest. I was supposed to set a path for the others. I have three younger brothers. My brother Andre is a teacher. Another one is a musician. None of them want to be writers.

**AL:** Wouldn't you like to write things in French or Creole?
**Edwidge:** I don't think it's odd. I came here when I was twelve. I adapted. I spoke Creole at home and French at school. I liked to write in English. When I first started writing, I wasn't thinking about publishing it. I was working and writing. It just happened. It wasn't very calculated. Writing in any language is difficult. Only about 20 percent of people in Haiti speak French every day of their life. I've written some stuff in Creole for the radio because radio is a strong medium in Haiti. I go back there whenever I can.

**AL:** Is there a publishing or writing scene in Haiti?
**Edwidge:** There's a lot of writers. The obstacle there is that you have to pay for it yourself. So if you are poor you can't really get published. There are musicians and performers.

**AL:** The Haitian immigration has been going on for how long?
**Edwidge:** There were a lot first in Savannah, Georgia. Then in the 1920s and 1930s, there were a lot of immigrants concentrated in Harlem. Not just from Haiti but all over the Caribbean. Then the biggest immigration from Haiti was in the 1960s when Papa Doc was in power. He drove a bunch of people out when he was dictator. Especially people who were professional. Some went to Africa, some came to France, but most came to the United States.

**AL:** Did the Castro revolution in 1957 affect anything there?
**Edwidge:** Papa Doc was already in power at that time. When Castro came in, it gave Papa Doc a scare. That might have given people an idea for revolution. Instead people started leaving in droves up until the 1980s. Poorer people left in the 1970s, when my parents left, then you had boat people in

the 1980s. Then you had the military, and economical and political pressures. My dad left in 1971 and my mother in 1975.

**AL:** How did they leave?
**Edwidge:** My father came out the normal way with a visa and stuff. He sent for my mother. My brother and I couldn't come until eight years later. I was talking to my brother about this last night. He was remembering things. I was poor but I didn't remember being poor. I just remember kid stuff and going to the countryside in the summer when it was really beautiful. We used to have kite wars. When it rained you would go outside.

**AL:** When did you start writing the books?
**Edwidge:** I came here in 1981. I went to high school in Crown Heights. I worked for a newspaper that was sent out to New York City public high schools. I wrote an essay about my experiences coming here. After that I started writing stories. I was writing all the time since I was sixteen. When I went to college I started taking some writing classes. I started showing it to people at Barnard. I had about seventy pages of it then. I put it away for a year. Then I finished it at graduate school.

**AL:** Were there any writers that you were influenced by?
**Edwidge:** You always look up to writers but you don't think that you can do the same thing. Writers are always like tired old baggage. I remember reading Jacques Roumain early on. He was the first person to write about the peasant life. It was the first time I had seen Haitian imagery. He had written the book in the 1930s. Most of the Haitian writers modeled themselves on French writers. Victor Hugo was big back then. We were stuck in a Romantic style for a while. I think that Roumain was one of the first writers to look at what was going on in Africa and his own environment, rather than relying on abstract models of the Symbolists. There was a whole moment happening at the same time of the Harlem Renaissance. That was the first time I read about people I knew. That made a strong impression on me.

**AL:** *Granta* picked you as one the best writers under forty. How do you feel about that?
**Edwidge:** It's always nice to be chosen. I didn't campaign for it. I'm not sure how it happened. It's fair to protest. For the people who were chosen: we had nothing to do with it. For me the most important thing is the writing

and the process and the enjoyment. I know that the *Granta* thing was controversial. This passes and people forget it. You go on by yourself and write.

**AL:** What are some of your other influences?

**Edwidge:** I like to walk and think things out. That is really inspiring. Also the movies. You really think about the economy about storytelling. Nothing is wasted. Even in the worst movie everything has a purpose. I prefer silence when writing. That was hard to come by when growing up with three boys. You can tune out.

# Edwidge Danticat

## Robert Birnbaum / 2004

From the *Morning News*, April 20, 2004. Copyright Robert Birnbaum, Our Man in Boston. Reprinted with permission.

America may believe in its own exceptionalism, but it's also been exceptionally involved in Haiti's history. Here is a conversation with American Book Award winner Edwidge Danticat about the current state of Haiti and the current state of her stories.

In a recent e-missive to Maud Newton, with whom I am privileged to correspond, I related that I had had a conversation with Edwidge Danticat and I wrote: "Edwidge brings a whole new dimension to dignity and compassion. I think that my occasional dark moods about the real world and going to hell in a hand truck are assuaged when I meet women like her and Barbara Ehrenreich and Azar Nafisi and read Arundhati Roy."

Haitian-born Edwidge Danticat grew up in that nation's capital, Port-au-Prince, and moved to Brooklyn when she was twelve years old. She received degrees from Barnard College and Brown University. Edwidge Danticat has taught creative writing at New York University and the University of Miami and has written a number of well-regarded books including, *Krik? Krak!*; *Breath, Eyes, Memory*; *The Farming of Bones*, which won the American Book Award; and recently, her latest book of interconnected stories, *The Dew Breaker*. She has also edited two anthologies, *The Butterfly's Way: Voices from the Haitian Dyaspora in the United States* and *The Beacon Best of 2000: Great Writing by Men and Women of All Colors and Cultures*. Her writings have been regularly anthologized and translated into many languages and won numerous awards and honors. She has also worked with filmmakers Patricia Benoit and Jonathan Demme on Haiti-related documentaries. She currently lives in Miami with her husband.

Edwidge Danticat has said of one of her books: "I wanted to raise the voice of a lot of the people that I knew growing up, and this was, for the most part, . . . poor people who had extraordinary dreams but also very amazing obstacles." With her newest book, her overarching interest continues to be giving voice and attention to the neglected and marginalized people and issues. Here is how Richard Eder in the *New York Times* sees Danticat's *The Dew Breaker*:

> Archimedes held that he could lift the earth if he had a lever long enough, and an extra-planetary fulcrum to rest it on. There are horrors so heavy that they seem untellable. To bear to tell them so that we can bear to read them, a writer must find somewhere outside—peaceful, unmarked—to project them from. Atrocity enters the imagination not as the violating point of the knife but as the fair flesh violated . . . [Danticat] has written a Haitian truth: prisoners all, even the jailers. With neither forgiveness nor contempt, she sets it upon a fulcrum from where she's had the courage and art to displace the world even as she is displaced by it.

**Robert Birnbaum:** Does anyone ever shorten your name to something else?
**Edwidge Danticat:** Edie.

**RB:** What do you think of that?
**ED:** It depends.

**RB:** It depends who it is?
**ED:** [both laugh]

**RB:** Well, I won't call you Edie. Anyway, I know a little bit about you, a very little bit, but I have your dossier here.
**ED:** Um huh.

**RB:** It has all sorts of clippings and the material your publisher sent me—which I haven't read yet, but I did read *The Dew Breaker* and I recently talked to a young writer, Ana Menendez.
**ED:** Oh yeah.

**RB:** She extolled your virtues as a teacher and that meant a lot to me. So in the spirit of that, let me ask, is it a burden, as part of your life's work, to talk about Haiti to people who have no idea where Haiti is?
**ED:** It's not a burden so much as that it is complicated. There are times when it is a pleasure because it is such a big part of my life and it's a place

that I truly, truly love—in all its complications and difficulties. But there are moments when it's painful. Especially moments when things are very difficult and complicated for me and I am still trying to grasp what is happening and I am still trying to understand and to reach family back home. And it can be very complicated and often people want to hear about it in sound bites. They want you to summarize something that is a lot harder to understand and very hard to explain. So, there are moments when it is pleasurable and moments when it is very difficult.

**RB:** I suspect that not only is there something unpleasant about being asked for sound bites about something complex but also that this attention only comes intermittently? Most of the time Haiti doesn't exist on the radar of the news organizations.

**ED:** That's one of the most frustrating things about it. People think that there is a country there that these people are only around when they are on CNN. I don't think that's limited to Haiti. That's whatever news topic, whatever political process any country is going through—whenever they are in the news, that's when they exist. If you don't see them they don't exist. I think Haiti is a place that suffers so much from neglect that people only want to hear about it when it's at its extreme. And that's what they end up knowing about it. There is a frustration too, that at moments when there's not a coup, when there are not people in the streets, that the country disappears from people's consciousness. On some level, now, we are joining the larger world and realizing that we are connected with people in these very scary ways, sometimes. What happened recently in Spain affects us here and brings questions up. It is too bad that people have to be shaken up that way.

**RB:** Do you think people remember Nicaragua?

**ED:** Or El Salvador or Guatemala or—they don't. In fact that is the struggle that most Americans—as rich as this country is, most Americans are very limited in their interaction with the world, unless the world comes to us in a very shocking way. People aren't really aware of what's happening in other places.

**RB:** Why do you think that is?

**ED:** I think we suffer in this country—and I say "we" because I am part of that now too—from this idea of exceptionalism, that we are separate and different from everybody else. On some level, they can know about us but we can't know about them. That's why at times when the world comes to us in shocking ways, things like 9/11 happen and people then start questioning and asking and finding out. How many Americans knew where Afghanistan was before Osama bin Laden? It's too bad that these are the ways we learn about things, continuously.

**RB:** I wonder about your description—though in effect I do think there is this attitude that reflects exceptionalism. But for the farmer in Iowa or the white supremacist in Idaho—I take that one back—for the cattle farmer in Montana; do you think that they consciously hold this idea? That they even think about Americans en masse and say, "Americans are such and such and I don't know or care about the rest of the world"?

**ED:** There is a funny Chris Rock movie where he is running for president and one of the opposition candidates, at the end of every speech, he says, "Well, God bless America and nowhere else." [both laugh] And Chris—this gives him an opportunity to have a riff on that whole idea of "nowhere else." I think along with that idea of the exceptional, that part of it, there is also the lack of information. People who want alternative information have to try so hard to find it.

**RB:** They really have to want to—

**ED:** Yeah, they really have to search for it.

**RB:** I don't want to belabor my point here but I think there is at the core of America a xenophobia that is different than this so-called exceptionalism. And it is somewhat benign.

**ED:** That's true.

**RB:** It's not like Americans particularly hate the rest of the world any more than they hate each other, their neighbors. [laughs] Something about their process, the media, about their education. They just don't know. Unless they see a Greek restaurant or some ethnic restaurant, their outward look is very limited. I mention it because I don't know that we can combat this defect in our civilization unless we really grasp what we are combating. Sometimes there is a suggestion that it is conspiratorial.

**ED:** Not conspiratorial. This feeling that we are exempt from certain things that happen. On some level, now, we are joining the larger world and realizing that we are connected with people in these very scary ways, sometimes. What happened recently in Spain affects us here and brings questions up. It is too bad that people have to be shaken up in that way.

**RB:** I am getting a growing sense that there is a greater anxiety that American voters have about their leadership than I have seen before. There is some impending evil that seems linked with the Bush regime that may be catalytic for real change, but also there is a fearful anxiety, a dread about what the administration is doing.

**ED:** People would understand it or would almost accept it more if there was this very different agenda than what we would see, if there was pure ideology behind it. But it is so mired in money and oil—in a nonconspiratorial way—in documented ways with Dick Cheney's connection to the oil industry and the Bush family's connection with the Kuwaitis. On some levels, you can also have this feeling that we are being duped, somehow. And that the world is at play for something you would understand more if it were pure ideology. It is a very strange time and also basic things are being taken away. Social Security—

**RB:** And also Medicare by 2019.

**ED:** Exactly, exactly. Actually, at the same time we are asking for the $80 billion or so from Congress, I was reading an article about a school in Oregon that couldn't afford to get light bulbs. They couldn't change the street lamps, they had to alternate them because they hadn't enough money. So there are concrete things in people's everyday lives that are being compromised.

**RB:** Well, this is a very big subject that we have embarked upon—let's not digress too far from you and your book. I must say I am fearful and anxious also and find the Bush people despicable in a way that resonates with Hannah Arendt's brilliant notion of the banality of evil, the likes of which we haven't seen in some time. I believe in the "anybody but Bush" position and I accept that John Kerry is also seriously flawed. But there does not seem to be a group of evil ogres around him. That aside, no matter who is elected, will anyone pay attention to the school in Oregon or the juvenile justice system or the failing health-care system? Will either candidate pay attention to these matters?

**ED:** Yeah. Or even the state of Florida, where they are prepared to execute children. Umm, well, you hope that at least that there is something there to be claimed. I think in very concrete ways even if the people in Oregon wanted to take the administration to the Supreme Court there might not be any money for their light bulbs even with trillion-dollar surpluses. I think daily that the country's future is being thrown to the wind.

**RB:** Let's talk about Haiti. What I know about Haiti comes from having reading Herbert Gold's odd travelogue, *Best Nightmare on Earth* and Graham Greene's *The Comedians* and Madison Smartt Bell wrote *All Souls' Rising*, a novel based on Toussaint L'Ouverture—didn't he write a second one, *Master of the Crossroads*?
**ED:** It's actually a trilogy, and the third one will be out this year.

**RB:** One of the great things about Smartt Bell's novel was that, like so many people, L'Ouverture, if there is any basis in fact for the character in the novel, sounds fascinating and brilliant and has the same kind of weight as someone like José Martí. And at some point in the nineties, Aperture put out a book of photographs about Haiti, *Dancing on Fire*. So that's what I know about Haiti.
**ED:** Um huh. You can see that people, if given an opportunity, would do wonderful things, would do great things with their lives. So, Haiti is a hard place to live, especially at moments like this where you have the political squabbling, which leads to actual battles with guns and shooting and so forth. But it's a place that hasn't really been given a good chance by our own horrific dictators and other forces that press on us.

**RB:** What would you think North Americans should know?
**ED:** To start with, for example this year, 2004, is the bicentennial of Haitian independence. Haiti was the first black republic in this hemisphere, the second republic along with the United States. And actually the Louisiana Purchase [less than a year earlier] gave the US a big part of this country from France. It happened as a result of the Revolution. Napoleon had been fighting this army of slaves and free people in Haiti and it depleted his forces. And after the Revolution, when the French were driven out, they stopped and sold this big chunk of North America to the Americans for very little money.

**RB:** $15 million?
**ED:** Something like that. It's the best real-estate deal ever in the history of the world. And [John James] Audubon from the Audubon Society was born in Haiti. He was born in Les Cayes and we have a man, Jean Baptiste du Sable, who was the founder of Chicago, a Haitian man. So his name lives on. All those connections and that one of the first presidents, Henri Christophe, who was considered one of the three fathers of the country along with Toussaint L'Ouverture and Jean Jacques Dessalines, he came here

with a group of men to fight in the American Revolution and they fought in the Battle of Savannah, Georgia. And the fact that Haiti was occupied for nineteen years by the United States, from 1915 to 1934. In terms of the idea of long-term occupation—I have been reading a little bit more about this period—and you can see in that occupation are many lessons for the current occupation of Iraq. So we have these connections that go way back that people aren't aware of. Also, people are not often aware of the way the United States' policies influence what happens in places like Haiti or El Salvador or Nicaragua. Or in Colombia right now. And how these policies sometimes—

**RB:** Sometimes?

**ED:** Most of them, they serve the interests of the United States but are not building any kind of permanent structure for the country they are affecting.

**RB:** They don't even come close to building democracy.

**ED:** Exactly, exactly. And then we have this recycling—we have Saddam Hussein, who [was] supported by US government interests for a very long time before this moment. And [Manuel] Noriega. And in our case, we had one of the generals who was responsible for the first Aristide coup in 1990, who was trained in Fort Benning—

**RB:** At the infamous School of the Americas.

**ED:** Yeah. And who was on the CIA payroll. And so all these things, and people wonder why are people angry with us and they'll see these images on the news and say, "Those Haitians just can't get it together." Not realizing there is a fundamental structure behind it.

**RB:** That would be the mythology that is relentlessly piped in. At primitive and subtle levels. We are the good guys and so when we show up anywhere we are doing good and why do these people hate us?

**ED:** That's what I meant by that notion of exceptionalism, in the sense that "God bless America and nowhere else." Creating these messes that go from administration to administration and then you swoop in and clean them up—with that heroic Delta force—people not realizing that they were always there but doing different things than what we see them doing at the moment.

**RB:** The Chris Rock anecdote reminded me of the Mexican proverb that goes something like, "So close to the United States and so far from God."

**ED:** Um huh, there is a wonderful book with that title, Ana Castillo's *So Far from God.*

**RB:** I am struck by the oddity of selective indifference and ignorance. People are outraged about Cuba and continue to be but in no way is Fidel Castro—though I wouldn't know how to quantify these things—as bad as the Papa Doc and Baby Doc Duvalier. François Duvalier and his son, Jean-Claude, were Haitian dictators one after another, from 1957 to 1986. And I never hear mainstream American voices lifted against those regimes and our complicity in supporting them.

**ED:** You have also at the same time Castro and the revolution being the glue that held the United States together with a lot of these dictators. In Haiti you had the Duvaliers for twenty-nine years and they were very well supported by the United States. People make the argument now that they couldn't bear Aristide in this hemisphere, when they supported the Duvaliers and at the same time they were supporting people like [Rafael] Trujillo in the Dominican Republic and maintaining him and fighting on his side against other forces who were more liberal. It's very complicated. Someone has said that nations have interests, they don't have friends, and you see that over and over in US policy.

**RB:** That's not part of the mythology of Uncle Sam, the doting avuncular cartoon character. So how do we combat this miscasting of so-called objective realities? If a constituency is not energized to look past the slogans and imagery, then the idea of America is just as creditable as the products in a beer or auto commercial and people won't care much about the truth.

**ED:** That's true. More and more people are able to access information—thank goodness we have the Internet and if you are interested you can find things. Which is different than even twenty years ago. So at least the people who have another voice and people who are interested in other things can have a place to put their information and be heard.

**RB:** So from what little I know it seems that Haiti is a horrific place to live.
**ED:** For the majority of the people it is a difficult place to live. That's a reality that we can't ignore. But there is also great beauty to it. For example I was there with my husband in January and we decided we wanted to be there for the bicentennial and we wanted to be near water and in the mountains. It was our attempt to be closer to what it might have been like during the

revolution. And we went to some beautiful places. They were very hard to get to—there are problems with roads.

**RB:** And fuel?
**ED:** Exactly. It was a time with very inflated fuel prices, as there always are. There is always a spike at different moments. We get a lot of fuel from Venezuela and there was a strike there at the time. Another interesting connection. But it was just gorgeous, the places we went to. Untouched because a lot of people can't get to them in a touristy way. So there is also great beauty in the country. You can see that people if given an opportunity would do wonderful things, would do great things with their lives. So it's a hard place to live, especially [at] moments like this where you have the political squabbling, which leads to actual battles with guns and shooting and so forth. But it's a place that hasn't really been given a good chance by our own horrific dictators and other forces that press on us.

**RB:** My contact with the Caribbean Basin, Cuba, Puerto Rico, Nicaragua, Costa Rica—it's clear that in the twentieth century, masses of people emigrated to the cities and left the countryside—in Puerto Rico, I don't think they grow anything anymore. In Cuba, Havana has four times more people than its infrastructure can rationally support.
**ED:** Exactly. There are a lot of people, especially in this current time—they will get very nostalgic for the dictatorship. They'll say, "Oh, it was so good then. And food was so cheap." And what people aren't taking into consideration is exactly what you are saying. In 1970 you had something like 150,000 people in the capital, Port-au-Prince. Now you have two million.

**RB:** Oh my.
**ED:** And very little has improved in terms of infrastructure to support that many people. So, of course, things are worse. And you have the erosion problem, which has only gotten worse. Back then the Duvaliers contributed to that—they were often attacked by people coming in and trying to unseat them. So the father, Papa Doc, was known to cut down an entire forest so that invaders wouldn't have a place to hide. So you have erosion and the land is not producing as much as it used to. You have all these people in the city and everything has become centralized. If you live outside the city and you need a birth certificate or some official paper from the government, you have to travel to the city. People feel like their kids won't get an education

unless they are in the city. So there is a strong centralization and you have overcrowding and it becomes very difficult. And we have that problem that people aren't growing anything. And globalization is killing us.

**RB:** Haiti used to manufacture baseballs.

**ED:** They don't make them anymore, that's moved on. Even when they were, that was something like ten cents a day. People were being paid that, with no benefits and ruining their health. But there's not many opportunities in the city and fewer now in the country. For example, someone who would spend a couple of months growing a chicken and now you can buy chicken legs from Miami that arrive the same day [as they are slaughtered] for less than that, so who is going to waste their time doing that? We had a *cochon oui*, the local pig, and that was, for a lot of people, that was a bank account. You grew your pig and if your child has to go to school, you sell the pig or you slaughter it and sell the meat. And in the 1990s the US had a campaign where they eradicated all the pigs because the FDA decided they had swine fever. So there was a complete eradication of that whole population. One of the last indigenous animals to this island.

**RB:** No replacement?

**ED:** There were replacements of these pigs from Iowa who couldn't live there. [both laugh] They had to build houses for those pigs. They had to buy grain from the US. So they killed the pigs and now you have to buy the Iowa pigs from the same people, buy the grains to feed them because they couldn't eat what local pigs had eaten. And it took more than a decade to replace some of them—now you see more of them because they also came from Jamaica and other places. But it was a valuable resource that was completely depleted.

**RB:** That kind of arrogance reminds me of a story I read recently in Todd Balf's *The Darkest Jungle* about a plan to cut another canal from the Atlantic to the Pacific in the Darien Gap, the area in Panama that borders what is now Colombia. Apparently in the seventies the plan was to cut the second canal using eight nuclear devices to blow up the channel way. This was a reserve that was inhabited by 40,000 to 50,000 indigenous people whose roots are prehistoric. And, of course, these people would be resettled.

**ED:** Yeah, yeah, it's collateral damage. And all the people who starved because their pigs were killed, they were collateral damage.

**RB:** I don't know if this is an apocryphal story but I was told that the border between the Dominican Republic and Haiti is clearly demarcated, with the Haitian side being barren and foreboding and the Dominican side being lush and green.

**ED:** That's true in a lot of places where you have the boundary. There was a very large program behind that. Trujillo, who was a president [of the Dominican Republic] for many decades, had a program specifically aimed at that, sprucing up a lot of the border towns in order to contrast them from Haiti—it was a very conscious effort. Haiti has a larger population, in a smaller area. Not that there isn't poverty in the Dominican Republic, but aside from that you have more tourism, so part of whatever preservation has been connected to that, too. Trujillo was interested in the contrast. And even for myself, when I have had to go there, if I am staying in Cap-Haitien, which is on the Haitian side close to the border, there are times when I, shamefacedly, need to make a phone call or something, [and] I have had to cross the border.

**RB:** And now what about the writing of a book about Haiti? Some parts of *The Dew Breaker* have appeared before, what was the very first story you wrote?

**ED:** The very first story was "The Book of the Dead."

**RB:** Did you know that you were going to write this as an interwoven collection of stories?

**ED:** No, I had just finished my book *The Farming of Bones*, the book about the Dominican Republic and Haiti, and I was going back to writing stories. I didn't feel like I could go into a novel just then. So I went back to writing stories and I started this one story about a father and a daughter who went on a trip. And the father makes this revelation to his daughter, that he was not a prisoner, as his family had thought, but was a "dew breaker," a sort of a torturer.

**RB:** That is an interesting phrase for such an odious thing.

**ED:** It comes from the Creole. It's an expression *choukèt laroze*; it really means somebody who breaks or shakes the dew. That's where that comes from. Creole is very forgiving of things like that. There is also an expression on the other side, *gouverneurs de la rosée*, people who govern the dew, who are kinder people, people of the land who nurture the land and try to control their destiny through the land. But that was the first one I wrote and I was very intrigued by the father so I started writing the very last story, which talked about his past and the last time he was in Haiti.

**RB:** That story that is called "The Dew Breaker." And so the stories in between?

**ED:** The stories in between really came in between. The third one was in the middle, which involved the family. So I was always circling around this family. But how do you write a book about Haiti? And this particular book, like a lot of the other books I have written, came from a kind of desire to go back to Haiti and to revisit and maybe to understand better some things from the past. I am very much intrigued by Haitian history and the way it is connected to current struggles. So the book is an attempt at exploring that.

**RB:** The notion of Creole being very forgiving is fascinating. In the very first story the father does something and—without giving it away—the daughter is clearly angered and she gets around to getting angry but first she says something to the effect that she had always thought anger was not a useful thing. I thought, "Oh really?"

**ED:** [laughs]

**RB:** All through the stories I have this sense of the Haitian ethos having so little malevolence.

**ED:** I'll give you an example of something very real and similar. In the 1990s we had a man who, again, was backed by the CIA and he was on *60 Minutes*, Emmanuel Constant, he started an organization called FRAPH. There was a point in the late nineties in New York where people would say, "Guess what? I was at a party . . ." and they would mention his name. For me, that was always extraordinary. How forgiving are we? Even the fact that people think now that they would accept Jean-Claude "Baby Doc" Duvalier coming back. How either forgetful or forgiving that Emmanuel Constant—whose organization killed five thousand, and if you hear five thousand in a Haitian estimation it's probably double that number—that he can feel safe to walk in the community, some of whom are wounded people. That to me was the kind of lack of malevolence—

**RB:** Danny in one of the stories has an opportunity to harm the dew breaker and doesn't.

**ED:** But he didn't want to be wrong—like many of the characters that felt they would want to repeat exactly this thing. Because on one level they were wrong about his parents—that there was a mistake made and his parents shouldn't have been killed.

**RB:** I have been thinking about forgiveness. I caught some piece of Elie Wiesel's speech at Auschwitz, where he said something like, "No, you cannot forgive these people"—
**ED:** Perhaps.

**RB:** My sense of the conditions in Haiti with these predatory dictators and their elite killers, the Tonton Macoute, sustains my sense of the horrific. You do mention one instance of a Tonton Macoute having gasoline poured down his throat and then ignited.
**ED:** There were many cases like that after the dictatorship ended in 1989. There was a term that was created around that—*dechoukaj*—"uprooting." Many of these Tonton Macoutes were killed. What interested me in the stories and in these people and in this era, because it was the last era that I lived consistently in Haiti, was to understand these people so at least try to get as close to understanding these people as possible. The country and other countries, too, where things are difficult, keeps repeating or keeps recreating this environment that creates these kind of people. Now we have a phenomenon with young men who are deported, many from the United States and were returned to Haiti and became what is called *chimé*—

**RB:** Like Claude?
**ED:** Yeah, they are stranded there. And they have assembled together [in gangs] to survive and some of them, not all of them, become involved in crime and are labeled this way in the country. The greatest of ironies is that you have some American soldiers from the country that deported them, some will be killing them. So you have this situation that keeps opening this opportunity to allow these types of people to be created or recreated. First you had the *Macoutes* under Duvalier, then in FRAPH and now the Chimé. There are people, I am sure, that have gone from group to group, because they don't have work. Because they don't have other things. So there is this culture and the lack of infrastructure that perpetuates this kind of system.

**RB:** What are you going to do next?
**ED:** I am taking it easy for a little while. I am doing a young adult book that I am almost done with [about] Anacaona, who was actually one of the few female indigenous leaders before Columbus came and she was a very

powerful leader and known to be a poet and she was one of the last ones. She was hung by Columbus's people a couple of decades after they landed on the island. She hung in there and fought and was a true warrior-queen. I don't like to use the word "queen" but a true warrior and leader in our history.

**RB:** And you chose to make this a young-adult story?

**ED:** Yeah, it's my first attempt at dealing with this story. It will be in a series called Royal Diaries that sort of positions it with other women who were leaders, but it concentrates on a particular time, like their teens. Maybe I will do something with her later but this was a way to approach it in a manageable way.

**RB:** Well, I hope we talk again.

**ED:** Likewise, thank you.

# Splintered Families, Enduring Connections: An Interview with Edwidge Danticat

## Katharine Capshaw Smith / 2005

From *Children's Literature Association Quarterly* 30, no. 2 (Summer 2005): 194–205.
Reprinted with permission.

Edwidge Danticat (b. 1969) is one of American literature's most exciting young writers. In novels, short stories, travel narrative, and young adult fiction, Danticat writes about Haitian American experience in graceful, imagistic prose, revealing the traumas of cultural dislocation and political violence through suggestion, fable, and metaphor. Born in Port-au-Prince, Haiti, Danticat was raised by an uncle and an aunt since her parents had emigrated to New York when Danticat was four years old. In childhood, Danticat experienced the variety of Haitian life; her home was in the urban capital, and she spent summers in a rural community with extended family. In some ways, then, she straddled two worlds even when living in Haiti. In 1981, Danticat left Haiti with two of her brothers to join their parents, and as an adolescent in Brooklyn she found some difficulty bridging the cultural divide between American and Haitian experience. Danticat discovered a way to articulate the difficulties and rewards of her bicultural position through writing. After graduating from Barnard College in 1990 with a degree in French literature, Danticat enrolled in the masters of fine arts program at Brown University where she wrote a draft of her first novel, *Breath, Eyes, Memory* (1994). A popular and critically acclaimed novel, *Breath, Eyes, Memory* drew on Danticat's own experience to depict the migration of a young woman from Haiti to New York. After graduating from Brown University, Danticat returned to the East Flatbush section of Brooklyn and published a collection of short stories entitled *Krik? Krak!* (1995), which became a National Book Award finalist. Her second novel, *The Farming of Bones* (1998), diverged from her interest in migration, emphasizing instead a particular moment in Haitian history: the 1937 massacre of Haitians at the border of the Dominican Republic. This text connects with Danticat's other work in its emphasis on the protagonist's cultural liminality, since she lives in close contact with Dominicans, and in its exploration of working-class Haitian subjectivity.

A travel narrative, *After the Dance* (2002), took Danticat into nonfiction in its description of Carnival celebrations in Jacmel, Haiti. Danticat recently published *The Dew Breaker* (2004), a collection of short stories which focuses on a man who worked as a torturer in Haiti under François Duvalier.

Danticat's first young adult novel, *Behind the Mountains* (2002), returns to her earlier interest in Haitian migration, drawing deeply on Danticat's experience as an adolescent. Written in a diary format, *Behind the Mountains* offers its reader an intimate portrait of its central character, Celiane, as she experiences the richness of Haitian cultural life and the threats of an unstable political system. When Celiane moves to New York with her family, she longs for connection to Haiti and discovers that her family must negotiate not only the new cultural context, but also new definitions of family relationships. In the interview below, Danticat talks about children's culture in Haiti and the tensions between folk culture and French-based educational and publishing structures. In discussing her own youth in Haiti and New York as a source for her fiction, Danticat stresses the centrality of childhood to her work and alludes to the cross-read nature of her books for adults. She also evades compartmentalization in terms of her own position as an ethnic writer, asserting that she is "a writer of the African Diaspora, Haitian, Caribbean, and African as well." Most of the interview focuses on *Behind the Mountains*, exploring its linkage of visual to literary arts, its depiction of physical and emotional trauma, and its attempts to make an American readership aware of Haitian investment in American history and identity. Danticat's second novel for young adults, *Anacaona, Golden Flower*, recently appeared from Scholastic. A major contemporary writer for adult readers, Danticat is committed to rendering complicated and realistic descriptions of ethnicity and historical incident for her young readership.

**KCS:** Thank you for allowing me to talk with you about your experience as a writer for younger readers. I would like to start by asking you to describe children's culture in Haiti. Could you tell us about the vitality of folk stories, traditions, and practices in Haiti? How does a child's experience of folk culture relate to her classroom life at school?

**ED:** Children's culture in Haiti is probably a lot more different now than it was when I was a child in Haiti. As I remember it, there was a very vibrant storytelling culture, particularly in the countryside. That experience was never really acknowledged in school because that education system was strongly based on a French educational system so that local culture was primarily ignored to highlight French culture, so often what a student experienced at home was never really echoed in the classroom. Even the language of home was not echoed in the classroom for most kids. We were told there were four seasons, for example, when really we could see two: the dry season and the rainy season, so the culture was never really echoed in school. I don't think that's changed too much, even though there are some schools now that use Creole texts written by Haitian authors that reflect Haitian realities. Also when I go back, even in the countryside, I see less storytelling and more television watching. Like children elsewhere, our children too are moving into a different age with less traditional storytelling and more television.

**KCS:** Are there texts for children produced in Haiti? If so, what are these texts like? Are they printed in Creole, or French, or English? Is there a Creole language movement for young readers in Haiti?

**ED:** There is some movement towards educating children in Creole. Mostly they're private efforts. We have a friend named Yves Dejean, a very well-known Haitian linguist who has written consistently about Creole education and how children can benefit from it. He has a school in the countryside, in the South, where this is practiced and he also has produced his own texts for the children to use in Creole, using the children themselves as characters in the stories he writes. There are now some companies that produce texts in Creole with Haitian themes inside Haiti; one of them is run by a woman who was a New York educator for years in bilingual education and went back to start a school in Haiti.

There's also a company in Miami called Educa Vision that produces culturally relevant materials in Creole and uses a combination of vibrant illustration and storytelling to teach children the basis, reading, writing, math, and even hygiene. Of course Haitian kids also have access to a lot of books in French, books that are written with children in mind. Those who can afford it can read the latest Harry Potter in French, for example, just like

French kids. Also many Haitian authors who write for adults have also written a couple of books of poetry and novels for children.

**KCS:** How did your experience growing up in the rural mountain community of Beauséjour and in urban Port-au-Prince influence your sense of identity?

**ED:** I mostly grew up in Port-au-Prince, the capital, where I was born. But my father and all his brothers and sisters were born in Beauséjour and left as adolescents for the capital. I did spend my summers in the countryside, in Beauséjour and elsewhere in the provinces. Being exposed to both city and rural life at an early age made me experience both sides of Haiti, the part that some call the *peyi andeyò*, the outside country, which is the countryside, as well as the capital, where most of the country's economic and political energies are unfairly concentrated.

**KCS**: How does this rich, diverse experience of Haitian life influence your vision of yourself as an artist?

**ED:** I still really don't think of myself as an artist. I see myself as a storyteller, someone who is always looking for different ways to tell a story. Haiti, though, is a very inspirational place for artists. I think the richness of the culture, the complexities of life there, the vibrancy of the place, including the difficulties, enrich one's vision of life and add several layers to the narrative and creative process.

**KCS:** In your books for adults as well as in your first young adult book, *Behind the Mountains* (2002), you frequently address childhood and adolescent experience, sometimes in first-person perspective. Could you talk a bit about your relationship to childhood as a subject? Do you see yourself addressing an adolescent audience even in books that have not been labeled as young adult?

**ED:** I was surprised that so many adolescents were reading my first book, *Breath, Eyes Memory*. I think on some level young people were already drawn to my adult books. People often say I look young. Maybe I also write young. I found childhood as a subject, I think, when I was away from my parents. They left me in Haiti to move to the United States when I was four, and I grew up with my aunt and uncle. There were some aspects of childhood that I missed in real life that I try very hard to recreate in my books, whether for kids or adults.

**KCS:** Since children as well as adults participate in communal and oral traditions in Haiti, the dividing lines (from what I understand) between adult and child cultural experience are not always as rigidly drawn as in the United States. Has that been your experience? What are your thoughts about designating written literature as either "for adults" or "for children"? Who do you consider your audience?

**ED:** The demarcation between children and adult books can sometimes feel artificial. There are plenty of adults reading the Harry Potter books, for example, and children who read Dickens early on, children who just pick up books like that and read them. So it depends on the child or the adult in question. But I don't think children should feel limited by the labeling of a book. If a book interests you and you feel you can read it, just read it. In places like Haiti certainly children take on adult-type responsibilities at a very young age so they sometimes have a view of the world that's closer to an adult's than a sheltered child's.

**KCS:** What do you hope to achieve as a writer for an audience that is explicitly "young adult"? Are your goals as a young adult writer different from your goals in your texts for adults?

**ED:** They're not really that different. In both cases, I hope to tell a good story that's both fulfilling and entertaining for my readers.

**KCS:** Your move from Port-au-Prince to Brooklyn, New York, in 1981 runs through many of your narratives. How did you transform that experience into fiction? What are your goals when writing about that experience for a young American audience?

**ED:** When I came here I was surprised how many similarities there were between myself and other immigrant children from all over the world. Using some of my own experiences in fiction helped me to understand "my story" in a much deeper way. I hope when young Americans read my stories and other stories like mine they can understand that we're not all that different from they are. Only our circumstances are.

**KCS:** I would like to ask you a few questions about *Behind the Mountains*. It is such a powerful story. And while it contends with weighty issues of political violence, physical and psychological trauma, migration, and adolescent identity crises, the narrative voice is so gentle; the story comes alive through the poetic descriptions of its narrator, Celiane. Could you talk about why you used a first- person narrator? Why is Celiane the best voice for this story?

**ED:** Celiane was the best voice for the story because she was the most sensitive and least hardened person in the family. She was also a great observer, a prolific note taker, someone who wanted to be a writer, so she was a natural choice for the telling.

**KCS:** The early sections describing Celiane's life in Beau Jour are beautiful. What are your goals in weaving folklore and proverbs into your narratives? Are you writing for an audience who is familiar with Haitian cultural life? Since the book is published for a national audience, do your descriptions of folk life or the natural landscape aim to shed new light on rural Haiti for an unfamiliar audience?

**ED:** I never really think about an audience outside of myself when I write. If anything, I think of writing for the girl I was when I was fifteen, a girl who was looking for images of herself. In describing Haiti, a Haiti that some may not know, I try to be as specific as possible, as visual as I can so not only can I travel back with the reader, but they can also travel along with me. I can't really write something unless I can see the moment and the place I'm writing about. I always want the reader to see it too so in describing the landscape I'm painting a picture that no matter who the reader is, he or she can see it as well as I do. And hopefully they can feel some of what I feel for the story, which is often a mixture of both sadness and hope.

**KCS:** Could you tell us about the role of the visual arts in the novel and, perhaps, in Haitian life in general? I found your description of the tap taps particularly suggestive since you emphasize that they employ both folk sayings and vibrant visual art. You seem to emphasize that tap taps fuse word and image in order to convey a populist Haitian perspective. Maybe I am pushing the point here, but the two main characters are artists: Celiane the writer, and Moy the painter. And since your literary art employs such beautiful imagistic descriptions, could you talk about the relatedness or interdependence of the visual and literary arts in your work and/or in Haitian life?

**ED:** Haiti is a strong visual art community. We have a large number of visual artists from all social groups and all classes. The public space for Haitian art includes walls and moving vehicles, like the tap taps. Sometimes when you see a tap tap, you think you're looking at a moving cathedral, practical stained glass. The themes range vastly too in tap tap art, from religious symbols to basketball and rap stars. So taps taps, I think, are the people's museum. They merge art and life in the most poignant way. They also have commentary and advice sometimes. I wanted the reader to see very well that aspect of Haitian life because if you go to Haiti, especially the capital, that's one of the first things you're likely to encounter. You're right in seeing the tap tap as a common medium for Moy and Celiane. It's a kind of thing that the two of them could have easily collaborated on. I see popular visual art especially the way it's used in Haiti as a kind of cousin to written art. Celiane and Moy do too. Just as you might tell a story with your voice. The tap taps also tell a story.

**KCS:** I was also affected by your description of the great love between Papa and Manman and their children. The book seems concerned with exploring the nature of the ties that link families, even across great distances. Although Papa has not been physically present in the family for years, he still knows them: he can describe their demeanor and mannerisms as they sit to listen to the cassette he sends each month. And yet, as Celiane explains, there remains a distance between Papa and the family; she repeatedly attempts to bridge that gap and finds that her efforts to communicate fail. Could you tell us why you emphasize the longing this family feels for each other?

**ED:** In most cases I think the saying absence makes the heart grow stronger is true. Especially if that absence is forced. A child would never want to be away from her parents, just as a parent would never want to be separated from his or her child. So the weight of that absence is supported by love, love across great barriers of time and distance. Papa has to keep them alive in his mind that way he knew them to bear the separation. They must do the same for him. That's how they can survive as a family even though they're miles apart. But reality imposes distance naturally. It's inevitable. I don't feel as though I am emphasizing that longing. What I am doing is acknowledging it as it is a strong part of this kind of family relationship.

**KCS:** In addition to family ties, the novel also stresses the importance of female friendships to Celiane. In fact, many of your texts for adults also feature fundamental connections between women. Could you talk about Celiane's affection for Thérèse and Immacula and the way these relationships help define her, offer her solace, or cause her to extend herself emotionally? Do you imagine that young readers are especially sensitive to the significance of friendships?

**ED:** These relationships are important to Celiane because really they keep her going. They keep her spirit up and give her something to cling to. I think young people, as well as adults, can understand that. We all love having someone who understands us exactly where we are, someone we don't have to explain ourselves to, and that's what Immacula and Thérèse offer to Celiane. Of course in migration we lose a lot of those ties. Ties that are not necessarily family ties, friendships that are easier to let slip away. But we also gain new ones as Celiane does in New York.

**KCS:** The narrative's overall political context also interests me. When describing the November 2000 elections in Haiti, what ideas were you aiming to foreground? In other words, what did you emphasize when you depicted the political background?

**ED:** I used actual events, which took place at the time. Just put the characters in the middle of them. Everything Celiane describes actually happened. Children were killed and some were hurt, as Celiane is, by pipe bombs. There were people who simply didn't want these elections to happen.

**KCS:** I especially appreciate the way *Behind the Mountains* uncovers children's inevitable political involvement. These children are not sheltered from the social context: Celiane listens to discussions about the elections and politics on the radio; Moy accompanies his aunt when she goes out to vote; two young people are killed in the violence that prefaces the election. Not only does Celiane seem interested in the events that surround her, the narrative emphasizes that she is necessarily implicated when her camion is bombed. What do you think about children's political involvement (in Haiti and in the United States)? How does the depiction of Celiane demonstrate your ideas?

**ED:** I think in a politically volatile environment, children can't help but find themselves in the middle of the situation. Children all over the world live with the same fears and worries that adults do. In the United States we spend a lot of time trying to protect children from these realities. After September 11, 2001, a lot of parents were scrambling trying to figure out how to make their children feel secure. But I think children have a natural curiosity that leads them to the truth. They know exactly what's going on, and if they are vulnerable in a situation, they know it. So it's better for us to help them protect themselves as much as we can rather than keep them in the dark.

**KCS:** Tante Rose's commitment to vote was also quite suggestive. Could you talk about the importance of that moment in the book? Her political involvement seems to be an extension of her commitment to the dead (to those who died voting in the 1987 election, to her parents), as well as to social justice.

**ED:** She's very determined to vote because so many people died so she could have the right to vote. She sees her vote as a way of honoring their sacrifice.

I think there are people who still feel that way in this country, especially the children and grandchildren of the civil rights era. If your right to vote was earned with someone else's blood, you must prove yourself worthy of that sacrifice. That's how Rose feels. I think a lot of Americans are a bit nonchalant about the vote because that sense of sacrifice is not so recent for a lot of people. Rose watched people die going to the polls so that left a powerful impression on her.

**KCS:** What do you keep in mind when you depict trauma? Do you have different goals in describing trauma to a young audience than when describing it to adults in, say, *The Farming of Bones* or *Breath, Eyes, Memory*? I was especially moved by the fact that Celiane, in the hospital, keeps asking after her mother: the potential loss of family affects her as much or more than the fact of the bombing.

**ED:** In Celiane's case, trauma is a natural development of the story. It's what prompts change in the story. I don't try to make the trauma even easier for children in my stories for younger people, but I try to make their reaction age appropriate. For example, the way Amabelle, an adult, reacts to a massacre in *The Farming of Bones* is not the way Celiane would to the same event. So I try to keep in mind the child's age and worldview in describing the event. Granted some children are precocious and others lag behind emotionally, but that should be clear before the child comes face to face with a life-changing event.

**KCS:** When Celiane and her mother and brother join Papa in New York, the novel begins to focus on the features of Haitian diasporic communities. Celiane writes, for example, of a religious service in New York attended by Haitians: "At Saint Jerome's, Haiti did not seem so far away. I felt that if I reached out and touched anyone at the mass, I could be back in Haiti again, as though every person there was carrying a piece of Haiti with them in the warmth of their skin, beneath their winter coats" (95). How do you imagine the role of the Haitian American community for new immigrants? What have "tenth department" communities in New York, Miami, Boston, and Providence meant to you?

**ED:** The Haitian American community can be a lifeline for a new immigrant. Right now I live in Little Haiti, in Miami, and I see it every day. People are able to start a new life a lot quicker if they have help. If they know someone who can take them somewhere for a job. If they have some guidance, which the community can provide in both formal and informal ways. This was crucial to my parents, having friends and family and a church that supported them and us. And it continues to be crucial to many new arrivals.

The diaspora communities, what we call the tenth department, have been wonderful models in that they offer examples of every kind of Haitian immigrant in the United Sates, all the steps from new arrivals to Haitian Americans of many generations now.

**KCS:** Like every migrant to a new country, Celiane must adjust to her new situation; her family must also redefine itself. How do you imagine Celiane's national identity? Is she a Haitian living in America, or does she become something new? A Haitian American?

**ED:** When she arrives, I think she simply sees herself as Haitian, as a Haitian immigrant. But like many young immigrants, her view of herself will probably change. In a few years she'll probably end up calling herself Haitian American, like a lot of us.

**KCS:** In the novel you mention Abraham Lincoln's relationship to Haiti and the significance of Martin Luther King Jr. to Celiane. How do you imagine the relationship between Haitian American communities and African American communities? (You could talk about the novel or about your point of view in general.) Do you consider yourself a Haitian American writer or an African American writer—or are those designations too reductive?

**ED:** There was a moment when there was a lot of misunderstanding between the Haitian American community and the African American community. When we didn't know that much about each other. Over the years I think there's been some movement towards filling in that gap. We've had common tragedies and causes in cases like Abner Louima's and Amadou Diallo's for example. When these immigrant black men were attacked and in Diallo's case, killed, I think Haitians realized that we were not exempt from racism and the violence it breeds, and African Americans realized that other communities were also being touched. So in those moments and others we have moved closer towards community building. Also, the more time goes by, the more we learn about each other, the easier it is to build bridges. I consider myself a writer of the African Diaspora—Haitian, Caribbean, and African as well. But often I find the question much more interesting than the answer. The range of possible answers is much more fascinating to me than any answer I could give to the question.

**KCS:** The novel also spotlights the contributions of Haitians to the foundation and development of America, mentioning Jean Baptiste Point du Sable (the first settler in what would become Chicago), John James Audubon (the famous naturalist and painter), and Haitian fighters in the Revolutionary War. What are your goals in highlighting the historical intersections between America and Haiti? Do you hope to change how the reader imagines or defines America? Do these descriptions enable Haitian American readers to claim a sense of place in America?

**ED:** I want the readers, both Haitian and American kids of other backgrounds, to understand that there have been times before when Haitian and American history have intersected. A lot of kids don't know that. I hope to change the way the reader defines Haiti as well as the way he or she defines America, to let them know that indeed Haitian Americans have earned themselves a place here. We've not only taken from this country, but we've given a lot of ourselves as well.

**KCS:** At several points in the story you seem to be implicitly educating your reader about Haitian history in particular and its legacy of political independence. Do you think that when writing for young people that you have more of an obligation to inform them about social history (and Haitian history in particular)? In other interviews you have talked about the stereotypes that Haitians in America have to face: do you see in your young adult work an opportunity to affect the reader's ideas and impressions about Haitians? Do you imagine young adult readers as being perhaps more malleable or more open to knowledge that would influence their perspective on minority communities?

**ED:** I hope to inspire the readers to learn more about their connection to the material they're reading. I hope to spark their interest and send them on that quest for more information. The best way to deal with stereotypes is to introduce folks to other folks from a group they know little about and perhaps misunderstand. A book is able to do that in a way that only a personal encounter can do, that even a personal encounter might not be able to do. So I hope my books do that for the readers, introduce them to a Haitian character that they might find surprisingly like themselves. I don't think young readers are more malleable than other readers, but these encounters are perhaps the first for them, so they count a lot because they can add layers to the way they look at a particular group.

**KCS:** I admire the way that *Behind the Mountains* acknowledges the depth, complications, and pain of young people's lives. At the end of the novel, Moy sums up this idea succinctly. When Papa suggests that manhood is difficult, Moy replies, "It is not been so easy being a boy, either" (152). Whether it is Celiane, who is injured by a pipe bomb; Gary, whose street life puts him at risk; or Thérèse, who "laughs like someone who thinks she may never laugh again" (22), all of the young characters lead difficult, complex lives. How do you imagine your responsibility to tell the truth about life (and adolescence) to a young adult audience?

**ED:** I think we have to tell the truth to a young audience. They know a lot more anyway than we think they do, so we have to talk to them in a way that does not speak down to them, but speaks to them in a way that shows respect for their interests and intelligence.

**KCS:** To continue this idea, I was wondering whether you might talk about how the novel compares New York to Port-au-Prince. Late in the book, Celiane describes the many threats awaiting young people in the American city: gangs, violence, parental neglect, etc. Then Celiane reflects on Thérèse's life as a restavec in Haiti. Are you drawing a comparison between the two urban sites and the threats they pose to young people?

**ED:** As children who grew up primarily in rural settings, I can see how an urban setting—wherever it is—would be equally frightening to both Thérèse and Celiane. This is why at the end of the book I talk about the migration taking place in three steps for Celiane, as it has recently for many children. First there is the journey from the country to the city and then form the city to another city. Some kids who come to the US by boat bypass the Haitian capital altogether and end up in a major American city, and of course they experience a triple shock. The problem of restavecs—children whose parents turn them over to friends or relatives to work for food and shelter—is a huge problem in our country. Many of our children are terribly mistreated in this situation. I simply wanted to highlight it in the story, that it is like gangs and prostitution and other menaces, one of the things that our children are at risk of living through in Haiti.

**KCS:** I was wondering whether you might tell us a bit about your new young adult title. What can we expect?

**ED:** It's called *Anacaona, Golden Flower*. It's about an indigenous woman leader named Anacaona. Along with her brother, Behechio, Anacaona ruled over a region in the south of Haiti called Xaragua. She was married to one of the most powerful caciques, or leaders, on the island. His name was Caonabo, which means Lord of the House of Gold. He was a fierce warrior as she was. But she was also a poet. She wrote ballads that her people sang at feast and designed pottery that they traded. She was one of the last Taíno leaders to be captured after Columbus, and his men came to a place the Taínos had called *Ayiti*, which in their language means land on high, mountainous and slippery. She was hanged by a Spanish governor at twenty-nine years old. To the Taínos, of course, we owe certain words: Jamaca, hammock, which was their creation, Jurakan, which means storm, hurricane. Tabacú, which is tobacco. Tuna, which to them simply meant "something from the water."

**KCS:** How does the new title connect with *Behind the Mountains*? Are there other young adult works in your future?

**ED:** They're both in the epistolary form. That's a form that interests me right now and they're both in a series. *Behind the Mountains* was part of the First Person fiction series at Scholastic and *Anacaona, Golden Flower* is in the Royal Diaries Series. I am glad that I started out writing for young adults this way because the books, though singular, are part of a larger story and when the reader's done with one book, he or she might be tempted to venture towards another. Are there other young adult works in my future? I sure would like to think so. I'd also like to tackle some picture books, but I find these a whole lot harder than adult books.

**KCS:** What do you think about other Haitian American children's and young adult writers, like Joanne Hyppolite (one of my favorites) and Jaira Placide? Is there interest among the Haitian American literary community in writing for young people?

**ED:** I know both Jaira and Joanne, and I admire their work very much. I think it's quite hard to write for young people, and they do it with such complexity and respect. I think they're wonderful. There are so many Haitian American children growing up without complex images of themselves, images that reflect their own reality. Both Joanne's book and Jaira's offer that. They're making such a wonderful contribution. I wish they were around when I was growing up.

**KCS:** Thank you so much for talking with me.

**ED:** My pleasure.

# An Interview with Edwidge Danticat

## E. Ethelbert Miller / 2007

From *Foreign Policy in Focus*, October 16, 2007. Copyright 2007, E. Ethelbert Miller, *Foreign Policy in Focus*. Reprinted with permission.

The noted Haitian American novelist Edwidge Danticat has recently published a memoir of her family, *Brother, I'm Dying*. When her parents went to New York to find work, the young Edwidge remained in Haiti with her brother, her aunt, and her uncle. There, her uncle Joseph builds a Baptist church that local gangs eventually loot and burn down. Joseph flees to the United States. At the age of eighty-one, he ends up at Krome detention facility in Miami. He falls sick and dies shortly after arriving. *Brother, I'm Dying* is a finalist for a National Book Award. FPIF's E. Ethelbert Miller talks with Edwidge Danticat about her new memoir, US immigration law, and US–Haitian relations.

**E. Ethelbert Miller:** When I think about the looting of your uncle's church in Haiti, I also think about the bombing of mosques in the Middle East. It seems as if we are destroying the things that are sacred to civilization. How can a writer restore hope to a society in which its basic moral fabric seems to be crumbling?

**Edwidge Danticat:** I worry that it would be overreaching to think of the trashing of my uncle's church in the same way as the bombing of a mosque. The looting of his church and the fire set in some parts of it was a personal matter, something that was seen by the people doing it as revenge against him for what they saw as his letting riot police and United Nations peacekeepers shoot from the roof of his church. It is interesting, though, the fact that his church was desacralized not just by the gangs who pillaged it but by the police and peacekeepers who stormed it to shoot from the roof.

When I was growing up in Haiti, churches were places where gendarmes, even during the dictatorship, were not supposed to enter. I remember once when the Tonton Macoutes, the henchmen enforcers of the Duvalier regime, wanted to attack a very popular preacher, they waited until he left the church to do it. Thus, even during the dictatorship, which was horrible and cruel, the church was still seen as a sanctuary. Obviously, in my uncle's case, and in the case of these mosques, this rule was broken. So you can say that a neighborhood, a society, is truly unraveling when these things happen. In my view, though, the body is sacred, yet people are raped, maimed, beaten, and killed. Breath is sacred, yet we smother it every day. We do not value people either as much as we should. A writer cannot really restore hope to any of that, at least not the kind of writer I am. All I can do is document it.

**Miller:** How is the Haitian community within the US dealing with proposed changes to immigration laws? How organized are Haitians?

**Danticat:** In Miami where I live, we are very organized around immigration issues primarily, I think, because they affect us a great deal. Miami is still the first place many Haitian migrants land, so it is ground zero. We have wonderful organizations like Haitian Women of Miami, the Haitian Neighborhood Center, and the Florida Immigrant Advocacy Center that help in that fight. We also have many Haitian elected officials here, mayors, judges, and others who help in that fight. We do have room to grow, but we are not complacent. We are fighting. While the new immigration laws were being proposed, there was a dialogue going on here both within the community and with elected officials. There were reactions from our community leaders at every step of it so we were part of the debate.

**Miller:** Why is a detention facility like Krome not being discussed in the media? These places seem to be invisible to the American public. Is this true?

**Danticat:** It's funny you should say that. The year my uncle died, Krome received an award as best detention center or something like that from some watchdog group. I think these things happen because few people, unless your loved ones are there, know that these places even exist. When my uncle died, I was told that there would be a general investigation of all these places, but unless a human rights group writes a report about a place like this, you don't hear very much about it.

**Miller:** What should the next president of the United States do to improve conditions with (and within) Haiti?

**Danticat:** I think he or she should support the leader the Haitian people have chosen for themselves and not impose US choices on the people. Haiti is a very close neighbor and should not be neglected. Aid should be given toward building infrastructure and long-term institutions so that every couple of years there is not a forced regime change that requires putting out more fires.

**Miller:** If your daughter, Mira, decides to become a writer, what stories are you leaving behind for her to tell? What lessons will she learn when she reads your books?

**Danticat:** I think she will have her own stories to tell, stories that are perhaps much more different than mine. I have been conscious since she was born that she will know me a whole lot better than I knew my parents because she will have these things I have written to read for herself, in her own time, in her own way. Most of us don't have that much access to our parents' minds and hearts. I can only hope that this would inspire her on whatever path she chooses to follow for herself.

# Up Close and Personal: Edwidge Danticat on Haitian Identity and the Writer's Life

## Opal Palmer Adisa / 2009

From *African-American Review*, Summer/Fall 2009, 345–55. Reprinted with permission by Opal Palmer Adisa, writer and Distinguished Professor at California College of the Arts.

I have met Edwidge Danticat several times, and always I come away thinking of her as a sweet, innocent, talented writer, who seems to be removed from it all. Since the appearance of her first novel *Breath, Eyes, Memory* (1994) at the tender age of twenty-five, the word was out that she was someone to watch, and indeed that prediction has proven true. Danticat has been prolific, producing a book or two yearly: *Krik? Krak!* (1996); *The Farming of Bones* (1998); *Behind the Mountains* (2002); *After the Dance: A Walk through Carnival in Jacmel* (2002); *The Dew Breaker* (2004); *Anacaona: Golden Flower, Haiti, 1490* (2005); and her most recent book, a memoir, *Brother, I'm Dying* (2007). She has also edited two important collections: *The Beacon Best of 2000: Great Writing by Men and Women of All Colors and Cultures* (2000) and *The Butterfly's Way: Voices from the Haitian Dyaspora in the United States* (2001). Edwidge Danticat is perhaps *the* most popular Caribbean writer. Her books are taught, both nationally and internationally, across many different disciplines: African American, ethnic and women's studies, and comparative literature. Countless papers and dissertations have been presented on her work, and at almost every conference within the last ten years, scholars have presented a wide array of critiques on one or more of her works.

Haitian by birth and affinity, Edwidge Danticat has received many awards, including the Fiction Award from *The Caribbean Writer*, 1994; the National Book Award nomination for *Krik? Krak!*, 1995; Best Young

American Novelists for *Breath, Eyes, Memory* by *Granta*, 1996; the American Book Award for *The Farming of Bones*, 1999; and the National Book Critics Circle Award for *Brother, I'm Dying*, 2008. The idea for this interview was hatched in 2006 when Danticat and I both participated in the Association of Caribbean Women Writers & Scholars Conference (ACWWS) in Miami. We began a conversation there, but were too distracted by the events to make it meaningful. I decided to put it off until we met up again, but Danticat and I each became consumed by our own projects. We decided that the Internet would be the most expedient way to get this done.

My approach to this interview was personal, as one Caribbean woman to another, whose works revolve around our love and commitment to the region. In this setting, I sought to discover the intersection of this woman and her writing.

**Opal Palmer Adisa:** You came to the USA when you were quite young, but still, I suspect, you were raised with Haitian cultural sensibilities even in the USA. Although this might be redundant or even obvious, what is your relationship to Haiti, not simply in the political realm, but on a more visceral, navel-string level? What does Haiti mean to you?

**Edwidge Danticat:** Haiti is and will always be one of the two places, the United States being the other, that I call home. Haiti is where I was born and Haiti was my first home. I am like most Haitians living with my feet in both worlds. I go to Haiti as much as I can. I still have a lot of family there. I have always lived in Haitian communities in the United States, so while I have left Haiti, it's never left me.

**OPA:** What are your hopes for Haiti, given its historical precedent, being the first country in the New World to earn its freedom, and now being considered one of the poorest nations in the world?

**ED:** Recently, there was an article in all the world's papers about people eating cookies made of clay in Haiti to quash hunger. Then Haiti was one of many places where people had demonstrations against hunger. This was quickly followed by a story about a group of Haitian sea migrants, so-called boat people, drowning off the coast of the Bahamas. You can't be Haitian, human, and not feel sad for all that. But you can't be human and not also hope, so we go on hoping. Haiti is sometimes the canary in the mine. The US occupation of Haiti between 1915 and 1934 can tell us a lot about what's going to happen in Iraq in a few years. These hunger demonstrations and migrations can tell us a lot about what might happen to the rest of the world given where we are now with high fuel and food prices and the political destabilizations and the migrations they will inevitably cause.

**OPA:** There seems to be a definite correlation in Caribbean literature between political turmoil and its literary traditions. What were the cultural, literary traditions that you remember as a child?

**ED:** Storytelling. Being told stories by my aunts and grandmothers. Going to the church run by my Baptist minister-uncle and reading my school lessons as though they were poems or songs. All that was part of my growing up.

**OPA:** Very often, many European American or Western writers can read-ily trace a literary tradition that gave birth or helped shaped their writing career. For me, as a Jamaican born in the fifties I have no such claim, but I have the storytelling tradition of my maternal great-grandmother and grandfather and others in my community. Alice Walker has two impor-tant essays, "Saving the Life That Is Your Own: The Importance of Models in the Artist's life" and "In Search of Our Mothers' Gardens." The latter is more instructive for us as women of the African diaspora, in which she talks about creativity in a more inclusive and domestic sphere—to help us trace the roots of our writing and/or creative process. Looking at your personal heritage, both familial and country, where do the roots of your writing begin? When did you begin writing?

**ED:** The roots of my writing also begin in storytelling. I was lucky enough to share a room as a small child with a great storyteller, my uncle's wife's mother, Granmè Melina. She was almost a hundred years old when she came to live with us. Her body was racked by illness. She had crippling arthritis, but she was a lively storyteller. Even now, I still think of one of her stories when I encounter certain situations. She seemed to have one for each situation. I was recently reading a book on child development that talked about the importance of storytelling in the development of imagina-tion. It's crucial, the author said, for children to have stories told to them, not just read to them. I was lucky enough to have stories told to me almost every day, so even when I started reading, I would compare what I was read-ing to all I had heard.

**OPA:** Did you always know that you wanted to write, that you were going to be a writer, that you would bring people, disparate people, home to Haiti?

**ED:** Because of that early exposure to storytelling and my love for it, I knew I wanted to be a storyteller. I was shy, so that was a problem. Nobody would want to hear the lively stories Granmè Melina told in my shy voice. So when I started reading, I saw a silent way to tell stories and I wanted to tell my stories the way they were in books. I don't remember how far back this goes, but that was my first realization that I wanted to be a writer. I had no idea it would come this far, but writing remains my life's passion, besides family, of course. I love it and can't imagine my life without it.

**OPA:** Do you think your works allow people to see you, the Haitian, not as an exception, but perhaps as the norm? Do you feel your work has contributed to Haiti and the Haitian being "seen" more often?
**ED:** I hope my work has made those contributions, made Haitians seem more complex, more present. I hope so, but I can't really know for sure. And I can't take credit for something like that. A lot of readers facing my work have a load of stereotypes in mind. Some are willing to release them. Others are not. I hate to say it, but some have them further reinforced by some of what I write. That's the complexity of the process, of the work, of any singular truth.

**OPA:** What was the environment in which you were raised? Was your family very nationalistic and proud? Did they tell you the history—that Haiti was the first to gain its independence and keep its name? That it defeated the largest European army sent abroad at the time? Are you proud to be Haitian?
**ED:** Of course I'm proud to be Haitian. That's a given. Everything I write about Haiti comes out of love for Haiti. I hope that shows in my work. I grew up during the Duvalier dictatorship, where nationalism was complicated. François Papa Doc Duvalier had made nationalism the same as noir-ism, that is, you're only truly Haitian, if you're dark-skinned. That was his way to stamp out the country's mulatto elite, exile and kill them. We were not part of the mulatto elite or the business elite, but we were also not nationalist in his way of defining it. We loved our country. Of course, my family knew our history. We learned it in school from the time we were quite young. People talked about the revolution like it happened the day before. We were proud of that. We went to Flag Day parades; everyone did.

**OPA:** Can you say more about the distinction you are making between noir-ism and nationalism? What are the distinction and/or similarity between nationalism and noir-ism?

**ED:** After the American occupation, one of our writers, in particular, Jean Price Mars, started telling Haitians to look homeward for inspiration. He urged our writers to turn away from European influences, especially French ones, which were very strong, and look homeward, in the Haitian country-side for inspiration for our novels and songs and other types of work. Two of our great Haitian novels, *Gouverneurs de la Rosée* (*Masters of the Dew*, 1944) and *Général Compère Soleil* (*General Sun, My Brother*, 1955) grew out of that period. They were written by Jacques Roumain and Jacques Stephen Alexis, respectively. Roumain was a great friend of Langston Hughes and Mercer Cook, who translated *Masters of the Dew*, and the Harlem Renaissance represented a homebound aesthetic that was a great inspiration for our writers at that time. Roumain, for example, wrote poems about lynching that echoed some of Langston's work. He wrote about Harlem and the American South, the horrors and pains there for black Americans. Noirism also grew out of this sense, after a long racist occupation, that everything black was good. I suppose it's a particular type of nationalism, which does not allow everyone in. Of course, we were poor and dark-skinned and would have supposedly been on the inside of that, but that, too, was an illusion because there were sayings in the general culture like if you're a rich black, you're a mulatto, and if you're a poor mulatto, you're black. Noirism means *Négritude*, pride in black culture. It has nothing to do with race or sovereignty or class. Duvalier twisted it to mean only dark skin. This is something with a lot more nuance than there is space or time here. I don't think I've made it all clear, but that's part of it.

**OPA:** As a pre-adolescent Haitian girl moving to New York in the 1980s, did race factor at all in your development? Have you had to deal with racism?
**ED:** I lived in an all-Haitian, all-black, all-Caribbean atmosphere until I went to college. I didn't really face a conscious racist act that I recognized until I went to Brown and was called a brown dog by some drunken football players who were walking behind me down the street one day. I remember thinking that day, so this is what it feels like. Maybe because I was shielded inside my community, I didn't recognize it as directed to me until it was that obvious.

**OPA:** As a young woman coming of age, whom did you read? What and when was your first exposure to black writers and which ones? Which writers have had an impact on you? Whom do you love to read now, though I know it probably changes.

**ED:** In Haiti, strangely enough, we never read our own writers in school when I was there. Before I moved to the US at twelve, I read Émile Zola, Flaubert, and others, but never Haitian writers. The first book I read when I moved here in French was Roumain's *Masters of the Dew*, then Marie Chauvet's *Amour, Colère, Folie*, and *Mémoire d'une Amnésique* by J. J. Dominique. All three are Haitian writers. Later, when I could read English, I also read all of James Baldwin's plays, essays, and novels in one summer.

I loved the early Amy Tan and her novel *The Joy Luck Club*. I also especially liked Sandra Cisneros, Jamaica Kincaid, Alice Walker, and, of course, Ms. Morrison, Toni Morrison, my favorite of all time being *Song of Solomon*.

**OPA:** *Song of Solomon* is also my favorite work of hers. Of all these writers that you have mentioned, whom do you think has influenced your work the most and in what ways?

**ED:** They all have in many ways. I can't really parcel it. It's a stew of influence and I'm lucky to have had them all and others who are slipping my mind right now.

**OPA:** These days, "feminism" and "womanism" are words that are not as potent as they were in the 1980s and '90s, but in your work you do explore, if but tentatively, issues that affect women—rape, virginity, prescribed roles, et cetera. Broadly speaking, what is your sense of women's place in the world in general, and in Haiti and the greater Caribbean, specifically?

**ED:** We have a Haitian saying: *Fanm se poto mitán.* Women are middle pillars of society. I think that's true of all societies. I agree to the often quoted maxim that we hold up half the sky. Sojourner Truth, in her famous speech, said that if Eve were able to change the course all alone we should be able to do more together today. Those are the foundations of my feminism, my activism as a feminist/womanist.

**OPA:** It is insightful that you should quote Sojourner Truth, clearly one of the first African American feminists. Could you thus elaborate on the Haitian saying, *Fanm se poto mitán*, specifically as you see your place and role as a woman today?

**ED:** I don't really think there's much more to say about it. It pretty much speaks for itself. For a lot of poor families, the men are abroad or the society has crushed them and they're absent for one reason or another. The women may not be labeling themselves feminists or womanists, but they're doing the work. They're keeping the children alive. They're keeping the family going. That's a developed-world, as well as a developing-world reality.

**OPA:** How have your views of feminism been affected by patriarchal privileges?
**ED:** That's an entire thesis. The entire world is patriarchal, isn't it? Except those rare matriarchal societies that every day are becoming extinct in some recently "discovered" part of the world. We've all benefited from patriarchal privileges and have suffered from them. From the hospital where I was born, the male doctor who delivered me—female doctors being rare in Haiti at the time—to Mr. Gates or whoever designed the Mac on which I am writing my books.

**OPA:** When you set out to write a novel, for example your first, *Breath, Eyes, Memory*, what served as the impetus? Is it somewhat autobiographical?
**ED:** I had written a short essay for a local high school paper in New York called *New Youth Connections*, and when I was done I continued with it as a short story, which became this book. I guess it's autobiographical in the way that all first novels are. We draw from personal experience and the experiences of people we know. Yes, I did move to the States when I was twelve. But no, my mother was not raped and I was not born as a result of a rape.

**OPA:** In *Breath, Eyes, Memory* you examine women's relationships, mother/daughter/generational, among others. As archetypes—who are Tante Ate, Sophie, Grandme Ife, and the mother?
**ED:** Maybe some novelists think like this, but I don't think of my characters as archetypes. I think of them as people, individuals like you and me. Otherwise, I'd be writing myth and not the types of stories I do.

**OPA:** This novel is about redress, and also, it seems to me, to be about return, a kind of *Sankofa*. Sophie seems stuck until she returns to Haiti. By returning, Sophie is able to heal the past that her mother was unable to confront, and this journey therefore allows her, Sophie, to move forward in her life. Can you speak to this notion of return to redress, and perhaps its larger reverberations of African people in the diaspora, or Haitian people outside of Haiti, returning to help rebuild?
**ED:** Again, I was just thinking of this one individual case of a girl coming back to look for herself. I probably did it very badly. Of course, we now live

in an age where people go back and forth all the time, where the home we left is not so far away. In most migration experiences now, people have a chance to return for whatever reasons they wish. And we're lucky in Haiti that a lot of people go back to help rebuild the country.

**OPA:** In this novel, the mother is raped, which produces Sophie, and in the end Sophie immolates herself when she takes the pestle to her hymen, but even more importantly, each time the mother tests her, the mother, in fingering her, also rapes her. Can you talk about rape as a trope in the text?
**ED:** I see rape as an actual act. I would never use it as a trope. Sophie's mother was raped as many women were during that period. Sophie is proof of that rape. I just read an article about UN soldiers raping girls in a corn field in Léogâne where my mother was born. It's still happening—the actual rape of girls and women by people in position of power and authority in Haiti, both foreign and local.

**OPA:** So through Sophie you wanted to highlight the plight of women and the terror of rape that has historically been used to silence and thwart women's empowerment, both locally and historically, as wars are waged worldwide?
**ED:** No. Again, if I wanted to do that, I would have written an op-ed instead. Being a spawn of storytellers, I simply wanted to tell a story. Obviously there are parallels in real life, but I am not well versed in theory. If I set out with these types of things in mind, I would never write.

**OPA:** Do you feel that some women are as distrustful of their bodies, as Sophie appears to be, as a result of being raped? And/or that some, even without being raped, are disconnected to their bodies as a result of the ways that the black woman's body has been commodified, historically?
**ED:** I don't know. I guess it depends on the women and the circumstances. Of course, women whose bodies have been violated like Sophie's and her mother's, these women are probably going to not only distrust but also hate their bodies.

**OPA:** In the same text, you evoke or tell the story of the woman whom Erzulie turns into a butterfly . . . what is your relationship to Vodou and the *loa* of Haitian cosmology?
**ED:** Vodou is part of my belief system as a Haitian. Erzulie, the goddess of love, has always intrigued me. She is the *loa* of Sophie's family, their

chosen protector, which is why she almost always stands by them as a character in their story.

**OPA:** Do you identify with a *loa*, and if so which one? What role does s/he play in your life?
**ED:** I identify with Erzulie in her many manifestations as young, old, loving, angry, beautiful woman and crow. I can't really answer that last part. Not to be mysterious, but it's really not possible.

**OPA:** More than any of your other works, *The Farming of the Bones* is a conscious rewriting of Haitian history or the devastation of Haitians at the hands of the Dominican Republic's dictator Rafael Trujillo in 1937. Why did you decide to take on this rewriting? Do you believe in ancestral memory?
**ED:** I believe strongly in ancestral memory. Often that's all some of our ancestors have to leave us. I decided to write that book because I visited the Massacre River where some of the killing took place and saw no markers whatsoever. A lot of the survivors were dying and I wanted to talk to them. Out of these conversations and a lot of reading emerged the character Amabelle, who is a Haitian with access to a Dominican family.

**OPA:** What is Amabelle's and other Haitians' relationship to victimhood in the text? What is the road towards healing? Where does the pain go? The rituals?
**ED:** I don't like the word "victimhood." The word "victim" has become so trite in our culture. Amabelle and the others are survivors of this massacre. "Survivors" is also a term that has become quite trite, but I prefer it in this context to the term "victim." The book itself, the story, the telling, is meant as a path towards healing. The pain goes into the telling of the story, just as we discussed before. The pain goes into the telling, both for me and for her. The rituals don't exist. No markers. We have to recreate them. Our words are the markers.

**OPA:** In *The Dew Breaker*, which is really a love story, about fate, it seems to me, about how despite our respective past we can connect, and in a moment of great need, love beyond the wretchedness—the words are not only markers, but also forgivers. Can you speak about this aspect of that novel, or rather elucidate on your concept of love, love as a balm, a healing agent to transform as evidence in the novel?

**ED:** I have not heard *The Dew Breaker* described as a love story before. I am extremely grateful for that. I do see it as a story about love, love between a father and daughter, and love between a husband and a wife, who were not supposed to have ever met, who were never supposed to be together, star-crossed lovers of the highest degree. It is indeed a story about fate, fate that sometimes brings about the kind of love we never accept, about connections that rise out of desperation and indeed need. Perhaps it is that kind of fate that leads us to a kind of love that transcends banalities, the present, and even the past. My concept of love in this book is, I guess, that it's sometimes way beyond our control and out of our hands. It's really not something we can always guide. It guides and controls us. It can heal indeed, but it can also place us far beyond healing and we see examples of both, or I hope we do, in the novel.

**OPA:** The ideal of this novel is "old-spirit," meaning wise beyond the boundaries of the society in which we live, which is so bent on revenge. You explore the theme of redemption, forgiveness, and transformation—how someone at one point could do sinful and reprehensible acts, but have something happen that causes them to change from vile behavior to kindness, even goodness. These are very complex moral issues, yet the conclusion of the novel seems to suggest that we should be cautious about condemning someone based on past experiences. Thinking globally, especially in light of the climate of distrust and fear based in the "war on terror," what kind of moral/social values do we need to promote between peoples of the world?

**ED:** I hoped as I was writing the book that it would not espouse one view or another in terms of the notion of revenge versus forgiveness. I think after one has suffered and has found oneself facing the cause of one's suffering, there's bound to be thoughts of revenge immediately. I sometimes see the mothers of murdered people sitting and speaking to the murderers and I marvel at that. It rips my heart in ways I can't even explain. I put myself in their place and I don't know that I'd be able to do it. The only way I feel I can explain something like this and the only way I approach an explanation in this book is that the murderer or torturer has a piece of that person's loved one that the loved one knows that he or she no longer has. The murderer or torturer was the last to see that person alive. Forgiveness, an act of erasure of the last fatal act, is maybe a way of reclaiming that person again. People kept asking me how Anne, the torturer's wife, could live with him. The daughter in the book asks her mother how she can love her father and that's the explanation I gave her, the back-story for her choice. I don't know how we can promote greater understanding among people of the world. I really don't, but I think in the climate we're in now, not killing each other either through war, terrorism, or world-televised hangings would be a good start.

**OPA:** So, are you against the death penalty?
**ED:** Yes.

**OPA:** Could you describe, briefly, the kind of world you would create for your child—all children—to inhabit?
**ED:** A peaceful one, with no war, hunger, or misery, a world where all "isms" are done with. Doesn't look like it's going to happen anytime soon, though.

**OPA:** In *The Dew Breaker*, you tread new ground in that you explore the relationship between an adult daughter and her father. You also explore the creative process and some of the challenges when the subject is family. What is your relationship to your father? What do you admire most about your father? What inspired this story? Do you believe men of your father's generation who suffered and struggled under Papa Doc and Baby Doc will carry the ghosts of their pain to their graves?
**ED:** My last book is called *Brother, I'm Dying* and it's a memoir of my two fathers, if you will—my dad, and my uncle who raised me. My uncle died two years ago in immigration custody in Miami after he escaped a gang in Haiti. He had a valid visa, but at eighty-one years old was put in jail in Miami by the Department of Homeland Security because he requested asylum. The book is about all that and the fact that after years of living separately, my father here, my uncle in Haiti, they died around the same time. I adored my father and uncle both.

Before *The Dew Breaker*, I hadn't addressed the issue of male influence in my work. This new book allowed me to do that. The Duvalier era took a lot of fathers from a lot of daughters and sons. In *The Dew Breaker*, I was trying to address this fact. Is it better to have a father who's faulty or not have one at all? In the memoir, I revisit my own relationship with the two men who were my fathers.

**OPA:** Your examination of fathers and fatherhood is particularly poignant via their role in the political arena of their society. In *The Dew Breaker*, where the mystery about Haiti still surfaces, it is centered more comfortably on the US mainland and explores what it means to a Haitian living in America. Moreover, the trajectory of your work moves from a rites-of-passage theme to that of being an independent young woman. It can be said that your protagonists, while not autobiographical, are closely aligned to your age. Are you conscious of the correlation?

**ED:** I think you're right. I hadn't thought about it before. I think it possibly has to do with knowing intimately what it's like to be that age and feeling more comfortable writing about someone who's at that same place in her life.

**OPA:** Immigration and migration, physical and psychological displacement, and overwhelming loss are some of the common themes in your work. In fact, it can be said to be the very issue that Haitians have been dealing with since their gallant run for freedom in 1803. Do you consciously set out to write the history of Haiti?

**ED:** I don't consciously set out to do it. I like to write characters that are touched by it, like most Haitians are. History is very present in Haiti. We're always talking about the past because the present is either a recycling of the past or an echo of it or is too painful itself to discuss as much as the victories, or hindsight failures, of the past. You meet even now people who are so nostalgic about the Duvalier dictatorship because things have gotten so bad. The past is always with us. History is, after all, just another story.

**OPA:** And this brings to mind Audre Lorde and her declaration that the personal and political are not separate. Would you say your work is political? Instructive?

**ED:** I hope it's all that, but I think if I set out to write it that way, I would end up writing a tract. That's why I write opinion pieces to purge the preaching from my work. I hope I am first telling an engaging story that then leads people to think and question and possibly act for change.

**OPA:** Your work is certainly creating a space for the so-called "other," which is so welcoming. Thus it was appropriate that you were a special guest at the last ACWWS Conference in 2006. What is your sense of what it means to be Caribbean? Does that feel different or similar to what it means to be Haitian? Do you identify with other Caribbean/West Indian women?

**ED:** Of course, as a person and as a writer I see myself as part of a tradition that strongly includes other Caribbean writers, particularly women. What would be the alternative? I can't say I am an island—forgive the pun—that grew out of the head of Zeus. Of course I belong to a tradition. Of course I identify with other Caribbean/West Indian women. But we're trivializing by generalizing here. What does it mean to say you identify with millions of women who in reality are all over the world and speak different languages? Of course, I am one of them. But how?

**OPA:** Do you belong to any cultural or political groups, and, if so, which ones, and why?

**ED:** I feel like I'm being asked for authenticity credentials here. To see if I am really a worker. Yes, I work with several groups. I work with groups that help people like the Florida Immigrant Advocacy Group. I work with Equality Now, a women's organization in New York. I just worked on a book on women's issues with Legal Momentum, the legal branch of NOW, the National Organization for Women. I just narrated a video for a group called Beyond Borders, which encourages dialogue among people of all levels in Haitian society. I also narrated a film on the mistreatment of children in the sugar industry in the Dominican Republic. I prefer to work with groups that act rather than just make speeches. I write opinion pieces on issues of concern to me and do such work. I also believe writers should be independent and express their opinions freely. They don't have to do any of these things if they don't want to. We're lucky enough to have writers who just write their books. That's a great service to society in itself.

**OPA:** My students, as have other readers, remark that your work is painful, so much about suffering, an unwillingness or inability to let go of the painful memories of the past: for example, the mother cannot forget her rape. As a young and beautiful writer, with a serene face, how do you reconcile with the difficulties that so much of your work explores? How do you keep it at bay from destroying or disrupting your personal life?

**ED:** Jamaica Kincaid has said that if she didn't write she'd be burning down buildings. My work allows me to exorcise my ghosts. I purge the pain from it. The words are my tears on the page. Perhaps I'd be less serene without it. I tend to be melancholy. The work helps me to put that on the page. I lost my father recently and my uncle. The only way I knew to grieve them was to write about them.

**OPA:** And by writing through your grief, you share these men, your fathers, with us. Some critics compare your work to Jamaica Kincaid, who, in many of her works, appears to be fixated on the difficult mother-daughter relationship. How has Kincaid influenced your work?

**ED:** I love her work. I think it's narrow-minded of people to say that she's fixated with mothers and daughters. Have people read her *My Brother* or *Mr. Potter*? Her gardening or travel book?

**OPA:** You have gained national and international success at a very young age. What impact has that had on you? How do you think it has changed your life? How do you deal with your success?

**ED:** Success for me is achieving the goals you've set out for yourself. When I started writing, I really wanted to be a good writer. I feel like I am still working at that. The way to deal with people's glare on you—which is what people often understand success to mean—is to keep working. Most people are actually waiting for you to dry out and fail, so I don't put much stock in that kind of success. Success for me is achieving what you set out to do in your work, daily, one word at a time. And when I have nothing else to say, I'll go to nursing school and become a nurse, which is a really hot profession right now.

**OPA:** Do you have a cadre of writers, your peers that you connect with, share ideas with, show each other work before submitting to a publisher?

**ED:** I have writer friends, but I am really a solitary writer. I don't show anyone unfinished work. Perhaps it's because I was in an MFA program and I saw how people's reactions, sometimes things causally said, can derail your work, so I work alone. I also don't want to have overlap, people's work slipping into mine.

**OPA:** Do you think a writer of your stature has any obligation to mentor others who want to be writers—to serve as inspiration, and so forth?

**ED:** I mentor other writers as much as I can. I have a small child and elderly parents and I teach. Time is scarce, so I have to squeeze in as much as I can, but in terms of mentoring, I work with some individual writers who reach out to me. Some are friends and some are strangers.

**OPA:** Do you ever offer free writing workshops for girls in Haiti or elsewhere?

**ED:** I have done some workshops in Haiti. I did a couple of seminars a few weeks ago in Jacmel. I do some of what are called master classes in high schools now and again, but these days with my daughter being so young, I have been taking on less.

**OPA:** Many writers teach as an occupation. I know you have taught at various universities. What are some of the positives of teaching? The negatives? What do you like about the classroom and/or interacting with students?

**ED:** The positives are that you interact with other writers and you learn as you are trying to come up with things to teach. I learn a lot from the reactions of students to each other's work. The negative is you have less time and mind-space for your own work and sometimes their voices get inside your head and it's harder for you to write.

**OPA:** You are now a mother and wife. How have these roles changed your writing process? How is motherhood affecting your writing, not just in terms of time, but also perhaps in more subtle ways, themes and subjects? Have you noticed any changes?

**ED:** Being a mother, more than being a wife, takes *a lot* of time. I find that I have to be better at planning my time in order to find any space to write. I do less outside now, less traveling, and so forth, so I can be there for my family and still find time to work. I think motherhood adds many layers to my work. My concerns about people, the world in general, are deeper. I now write imagining my daughter reading my books as a college freshman and possibly taking them apart.

**OPA:** What insights have you gleaned from this relatively new role as mother?
**ED:** I am still too sleep-deprived to have learned anything. I find that I have less patience with anyone and anything but my daughter, so I understand the bitchy mothers in novels a lot better.

**OPA:** What are you telling your daughter about what it means to be a girl? To be Haitian or Haitian American?
**ED:** I don't plan to really tell my daughter how to be anything. I'll do my best to be a fun model to watch. Hopefully, we'll travel a lot, read a lot together. I'll try to expose her to as many things, as many aspects of life, as I can. We live in Little Haiti in Miami, so she will learn by walking out of the house what it's like to be Haitian.

**OPA:** What stories do you want to write for your daughter?
**ED:** I tell her a lot of stories that rise out of the moment we're together. I tell her a lot of the stories I was told. Most of them are written down somewhere. I wrote them in a notebook before she was born.

**OPA:** What special mother/daughter or family activity do you engage in?
**ED:** We do a lot of reading. Already she loves books.

**OPA:** What does Danticat like to do when she is not preoccupied with writing?
**ED:** More writing. I have no hobbies.

**OPA:** Really? All the time? Do you begin with pen and paper or directly on the computer?
**ED:** Not all the time, but whenever I have time. I start with pen and paper then move to the computer.

**OPA:** Do you work on several projects simultaneously?
**ED:** I usually do one project at a time, but will stop to write an essay or a shorter piece if I'm working on a long project.

**OPA:** Where in the Caribbean and Africa have your traveled?
**ED:** I've been to Jamaica, Trinidad, the Bahamas, Barbados, Martinique, and Guadeloupe, and South Africa.

**OPA:** Describe briefly your travel to one of these places, your response to the people, the food, and the society.
**ED:** I don't have space to go into every one. But something special brought me to each place and when I got there I found it.

**OPA:** Where in the world do you like to go to be at peace?
**ED:** A place I describe in my book *After the Dance,* a mountaintop retreat in a town called Seguin in Haiti. It's a quiet place, cool at night and hot in the daytime, surrounded by a forest of pine trees, which you'd never expect in Haiti.

**OPA:** Do you plan, at some point, to live in Haiti?
**ED:** I would love to live in the south in Les Cayes, where my husband is from and where my mother-in-law has a house. We've spent Christmas there every year except the last two. No electricity or running water. Just streams and hills and the sweetest neighbors ever. And a state-of-the-art hospital not far away. In my old age, after the kids have moved away, my husband and I might move there.

**OPA**: As a writer very much in the public eye, your readers are curious to know more about your personal life. How challenging is it to keep your private and public life separate?

**ED:** Frankly, I don't think readers are that curious. I did write a memoir and there's more in there than most writers reveal. I've already told too much.

**OPA**: You seem to have a very close-knit family, with intimate relationships with not only your mother and father, but also your brothers. What position do you occupy in the family? What is your relationship with your parents and your siblings?

**ED:** I am the eldest and have three brothers, so I've always been kind of a substitute mom in the family, I suppose.

**OPA**: Can you say what next we can expect to read from you? What projects are you pursuing now?

**ED:** A collection of short stories, then a book-length essay called *Create Dangerously: The Immigrant Writer at Work*, which began as a lecture I delivered at Princeton University as part of the Toni Morrison Lecture series.

**OPA**: Thank you for your time and sharing so freely. Is there anything else you would like readers to know about you or your work that has not been addressed in this or in other interviews?

**ED:** Nope. I think we've covered it all.

# An Interview with Edwidge Danticat

## Rose Marie Berger / 2010

From *Sojourners*, March 2010. Reprinted with permission from *Sojourners*, (800) 714.7474, www.sojo.net.

**Editor's Note:** Edwidge Danticat, author of six books, including *Brother, I'm Dying*, was born in Port-au-Prince, Haiti. She now lives in the US. Danticat engaged in an e-mail interview with *Sojourners* associate editor Rose Marie Berger.

**Rose Marie Berger:** Describe how you heard the news about the earthquake and what happened after that.

**Edwidge Danticat:** I was at the supermarket with my two young daughters and my sister-in-law called and asked if I'd heard that there had been an earthquake in Haiti. I was a bit stunned. "Earthquake?" I said. "Are you sure?" She said it was 7.0. That didn't quite register for me.

Then she said it was catastrophic.

It was dark already, so they were not sure of the damage, she said. I rushed home and parked myself in front of the television, but there wasn't much information coming through. Immediately we started calling every family member in Haiti nonstop. The phones were not working. My brother-in-law came over and he worked the Internet for information while answering calls. Then another friend came over and did the same.

Between calling Haiti, we kept calling other family members in the US and Canada to find out what they had heard, which was nothing at that point. Someone pointed out to me that my friend Richard Morse, a musician in Haiti who runs the Olofson Hotel, was on Twitter giving updates. Even though I'm not on Twitter, I was told how to follow his updates and we did. At some point, he seemed like our only link to the situation.

Then some media people started calling and that night I was on the Anderson Cooper show with Wyclef Jean. At that point I was still numb, because frankly I was assuming the worst. It just seemed so bad from what little was coming through. I was numb and scared and I don't even remember, frankly, what I said there.

I was just thinking of my relatives who don't necessarily live in the most secure or affluent parts of Haiti. I knew they would be very vulnerable to this. Like millions of other Haitians in and outside of Haiti, I was nearly out of my mind with worry.

**RMB:** What are you hearing from contacts in the region?

**ED:** We are talking now exactly two weeks after all this happened. I think everyone has seen the images. The fallen buildings. The dead bodies covered with sheets on the street. The amputees. The orphans.

We have also seen the resilient Haitian spirit. People singing during their worst hours. That's one of the things that Richard Morse first tweeted as night fell on a crushed Port-au-Prince, that people were singing. Now the world is more intimately acquainted with that Haitian spirit than it has ever been in the past. The best of Haiti, I think, has been on display even as the country has suffered and continues to suffer a great deal.

What I hear from the people on the ground is that they are sleeping outside for the most part. Some of them are still hurt or waiting for their wounds to heal. Many are hungry or thirsty. The very young and the very old have a hard time in the food distribution lines. Those who live outside of the capital have still not gotten a lot of aid.

My mother-in-law, who lives outside of Port-au-Prince in a town called Gros Marin, has seen the population of her town double with people who are fleeing Port-au-Prince. Of course, many people have begun to worry about the rainy season, then the hurricane season that are only a few months away. With so many people homeless—the UN now says, a million-plus people— the hurricane season can become another huge catastrophe for Haiti.

**RMB:** What misconceptions are you hearing repeated in news coverage?

**ED:** The news media keeps stressing looting and violence—almost inciting it at times when a news reporter throws himself in a crowd of hungry people who are, of course, eager to get something to eat. We saw it with Katrina. When black people get desperate and some lose their calm, it's seen as the most menacing thing in the world.

Given what everyone has suffered and lost, given the level of desperation that exists and can exist, I think the population in general has acted very dignified. When I speak to my relatives, even those who have homes, but are too afraid to sleep in them, they are saddened and humiliated to have to wait to be given food. They want to buy or earn their own food, but that's the situation some of them find themselves in now after this disaster. Whether they are getting help from the international community or from relatives who themselves might be in a precarious financial situation during these hard times in the United States, they would rather be earning their own way. They don't want to fight for food. They would rather earn it as they had been trying to do before.

**RMB:** What's the most important piece of information that is not making it into the media coverage?

**ED:** I suppose it depends on what you watch. If you watch Amy Goodman of *Democracy Now*, for example, she has the time and inclination to tell a larger story. The history of Haiti, for example, with so-called "donors and debt," the neglect of the countryside. No matter what you feel is missing from one outlet though, you can find in another.

The *Haitian Times*, for example. *Haiti Liberté* and other Haitian newspapers that publish in the United States and have some English articles can give you a different perspective.

In this day and age of the Internet and all other media, I think we have to look for our own information. Don't count on one media outlet to bring everything to you. One of the things I *did* like in the print coverage was the effort made to bring in voices from Haiti. So if you read *Le Point*, you can see essays there by Haitian writers in Haiti writing about what's going on right now. The *New York Times* also had some Haiti-based artists on its opinion pages.

**RMB:** What images/stories/voices from the earthquake are already standing out to you?

**ED:** The stand-out media image for me is of a little boy named Kiki coming out of the rubble with both his hands raised in the air and a mile-wide smile on his face.

I choose to remember that first, but of course there are so many other sad images, of the hands sticking out of the rubble as if reaching towards heaven. The children. The dead children. The orphaned children. The wounded children. As a mother, of course, those images haunt you. That's why Little Kiki was so comforting to see.

The stories that stand out to me are what I mentioned before. For example, of Évelyne Trouillot's essay in the *New York Times*, which ends with her saying that she is busy loving her country. There are so many other voices.

Regine Chassagne in the *Observer*, describing her first reaction to the earthquake. Crying, I think she says, as though everyone she knew had died.

**RMB:** How much of this disaster is "human-made," and how much is natural?
**ED:** I will venture to say that it's a natural disaster that could have happened anywhere else. The fact that this fault line was lying beneath Haiti was not something we could control. However the fact that Port-au-Prince was so crowded and had so many homes built on slopes and certainly not with earthquakes in mind, made this a bigger disaster.

Now why was Port-au-Prince so crowded? Haitian agriculture has been on the decline for years because of policies that favor import. The demise of the Haitian sugar and rice industries, and even livestock—with the United States Department of Agriculture wiping the Haitian pig population that it said had swine fever, which I suppose was a precursor to swine flu—left farmers with no choice but to migrate to Port-au-Prince and try to make a life for themselves in these houses that didn't stand a chance against this earthquake.

**RMB:** What can be done, medium and long term, so that Haiti can become less vulnerable to natural and other disasters?
**ED:** I am not an expert, but I think reforestation is one thing. In the wake of this disaster, you have a lot of people moving back to the countryside. I hope this will mean a renewal for Haitian agriculture, with the international community involved, with Haiti exporting, after the county has fed itself, more than it imports.

I can see now that people might be tempted to build, say, lighter houses. I have a cousin for example, who is rebuilding his house in Léogâne and he says he will build it with wood only, but people were building these cement houses to protect themselves from hurricanes. So in the long run, Haitians will need help in building homes that can be both resistant to hurricanes and now these earthquakes that we are being told might continue to recur now and again.

**RMB:** How have Haitians dealt with these kinds of natural disasters in the past?
**ED:** In the past we have mostly dealt with hurricanes. Two years ago, Haiti had four in a row in just one deadly summer. People rally and start again, because they have no choice. This is a lot more daunting, this earthquake, but people have already shown in the way that they've organized themselves

that they will rally and start again. Think of it, as we are speaking now, two weeks after this earthquake, no one has built a single tent city for the people who lost their homes in the earthquake. They have done it themselves, a lot of them with bed sheets. They are the ones relocating themselves, mostly. Not the international community. Not the government. So Haitians have learned to be very resilient—it almost sounds like a cliché now—because they've had no choice but to be resilient.

**RMB:** How can church folk stand in solidarity with our sisters and brothers in Haiti and the whole region affected by this tragedy?

**ED:** Do not malign them for one thing. It's heart-breaking to see people of faith say things like Haiti made a pact with the devil and that's why Haitians are suffering like they are. That's nonsense and it's heartless.

Haitians are very religious and spiritual people. Whether we are Catholic, Protestant, or Vodou practitioners, we believe in the Gran Mèt, a greater spirit who oversees everything good or bad. People of faith more than anyone else should not be blaming those who suffer for their suffering. Love thy neighbor as thyself is what the scripture says, and in these camps where people are living outside they are truly living up to that creed.

When the financial institutions opened and we were finally able to send help to our relatives, I can't tell you how many of them told us that they were given some food, some water by a neighbor who helped sustain them until they could get their own. How can someone who claims to be a Christian not see it when people are living the Gospel before their eyes? They are living the Apocalypse. They are each living Job. Yet they still manage to love their neighbors. I think that's an extraordinary example for everyone who is willing to open their eyes and hearts to witness it.

# Edwidge Danticat:
# The *Create Dangerously* Interview

## Lloyd "Kam" Williams / 2010

From the African American Literature Book Club (AALBC.com), September 1, 2010. Copyright 2010. Reprinted with permission by Lloyd "Kam" Williams.

Edwidge Danticat was born in Haiti in 1969 and moved to the United States when she was twelve. She is the author of two novels, two collections of stories, two books for young adults, and two nonfiction books, one of which, *Brother, I'm Dying*, was a finalist for the National Book Award and winner of the National Book Critics Circle Award for autobiography. In 2009, she received a MacArthur Genius Fellowship.

Here, Edwidge talks about her latest opus, *Create Dangerously*, a collection of essays based on a series of lectures she delivered at Princeton University last year.

**Kam Williams:** Hi, Edwidge, thanks for the time.
**Edwidge Danticat:** I hope you don't mind that I have my baby daughter with me. Usually, I make some sort of arrangements.

**KW:** No need to apologize. I once interviewed Soledad O'Brien while she was surrounded by her kids in the kitchen, and the children only added to the experience. First, let me say I enjoyed *Create Dangerously* immensely. When did you arrive at an understanding that your aesthetic coincided with that of Albert Camus in his essay of the same name, which served as the inspiration for your book's title?
**ED:** You ask that question in such a very, very serious way. I've always enjoyed the work of Camus, and found it very thought-provoking, especially his novels. But less universally read are his essays which are very beautiful. I read that one when I was in college and starting to think seriously

59

about writing. He always seemed to express more ambivalence than certainty. That's certainly how I feel, that this is all a kind of quest, and that things change in terms of what you're trying to accomplish as you go along. I like the fact that he talks about both sides and the ambivalence of artists.

**KW:** FSU grad Laz Lyles says: I heard a *New Yorker Magazine* podcast that mentioned you and Junot Diaz in tandem as the frontrunner "immigrant" writers. I'd like to know if there are any other writers we should be looking out for who are creating and writing in this tradition.
**ED:** [Laughs] I don't know if it's true that we're at the forefront. I think we are just part of a big and emerging group. Two of the people I'm most actively reading right now are Dinaw Mengestu and Jhumpa Lahiri. Also, Tiphanie Yanique, who wrote an absolutely amazing novella and collection of short stories called *How to Escape from a Leper Colony.*

**KW:** Rudy Lewis says: I have read several of your books and think that you are the finest and most courageous writer living today, on par with the late South African poet Dennis Brutus. Do you think it a waste of energy to protest for the return of President Aristide to Haiti when it is almost certain that the United States, Canada, and France will not allow his return?
**ED:** Rudy is right that it would be very difficult for Aristide to return as a leader because the larger powers won't allow it, but I don't think the people in Haiti who support his return would consider it a waste of energy because he is a citizen of Haiti.

**KW:** Rudy also says: South Africa was a cause célèbre. Why do you think that Haiti has not risen to that level in the African American political imagination, in their churches and other social and political arenas? Is it the problem of language or some other factors?
**ED:** There has long been an ideological and intellectual engagement with Haiti as the first black republic by people like Harry Belafonte, Danny Glover, Randall Robinson, Zora Neale Hurston, Langston Hughes, Katherine Dunham, Frederick Douglass, and Ntozake Shange. And since the earthquake, we've witnessed a very visceral reaction and a new wave of engagement on the part of many African American communities all across the country.

**KW:** Speaking of the earthquake, *Heritage Konpa* publisher Rene Davis wants to know if there's an earthquake relief charity you recommend.

**ED:** There are two. Haitian Women for Haitian Refugees (http://haitian-women.wordpress.com/) has been on the ground since the beginning. The majority of Haitian households are female-headed because of politics and migration. The other is the Lambi Fund of Haiti (http://www.lambifund.org/). Both work primarily in areas outside of Port-au-Prince, which get less aid.

**KW:** Rene also wants to know whether you have any political aspirations in Haiti, à la Wyclef Jean?
**ED:** No, no, no, no, no! The only thing I will ever run for is a bus.

**KW:** Harriet Pakula Teweles says: First of all, I want to say how very much I appreciated *The Dew Breaker*. How has winning a MacArthur Award and being dubbed a genius affected your writing process?
**ED:** It hasn't made it easier, strangely enough. Writing is the same, no matter what else happened with your previous book, because ultimately you have to sit down with a blank page and wrestle with an idea. It hasn't changed that process in terms of the anxiety. Once you're involved in the work, it's really just you and the characters and the words. What does change is that the more you do it, the more practice you have, the less stressful writing is. You know how that is, Kam.

**KW:** Yeah. What did being named an Oprah Book Club selection do for you?
**ED:** It gave me a lot of time. What it did was allow me the time to concentrate on writing so I did not have to do so many other jobs. The greatest gift anyone can give to a writer is time, as you very well know.

**KW:** Attorney Bernadette Beekman says: I am always so incredibly moved by your writing, especially *Krik? Krak!*, *The Farming of Bones*, and *The Dew Breaker*. I see that your new work is once again about life's challenges respecting immigrants. I wonder if one day you will write an extended work which will examine happiness instead of suffering.
**ED:** I think I'm just melancholy by nature, and a lot of that gets into my writing. But on a practical level, I think it's hard to write a book about happiness because fiction requires tension and complication.

**KW:** Bernadette asks: When was the last time you were in Haiti?
**ED:** I was there towards the end of the summer to visit family and to work at a camp called "Li Li Li" (http://www.lililiread.org), which means "Read Read Read."

**KW:** Yale grad Tommy Russell asks: Were you surprised at the outpouring of support after the earthquake? Are things getting better? And what more needs to be done down there?

**ED:** I was surprised at how broad the recovery was. Everyone was doing something. On another level, I probably shouldn't have been surprised because there is something human about the way people react to and identify with suffering. There's a lot more empathy in the world than we perhaps realize. The response to the earthquake proved that. Unfortunately, many of the donations haven't been used, and we still have a million and a half people homeless, plus the recent cholera outbreak shows the vulnerability of the situation. So, I think there needs to be a renewed urgency.

**KW:** Marcia Evans is a person who grew up in the Cambria Heights section of New York City. She asks: Why is this lovely neighborhood never discussed by the media when covering the Haitian community?

**ED:** Marcia's right about that, although since the earthquake there's a reporter from the *New York Times*, Anne Barnard, who's been writing a very extensive series about that particular community in Queens. I think it's hard for an outsider to capture the flavor of a community and all its nuances, so ultimately Haitian Americans need to start sharing intimate accounts of their stories. But, Marcia's right, there are many wonderful stories waiting to be told. We also have to support Haitian American media, like *Heritage Konpa* and the *Haitian Times*, because they not only link Haitian communities to each other, but they are the portals from the Haitian community to the greater community.

**KW:** Is there any question no one ever asks you, that you wish someone would?

**ED:** No.

**KW:** The Tasha Smith question: Are you ever afraid?

**ED:** Yes, I've been afraid a few times, especially now that I have kids. I'm more afraid for them than for myself.

**KW:** The Columbus Short question: Are you happy?

**ED:** Yes, most of the time.

**KW:** The Teri Emerson question: When was the last time you had a good laugh?

**ED:** Just now, with you.

**KW:** What is your guiltiest pleasure?
**ED:** That reality show, *Basketball Wives.*

**KW:** The bookworm, Troy Johnson, question: What was the last book you read?
**ED:** Dinaw Mengestu's new book, *How to Read the Air.*

**KW:** The music maven, Heather Covington, question: What are you listening to on your iPod?
**ED:** *The Suburbs*, the new album from an indie rock group called Arcade Fire.

**KW:** What is your favorite dish to cook?
**ED:** Diri ak djon-djon. It's Haitian rice with mushroom.

**KW:** The Uduak Oduok question: Who is your favorite clothes designer?
**ED:** My mama. She sews.

**KW:** When you look in the mirror, what do you see?
**ED:** A forty-plus-year-old woman.

**KW:** If you could have one wish instantly granted, what would that be for?
**ED:** A true rebuilding of Haiti.

**KW:** The Ling-Ju Yen question: What is your earliest childhood memory?
**ED:** My mother cooking. I think I was about two years old.

**KW:** The Nancy Lovell Question: Why do you love doing what you do?
**ED:** Because it's fun.

**KW:** The Flex Alexander question: How do you get through the tough times?
**ED:** By praying and reading.

**KW:** The Rudy Lewis question: Who's at the top of your hero list?
**ED:** Barack Obama.

**KW:** What has been the biggest obstacle you have had to overcome?
**ED:** That's a tricky one.

**KW:** What advice do you have for anyone who wants to follow in your footsteps?

**ED:** Just do it.

**KW:** The Tavis Smiley questions. First, how introspective are you?

**ED:** You know I have to be very introspective to do the work that I do, so I'll say quite a bit.

**KW:** Finally, how do you want to be remembered? What do you want your legacy to be, and where are you in relation to that at this point in your life?

**ED:** That's funny, because that was also Tavis's last question when I was on his show recently. I have young daughters, and I want my legacy to be more connected to them. I hope to be a good role model for my daughters. I'm only at the beginning of the process, because they're young.

**KW:** Thanks again, Edwidge, and best of luck with the book.

**ED:** Thank you, Kam. It was a lot of fun talking to you.

# Edwidge Danticat Responds to the "Five Questions pour Ile en Ile" (in Creole, English, and French)

## Thomas Spear / 2010

Printed with permission from "5 Questions pour Ile en Ile," filmed in New York by Yves Dossous for Ile en Ile (video available online). Transcription: Coutecheve Lavoie Aupont. Ile en Ile, April 2, 2010.

## Mes influences (in English)

It's not a *written* influence, but storytelling is my first influence. Some people think of storytelling as a cliché, and probably it is a cliché, but it's true. I grew up listening to stories and that's the first I realized I wanted to tell stories in some way: by listening to stories of my grandmothers, my aunts, and from the neighborhood in Haiti where I grew up. Bel Air was very lively, where storytelling was done beyond the structured way that we know; everything became a story. There were also many loud, verbal exchanges that as a child you don't understand—*Voye pwen, Goumen*—with words like agile weapons. That kind of daily storytelling, as well as more structured storytelling, were big literary influences.

The first book I remember was the Madeleine book my uncle gave me when I was very little. I remember reading that and thinking the book was sort of a parallel to storytelling, but was something you could take with you. Every schoolchild in Haiti learns to recite "Le Lièvre et la Tortue" by Jean de La Fontaine; we recite it the way we learn it, in a sing-song manner, which is another kind of storytelling. In school, everything was rote memorization, so you had such words stuck in your mind. You can see dramatically the last words of Toussaint Louverture, "*En me renversant . . .*"

I started to read on my own, I started reading really, ironically, at age twelve when I came to the US. Suddenly I didn't have texts in French to read, so I went and sought them out at the public library. The first was Jan J. Dominique's *Mémoire d'une amnésique*, which I thought was so brilliantly told in an unconventional way; her engaging confrontation, or mixture, of memory—*mémoire*—with writing. Before then, I had never been beyond childhood books for pleasure. Then there were works such as Marie Chauvet's *Amour, colère, folie* and Jacques Roumain's *Gouverneurs de la Rosée* . . . "*Nap mouri, nap mouri*" is an interesting connection: I hear from memory the Creole soundtrack from Roumain's *Gouverneurs de la Rosée* that was re-broadcast occasionally on the radio in Haiti; it had become something like the story of the Passion of Christ they would re-air every year on TV. I could hear that echo of "*Nap mouri, nap mouri*" when reading the novel again, and then later when rereading it in English in the Langston Hughes translation.

In English, the first book I read was Maya Angelou's *I Know Why the Caged Bird Sings*. I read it with a dictionary. I remember it was very interesting to me because it was so glaringly honest and it was a memoir, an autobiography. Once I started reading in English, I became a reading vampire. In college, I majored in French literature; I trace that interest to a French literature teacher I had in Haiti whom I idolized. She would say, "*il n'y a pas de civilisation sans littérature*"; of course, *sans le préciser*, she meant *French* literature. All these things encouraged me to read the French classics, which felt like a part of Haitian literature. At the time, I was moving away from French writers and was reading more American writers, especially African American writers, such as James Baldwin, Toni Morrison, and Alice Walker. Reading them was also a way of better knowing this country.

In college, I wanted to know [classic writers] better, including Haitian writers such as Jacques-Stephen Alexis. I worked on the translation of his novel, *L'Espace d'un Cillement* [*In the Flickering of an Eyelid*]. *Compère Général Soleil* gets so much attention, but *L'Espace d'un Cillement* is a brilliant, nuanced, and layered book, with less of an agenda. It's more of a novel and is a book I greatly love.

## Mon quartier (in English and Kreyol)

*Little Haiti*

I live in the Little Haiti neighborhood of Miami, a very interesting neighborhood. When we first moved there, it was on the cusp of gentrification, with arguments about what the neighborhood was losing and what it was keeping. This gave us a lot of thoughts, coming from New York. My husband, who has lived in Miami longer than I, was coming from Broward, outside of the city. But we wanted to live in a real neighborhood, like the neighborhoods where we grew up in Haiti and Brooklyn, the neighborhood of my later childhood. Little Haiti is fascinating; you sometimes feel as though you are in Haiti: you can look out your window and see a kind of tap-tap going by. Some Haitian artists in Miami have painted their pickups very beautifully; some of the tap-taps belong to the restaurant in Miami Beach called Tap-Tap; others are just *camions* that do the rounds in the neighborhood every morning. If you wake up very early, you will see the *camions* make the rounds to the different corners where they pick up agricultural workers on their way to Apopka or further out to Homestead. Literally, on their sides, you'll see the names of cities (such as Gonaïves and Léogâne) and all the paintings that cover these buses in Haiti. We call them *"Dignités"*; they resemble school buses that have become public transportation. Sights like that make you think you are in Haiti.

Two other things that are not lacking in equal measure in our neighborhood are botanicas and evangelical churches; all along 54th Street—the heart of Little Haiti—there are many. Other things that bring me back to Haiti, the skinny little old ladies walking long stretches, either going to church or to a botanica, or people dressed in white coming from evangelical services or vodou ceremonies. There are some *péristyl* in the area. It's one of the few places people have managed to recreate very strongly and visually a little bit of Haiti. Before the recent economic downturn, people worried that we were losing all of that [Haitian flavor] because the city [with gentrification] was shrinking what was considered Little Haiti. It would be hard in New York to have a Little Haiti, where, rather than a dense concentration of mostly Haitians in the neighborhood, you have mixed Caribbean neighborhoods. In Miami, and Little Haiti, even if other people live in predominately Haitian neighborhoods, as in North Miami where there are [Haitian American] elected officials, there is a strong sense of a neighborhood, and people identify it as such. We like living there.

When we go to Haiti, our five-year-old daughter will say it is "Big Haiti," because we live in "Little Haiti"!

*East Flatbush, Brooklyn*

The other neighborhood that was an important part of my life was the Brooklyn neighborhood where I grew up, East Flatbush. East Flatbush was the first place I lived when I arrived from Haiti, in an apartment in a six-story building on Westbury Court, near Church Avenue and Ocean Parkway. Our building towered over the avenue D train station. After a while you don't hear it, but this train was the constant backdrop to our lives. East Flatbush has also a large Haitian population; you can go the Korean market and buy *tritri*, *andwi*, chicken feet, all things Haitian, really. It's similar to Little Haiti, but in concentrated bits, with ladies who sell cashews or *dyondyon* on street corners, that sort of thing.

*Bèlè (Le Bel Air)*

Bèlè nan tan sa a se te yon katye entèresan tou. Paske li te politize men pa jan li vin ye kounye a. Se te yon kote kite trè entèresan nan sans li te gen anpil atis, atis vizyèl, te gen anpil mizisyen, te genyen kèk gro Tonton Makout tou kite nan Bèlè. Se te yon kote trè entèresan pou timoun, te gen anpil vwazen, te gen perestil, te gen ligliz, kidonk se te yon katye toujou anime. M sonje pa ekszanp vandredi sen, nan peryòd timoun monte sou do kay nan monte kap. Te gen rara, kanaval. Te gen anmenm tan bagay legliz. Te toujou gen radyo k-ap pale fò yon kote. Se te yon katye trè anime, ki te rete konsa, pa trò lontan, li te vin politize, vin gen plis *friksyon*. Men jiskamentnan lè mwen retoune kèk semèn nan moman nap pale la a, ki toujou gen menm karaktè sa. Men si yon ti kras detwi aprè tranbleman de tè a, men ki toujou gen karaktè kwense, moun ap fè sa yo kapab.

## Mon enfance (in Kreyol)

Premye mimwa anfans. Se yon tikras difisil, paske anfans mwen te kase an de paske m te gen yon premye pati kote m te avèk manman m ak papa m. Epi papa m te kite Ayiti lè te gen de zan. Donk m pa twò sonje pati sa a. Mwen jis sonje ke papa-m te la yon jou. Epi sa-m plis sonje nan anfans mwen avèk pati sa a ; se sa moun rakonte-m ke papa te konn sot travay, pote bonbon pou mwen. Men se vrèman yon memwa prete. Epi de de zan a kat tran, m te pase avèk manman-m, avèk frè-m, ke nou te ansanm, ke-m sonje vagman. Men mwen plis sonje dènye pati lè manman-m tap kite Ayiti, ke li te koud bagay twò gran kite pou mwen, pou-m te ka mete aprè. Frè-m ki te maladif. Epi a kat tran manman-m vin kite Ayiti. M te avèk tonton-m ak matant mwen, yo menm ki te nan kay la avèk anpil timoun ke lot paran te kite. Te gen kouzen, te gen lot timoun avèk nou. Chak ane nou te oblije al fè yon foto pou voye bay manman-m ak papa-m. Detanzantan nou te konn al nan Teleco pou-n pale avèk yo nan telefon. Chak lè lekòl pral komanse te gen yon kote nan zòn nou te abite a, kote te gen kodonye pou bay fè soulye pou nou. Al pran mezi pye. Mon nonk mwen te konn fè bòt pou mwen kòm fi menm jan ak sa frè-m ak kouzen-m yo te konn mete. Pat gen anyen de *sexy* nan bòt yo. Se youn nan bagay kounye a ki manke-m lè m-al Ayiti. Ou pa wè kòdonye. Sa mankem vrèman. Avèk bagay pèpè yo, ou pa wè sa ankò, kote te gen tou yon « *art* » sou sa. Kote pou al bay koud, al mezire inifom. M te nan yon lekòl ki te rele Collège Eliode Pierre. Kidonk, yo te gen yon sòt inifòm avèk jip mawon, yon kòsaj a karo mawon e blan. Epi nan pòch la te gen C.E.P. pou Collège Eliode Pierre. Timoun te konn rele nou Cochon Elve nan Pak ! Lòt souvni mwen genyen : manman-m te mete-m lekòl bonè. Li te difisil paske lekòl la te trè di. Te gen bat sou do men paske a twa zan y'ap eseye montre-ou ekri. Sa te trè difisil profesè te toujou ap di : tèt ou di ! Tèt ou di ! Kounye a map panse m gen yon timoun kat tran, lè-m sonje yon timoun twa zan yap fòse aprann yo ekri pase ke sa te trè difisil. Men aprè m te vin vrèman akselere. Yo te konn sote-m klas. A douz zan m te pase sa yo rele sètifika an Ayiti C.E.P. (Certificat d'Études Primaires) donk m te vrèman ap pouse.

Gen yon bagay m te panse nan tout anfans mwen. Se yon bagay m te reyalize aprè manman-m te pati. M te prèske pase tout tan sa a ap panse ke nenpòt jou m ka pati. Donk vrèman ou gen yon sans ke wap tann. W ap pase tout tan anfans ou w atann ke ou pral abite yon lot kote. Se kòm si ou la, men ou pa la. Sa pat afekte-m nan lekòl. Men gen anpil timoun m' konnen kite nan menm kay avè-m. M te gen yon kouzen ki te gen fanmi Kanada ki te nan menm sitiyasyon an men ki pat vrèman fè anyen lekòl. Paske l te toujou panse yon jou konsa l'ap pati. Ane pwochèn m ka pa la, mwa pwochen m ka pati. Se te toujou sa a, menm lè nan kay la lè yap pale avè-ou yo konn di « lè-ou al jwenn manman-ou l'ap regle-ou, papa-ou l'ap regle-ou ». Ou toujou panse ou gen yon vi yon lòt kote. M panse sa s'on aspè nan anfans ki trè empòtan. Timoun toujou ap reve. Men lè ou avèk vrè paran-ou. Menm lè ou avèk manman-ou ak papa-ou ; ou toujou ap reve m ; ou gen dè paran ideyal yon lòt kote. Timoun paran yo pa la toujou ap envante *des attributs* ki petèt lè ou reyini avèk yo ki fè ou vin yon tikras desi paske ou ideyalize yo yon kote, epi aprè lè ou al jwenn yo ou wè se de pèsonaj reyèl. Kounye a wap ideyalize moun kote ou te ye a. Sa a se te yon aspè ki te trè fò nan anfans la. Sa te pran-m anpil tan pou m reyalize ke m te pase tout tan sa a ap imajine lavi-m te yon lòt kote. Donk pat gen pèmanans vrèman nan kote m te ye a. Men nou te gen yon bon strikti, yon bon raprochman avèk tonton-m avèk matant mwen, ki te avèk nou. Epi m te konn anpil timoun nan menm siti-yasyon sa a. Sa se te anfans nou pat santi nou nesesèman abandone. Men nou te santi nou pafwa privilejye. Tan moun te konn ap di nou se privilejye. Nou gen paran isit. Nou gen paran lòt bò. Yo voye lajan lekòl. Yo voye lajan pou manje. Epi tou, te gen aspè sa a ladan-l tout kote ou te *hors de la réalité* ke lòt moun genyen. Epi tou ou gen yon vi ki pral kontinye lè ou pa timoun ankò ki pral kontinye yon lòt kote.

## Mon œuvre (in English)

I am primarily a fiction writer. I started out writing novels and short stories. My first novel, *Breath, Eyes, Memory*, is a story of a young girl who comes from Haiti at age twelve to the United States. My next book was a collection of short stories, *Krik? Krak!*, then I wrote a novel, *The Farming of Bones*, about the massacre of Haitian cane workers in the Dominican Republic. I have also written nonfiction. One is a travel narrative about Jacmel's annual carnival, called *After the Dance: A Walk through Carnival in Jacmel, Haiti*. I also wrote two young adult novels, *Behind the Mountains* and *Anacaona, Golden Flower*, about the life of our Haitian and Dominican icon, Anacaona. I had heard about Anacaona all my life and had always wanted to write about her. She was from Léogâne, as is some of my family (many things in Léogâne are named Anacaona: The Anacaona School, The Anacaona Hospital and so forth). Next, I wrote *The Dew Breaker*, a collection of linked stories. My most recent book was a memoir, *Brother, I'm Dying*, about the death of my father, who died of pulmonary fibrosis within a few months of my uncle, who died in an immigration jail. So it is their story and a bit my story, as all this was happening as my daughter was about to be born.

I am currently wrapping up a collection, called *Create Dangerously: The Immigrant Artist at Work*. The title is from a lecture that Albert Camus gave in the 1950s about engagement in creation. My collection of essays talks about the immigrant artist in a time of crisis in his or her country. The first essay is about the execution of two young men in the 1960s in Haiti, Louis Drouin and Marcel Dumas, and the reaction of many writers to that event. The recent earthquake is the subject of the last essay of the collection. I also have two picture books forthcoming. One is a fun book I am doing with Scholastic as a fund raiser for children's charities in Haiti (especially those that promote reading), called *Eight Days*. It's the story of a little boy who survives eight days under the rubble, and how he uses his imagination to survive. The other picture book is one I have been working on for a long time, about a child whose mother is in immigration detention [and it should be published in 2011].

## La préfacière (in French)

Oui, j'écris des préfaces. Ce sont toujours les livres que je connais, que j'aime, et qui ont vraiment compté pour moi. La plus récente de ces préfaces est pour une collection de nouvelles de Yanick Lahens. Ce sont des auteurs qui ont beaucoup compté pour moi : Marie Chauvet, Jan J. Dominique, Paulette Poujol Oriol, par exemple, comme *L'espace d'un cillement* de Jacques-Stephen Alexis, où j'ai participé à la traduction. C'est un grand plaisir d'introduire ces livres—ces romans et ces nouvelles—aux personnes qui aimeraient bien lire la littérature haïtienne, mais qui ne lisent pas en créole ou en français, qui ne lisent qu'en anglais. Il y a de plus en plus de traductions (Lyonel Trouillot, etc.) . . . Quand j'avais quinze ans, il n'y avait que Dany Laferrière traduit en anglais. La littérature latino-américaine est bien traduite ; pour la littérature haïtienne, cela commence.

Après avoir lu mes livres, des lecteurs me demandent de leur proposer d'autres livres haïtiens pour mieux connaître Haïti. C'est un plaisir d'introduire par mes préfaces les romanciers haïtiens contemporains et classiques.

## L'Insularité (in English)

I think there is less and less insularity, in terms of media that are available, and the new ways people have to directly communicate with their readers. The recent earthquake in Haiti is an interesting example. Whereas before, when you had a tragedy, you had to go through the traditional media to have your story told. Now, with writers who blog for journals in French, who write op-eds directly from Haiti in English . . . I think there is more direct communication and more direct access to readers for writers on *all* islands. If anything, tragic events show us we are engaging each other not only from *île en île*, but also *île* to *métropole*, and *île* and *elsewhere*. A democratization and opening up are perhaps positive sides of globalization. There is less insularity, in terms of being able to connect directly with readers. Whether poets, novelists, essayists, or ordinary people, writers are able to tell their stories, write blogs, and testify to the rest of the world.

Insularity? With traditional publications, perhaps we still have the same obstacles, but I think new media is opening that up. It's like what we're doing [in this recorded interview], it makes us all less insular!

# Edwidge Danticat: In Conversation

## Paul Holdengräber / 2010

From the New York Public Library, November 10, 2010. Reprinted with permission by
Paul Holdengräber and the New York Public Library.

**Paul Holdengräber:** Good evening. My name is Paul Holdengräber, and
I'm the director of LIVE from the New York Public Library. I say this a hundred times. My goal here at the Library is simply to make the lions roar, to
make a heavy institution levitate when I am successful. I will, though, not
say very much tonight. I would rather put you immediately in the presence
of Edwidge Danticat. I would like her to read, which is something we rarely
do. I rarely ask writers to come and read. I usually interview them, or we
have a conversation. But in this particular case I felt it would be powerful as well as necessary for Edwidge Danticat to read, and she will herself
contextualize what she is reading, and after that, we'll have a conversation
together. So here is Edwidge Danticat.

**Edwidge Danticat:** Good evening. I have both the great pleasure and the
mild discomfort of reading about someone who is here tonight, so it will
be interesting. But first I wanted to read a little bit from Camus, "Create
Dangerously," the essay that inspired this book.

It is said that Nietzsche after the break with Lou Salome, in a period of complete
solitude, crushed and uplifted at the same time by the perspective of the huge
work he had to carry on without any help, used to walk at night on the mountains overlooking the gulf of Genoa and light great bonfires of leaves and branches
which he would watch as they burned. I have often dreamed of those fires and
have occasionally imagined certain men and certain works in front of those fires,
as a way of testing men and works. Well, our era is one of those fires whose un-
bearable heat will doubtless reduce many a work to ashes! But as for those which
remain, their metal will be intact, and, looking at them, we shall be able to indulge
without restraint in the supreme joy of the intelligence which we call "admiration."

One may long, as I do, for a gentler flame, a respite, a pause for musing. But perhaps there is no other peace for the artist than that he finds in the heat of combat. "Every wall is a door," Emerson correctly said. Let us not look for the door, and the way out, anywhere but in the wall against which we are living. Instead, let us seek the respite where it is—in the very thick of the battle. For in my opinion, it is there. Great ideas, it has been said, come into the world as gently as doves. Perhaps then, if we listen attentively, we shall hear, amid the uproar of empires and nations, a faint flutter of wings, the gentle stirring of life and hope. Some will say that this hope lies in a nation; others, in a man. I believe rather that it is awakened, revived, nourished by millions of solitary individuals whose deeds and works every day negate frontiers and the crudest implications of history. As a result, there shines forth fleetingly the ever-threatened truth that each and every man, on the foundation of his own sufferings and joy, builds for all.

So now I will read about someone who attempts to build for all. And this essay and the book is called *Create Dangerously*.

On November 12, 1964, in Port-au-Prince, Haiti, a huge crowd gathered to witness an execution. The president of Haiti at that time was the dictator François "Papa Doc" Duvalier, who was seven years into what would be a fifteen-year term. On the day of the execution, he decreed that government offices be closed so that hundreds of state employees could be in the crowd. Schools were shut down, and principals ordered to bring their students. Hundreds of people from outside the capital were bused in to watch.

The two men to be executed were Marcel Numa and Louis Drouin. Marcel Numa was a tall, dark-skinned twenty-one-year-old. He was from a family of coffee planters in a beautiful southern Haitian town called Jérémie, which is often dubbed the "city of poets." Numa had studied engineering at the Bronx Merchant Academy in New York and had worked for an American shipping company.

Louis Drouin was a thirty-one-year-old light-skinned man who was also from Jérémie. He had served in the U.S. army and had studied finance before working for several banks here in New York. Marcel Numa and Louis Drouin had been childhood friends in Jérémie.

The men had remained friends when they'd both moved to New York in the 1950s, after François Duvalier came to power. There they had joined a group called Jeune Haiti, or Young Haiti, and were two of thirteen Haitians who left the United States in 1964 to engage in a guerrilla war that they hoped would eventually topple the dictatorship.

The men of Jeune Haiti spent three months fighting in the hills and mountains of southern Haiti and eventually most of them died in battle. Marcel Numa was captured by members of Duvalier's army while he was shopping for food in an open market, dressed as a peasant. Louis Drouin was wounded in battle and asked his friends to leave him behind in the woods.

"According to our principles I should have committed suicide," Drouin reportedly declared in a final statement at his secret military trial. Chandler and Guerdes (two other Jeune Haiti members) were wounded. Chandler asked his friend to finish him off; Guerdes committed suicide after destroying a case of ammunition and all the documents. "That did not affect me," said Drouin. "I reacted only after the disappearance of Marcel Numa, who had been sent to look for food and for some means of escape by sea. We were very close, and our parents were friends."

After months of attempting to capture the men of Jeune Haiti and after imprisoning and murdering hundreds of their relatives, Papa Doc Duvalier wanted to make a spectacle of Numa and Drouin's deaths.

So on November 12, 1964, two pine poles are erected outside the national cemetery. Radio, print, and television journalists are summoned. Numa and Drouin are dressed in what in an old black-and-white film seems to be the clothes in which they had been captured.

Numa, the taller and thinner of the two, stands erect, in perfect profile, barely leaning against the square piece of wood behind him. Drouin, who wears browline eyeglasses, looks down into the film camera that is taping his final moments.

Time is slightly compressed on the copy of the film I have, and in some places the images skip. There is no sound. A large crowd stretches out far beyond the cement wall behind the bound Numa and Drouin. To the side is a balcony filled with schoolchildren.

A young white priest in a long robe walks out of the crowd with a prayer book in his hands. The priest spends some time with Numa, who bobs his head as the priest speaks. The priest then returns to Drouin and is joined there by two uniformed policemen, who lean in to listen to what the priest is saying to Drouin.

The firing squad, seven helmeted men in khaki military uniforms, then stretch out their hands on either side of their bodies. They touch each other's shoulders to position and space themselves. The police and army move the crowd back, perhaps to keep them from being hit by ricocheted bullets. The members of the firing squad pick up their Springfield rifles, load their ammunition, then place their weapons on their shoulders. Off screen someone probably shouts, "Fire!" and they do. Numa and Drouin's heads slump sideways at the same time, showing that the shots have hit home.

Drouin's glasses fall to the ground, pieces of blood and brain matter clouding the cracked lenses.

On November 12, 1964, after Marcel Numa and Louis Drouin's bodies were carried away, some say to the national palace to be personally inspected by Francois Papa Doc Duvalier, a lanky thirteen-year-old boy who had been standing in the back of the crowd to avoid the thunderous sounds of the executioners' guns, stepped forward as the spectators and soldiers scattered. He walked toward the bullet-ridden poles, bent down in the blood-soaked earth, and picked up the eyeglasses that Louis Drouin had been wearing. The young man, the photojournalist Daniel Morel, only momentarily held the eyeglasses in his hands before they were snatched away by another boy, but in the moment he had them, he'd noticed tiny chunks of Drouin's brains splattered on the cracked lenses.

Perhaps if he had kept them, he might have cleaned the lenses and raised them to his face, to try to see the world the way it might have been reflected in a dead man's eyes. Sometimes in Haiti, the eyes of murder victims are gouged out by their murderers because it is believed that even after death, the last image a person sees remains imprinted in his or her cornea, as clearly as a photograph.

Before witnessing the execution of Marcel Numa and Louis Drouin, Daniel Morel was not particularly interested in dead men's eyes. He had been like any other boy, going for long walks all over Port-au-Prince and playing soccer with his friends. He sometimes worked in his father's bakery and tried to climb aboard Haiti's commercial train, which brought sugarcane stalks from the southern fields of Léogâne to the sugar-making plant in Port-au-Prince. But the execution changed everything.

The next day, Daniel walked by a photographer's studio near his father's bakery in downtown Port-au-Prince, and on the open paneled doors were enlarged photographs of Marcel Numa and Louis Drouin's corpses, purposely put on display as deterrent for the country's potential dissenters. These pictures were exhibited there and elsewhere for weeks, and young Daniel Morel would walk past them, and even though he had been at the execution, he saw them each day as if for the first time and was unable to look away.

"Photography is an elegiac art," the novelist and essayist Susan Sontag writes in *On Photography*. "All photographs are memento mori." That is, they remind us that sooner or later the subject will no longer exist.

"To take a photograph," Sontag continues, "is to participate in another person's (or thing's) mortality, vulnerability, and mutability." "Photography has something to do with resurrection," Roland Barthes wrote. "Might we not say of it what the Byzantines said of the image of Christ which impregnated St. Veronica's napkin: that it was not made by the hand of man, *acheiropoietos*?"

"I never intended to become a photojournalist," Daniel Morel tells me more than once in the time that we have known each other. "I became a photojournalist because at Numa and Drouin's execution, I felt afraid, and I never wanted to feel afraid again. I take pictures so I am never afraid of anyone or anything. When I take pictures, I feel like something is shielding me, like the camera is protecting me."

Did he, as a boy, want to protect Numa and Drouin?, I ask.

He could not protect them, he said, but over the years he felt as though he had managed to protect other Numas and other Drouins with his photographs. And he makes me even more certain that to create dangerously is to create fearlessly, boldly embracing the public and private horrors that would silence us, then bravely moving forward even when it feels as though we are chasing ghosts or being chased by ghosts, even when it seems as though we full-heartedly believe in *acheiropoietos.*

Thank you.

**Holdengräber:** Edwidge, it's really a great pleasure to have you here tonight. We now know or at least in your rendition we know why Daniel Morel became a photographer. He became a photographer because of an extreme situation in some way that called and beckoned him. Do you feel there's a parallel between his urgency to capture a moment in time and archive it in some way and make it live and make it continue to live and resurrect it and your own work, your own need perhaps, urgency, to become a writer and to create dangerously?

**Danticat:** First up, I just want to say it's a great pleasure. When I kept telling people that I was coming to be interviewed by you they were saying things like, "He rocks," and—

**Holdengräber:** Well, I am interviewing Jay-Z next week.
**Danticat:** You are so cool.

**Holdengräber:** And I actually think in some way this interview is a very good prelude.
**Danticat:** Okay. Can you tell Jay-Z that?

**Holdengräber:** I will, I promise you.
**Danticat:** So thank you for having me and I also want to acknowledge Daniel, who is here. I told him I was going to embarrass him. So—

**Holdengräber:** I must say that chapter—that Chapter 11 of *Create Dangerously* on Daniel Morel is perhaps one of the most extraordinary

essays I've read in a long time actually. It leaves you virtually speechless, but let's continue, because we have a lot to talk about, so I cannot be speechless.
**Danticat:** I don't think that's going to happen with you.

**Holdengräber:** Actually, Edwidge said, "I'll be fine as long as you don't bring up some obscure Camus quotation, or if you do, read it twice so that we know what you're saying."
**Danticat:** I think what I had always been so curious about—how people come to their art, and because I always felt in a way—I grew up in this family with a lot of storytellers with a lot of stories, some of them good, some of them bad, but it was always something that fascinated me, if one is able to even trace, I mean, there's this whole mystery of art, and I remember having this fascination myself with these two men who had lived here and then went back and just lost everything, you know, just really, literally lost everything, and they had lost family members, which had driven them out of Haiti, and then they had gone back to kind of save us all, and the story was for me epic and amazing, and I had never met someone who had this similar connection to it, and when Daniel and I talked about it, it was like, wow, and it was amazing that how, his being able to trace what he does to that moment, and I think we all have—sometimes you feel you have a compulsion to do something, but you don't know where it comes from, and it doesn't need to be the quest of your entire oeuvre, but it becomes the—you have a couple of images that reoccur again and that might have something to do with sort of what you're trying to arrive at in the creation of your art.

**Holdengräber:** And let's pursue that. What are those images for you? I know it's a very difficult question to ask of anybody and to ask of writers in particular, namely where it all started. In your case, you spent the first twelve years in Haiti—is that correct?—and then you came to the United States. Where did the urgency to write come from? What were those first obsessive images? You were mentioning Roland Barthes and he quite beautifully talks about creating an organized web of obsessions. What was your organized web of obsessions early on?
**Danticat:** Well, on some level, I feel like that's always changing, you know, these obsessions, and maybe they're sort of different formulations of the same obsession, which is—I think it has a lot to do with separation, silence because for a lot of us, when you were kids growing up in a dictatorship, for example, and my time overlapped, some father, some son, the father and son Duvaliers, and there's always sort of this code of silence of things that

couldn't slip, so I'm intrigued by silence, silence that's forced by outside and circumstances, but also I grew up with an uncle who had had throat surgery and who maneuvered around silence. He was a minister who couldn't speak. So, sort of the contradiction of that, so silence, I think separation is how families reformulate themselves, and violence, I think this type of violence, too, and how, on some level, certain people are victims, if you will, of it, or taken up in it or sacrificed in it, but this notion how others who could escape, orphan themselves—and I think that's why this image of this execution is such a reoccurring puzzle for me.

**Holdengräber:** What struck you at first when you read Camus's essay, misnamed, as I mentioned to you, "Create Dangerously"? It's an editor's choice, a translator chose to call it "Create Dangerously," which then became a very good title for your own book.
**Danticat:** Lucky for me.

**Holdengräber:** Lucky for you that an editor made this choice, because in French this lecture he gave in Sweden in 1957 was simply called "The Artist and His Time." What was anchoring for you in this essay?
**Danticat:** Well, there were several things. One of the things that he talks about in this essay and that reoccurs in some of the other essays, is that he says "*l'artiste ne meprise* rien," this sense that—and I think it's hardest to translate *meprise* in English—so like, not ignore—this thing of—

**Holdengräber:** Denigrate?
**Danticat:** Yeah, but denigrate, maybe it's like one aspect, but it's the sense of—

**Holdengräber:** Devalue. Devalue because *mepriser* means to give a bad price to, to devalue.
**Danticat:** To devalue, exactly. And I think part of what was intriguing, too, is that I think coming—and when we're talking about this issue of literacy or people who read and it's a privilege in a way if you come from a place where most people don't generally have—not everybody has access to an education. The sense also of how a large number of people are devalued, whether socially, culturally, financially, and that's one element of it, but also this ambivalence of—this wrestling with the place—this issue of the place of art, and he talks about the sense of artists—you're in trouble if you're silent. People get mad if you're silent, people get mad if you speak. It's this place where you end, and I think he had sort of—he seemed to have had more

than Sartre or the others, more ambivalence, and you felt like there was a sense of all these essays about art, his sense of trying to understand a little bit what he was doing, and that appealed greatly to me because I often felt, especially when I was starting, that this wasn't even—this is not—it's not my birthright in a way. I think that people who grew up in a certain way, come from a certain place, you feel like—

**Holdengräber:** What is not your birthright?
**Danticat:** Talking to you here at the Public Library, you know, all of it, and it feels almost like an accident. I often say it's like an accident of literacy. You know the fact that—

**Holdengräber:** You have that very sentence in the book. It's very haunting.
**Danticat:** It feels as though then this constant exploration of what it means and what you should use it for and all that is sort of this constant question.

**Holdengräber:** It's so interesting you say this, because for me—for you it isn't a birthright to be here, you seem to feel at least briefly, on this stage at the library. For me, I'm thinking, my goodness, on Monday I'm interviewing Jay-Z. What does this white kid with, you know, Mitteleuropa parents from Vienna know about hip-hop? It's the exact inverse in some very strange way, and I'm learning about hip-hop because I have an eight-year-old boy who's teaching me about the world that he inhabits now. And so in some way what fascinates me about this is that through different forms of reading—and I'd like to anchor our conversation to some extent on the importance of reading because in some way your book, I keep referring to it as if it were here, but it's in my hand actually, *Create Dangerously*, is an elegy in the power and the glory of reading in some way for an island where, I think you quote a number of less than half people are able to read. More than half of the population is illiterate, and in—or not able to read, read in different ways, but not able to read books. So I'm wondering for you if this possibility made you feel like a true outsider.
**Danticat:** I think after you interview Jay-Z you'll become an accident of hip-hop. What's also fascinating—because in the book I also talk about many of our writers and it's extraordinary the number that we have, you know, given all the difficulties and given the circumstances. And I don't think it—it doesn't feel necessarily—part of one of the clichés of the immigrant dilemma is that if the kids get super-educated and they're alienated from their community, I've never felt that thing, and though I live in a different country even from many of my family members and so forth, so I've felt—I mean I feel

the privilege of this back and forth, but there is this feeling of—people often think with me it's language because I write in English, but I think there is a feeling that all people who write, for example, must feel this sense that a lot of people won't be—a lot of people dear to you, you know, in my case, even in my family, won't be able to participate in the story this particular way.

But it's one of the constants of it, it's sort of one of the many pillars in the room as you're writing, and I guess part of this effort at creation is that to do it despite all these things, which some of the writers I mention in the book, too, a lot of them have been able to do—and their voice in a way.

There's a writer like Jacques Roumain, who wrote a book called *Masters of the Dew*, and it's interesting this whole journey that *Masters of the Dew* traveled, because it's a novel set in the Haitian countryside by Jacques Roumain, a Haitian writer who was not from the countryside, and then Langston Hughes translated it into English, and then it was made into this radio play that aired on Radio Haiti, and people in the countryside then heard it, and it was as if this voice that had traveled through this writer had gone back, and they could recognize it and people named themselves—they named their children after the characters in the novel, which is I think the height of—it's probably the greatest honor any writer can have. So there are these possibilities—I mean there are these bridges.

**Holdengräber:** There are these possibilities and in some way I'm wondering whether the writer, the figure of the writer, in Haiti doesn't have great credence and is respected in some form or fashion, is viewed as an important presence.

**Danticat:** Absolutely, but interesting, much more interesting to me, too, has always been the figure of the reader and, you know, my dad used to tell stories about young men, and maybe he was talking about himself, I don't know, who would go around trying to seduce young women by going around carrying a book under their arm. It was kind of sexy to be a *philosophe*, you know, and so this whole appeal of—

**Holdengräber:** Did he ever mention which book?
**Danticat:** Would you like—

**Holdengräber:** No, I mean, certainly there was a time in my life where I would carry around Kierkegaard, *The Diary of the Seducer*, that was a very good one.
**Danticat:** No, he never, he didn't mention. I don't think it worked that well for him. But we do have all these—I just remember even in my time in Haiti

like people who—like true sophistication was—like people would say, you know, "*comme dit l'auteur*," as the author said, and it didn't matter who the author was, you know, and the quote would come out and then you knew they were learned, so it was this whole notion of the appeal of the reader. I mean, the writer, too, because there were some—we had some sort of giant figures in the literature like Jacques Roumain, and even some like Félix Morisseau-Leroy, who walked among us—he was with us in Miami, for example, until he died, and people would sort of revere that presence. But there was also a kind of reverence, I find, for readers and for reading.

**Holdengräber:** And in *Create Dangerously* you spend some pages on the reader and even the title of the book, the way you interpret Camus's lecture is also not only the notion of creating dangerously but reading dangerously, exposing yourself, as Morel did, to some ugly parts of the world, and in some way by photographing them and by writing about the ugliness you speak truth to power and I was—when reading those passages I was reminded of this line which I'd like to read to you and have you react to, since you do mention a lot of European writers and some American writers—you mention Ralph Waldo Emerson and you mention Ralph Waldo Ellison—I like that. But there's a line that struck as perhaps working very well with your work, and I wonder if you know it. It's a line by Kafka where he says, "if the book we are reading does not wake us as with a fist hammering on our skulls, then why do we read it? Good God, we also would be happy if we had no books and such books that make us happy we could if we need be write ourselves." What we must have are those books, and I would say that to some extent you've offered us that book that Kafka is describing is this book. "What we must have are those books that come on us like ill fortune, like the death of one we love better than ourselves, like suicide. A book must be an ice ax to break the sea frozen inside us."
**Danticat:** That's fantastic. I mean, I think we all know when we've read those types of books because we mourn them, we sort of wonder, you know, when you emerge from that book, and you're just like, when will I ever read again. We're sort of book orphans, after you read those books that mean that to you.

**Holdengräber:** But did you try to do—that—Dany Laferrière—I'm sorry—
**Danticat:** I didn't try to do that. I took hammers to my head at times—

**Holdengräber:** But what I mean to say actually, Edwidge, quite seriously, is that the chapter 11 I mentioned and the way you describe real pain and real suffering seems to me to have an urgency of trying to do what Sontag talks about when she talks about photography, trying also to reawaken, to untarnish the wound and show it clearly and actually make us shiver.

**Danticat:** No, I always feel—and it goes back to this issue of accidents of literacy. I always feel the weight and my pleasure of having that experience of completely being lost, being lost in something and I think sometimes it goes both for reading and for writing, you know, when you feel so lucky when you're writing where you're completely lost in it. But one experience—Dany Laferrière, a Haitian Canadian writer, he talks often about this experience of the reader, of a reader who repatriates the writers, because he says, you know, he says when he wrote a novel called *Je suis un écrivain japonais*, "I'm a Japanese Writer," saying that if I'm read by a Japanese reader, I become a Japanese writer, but he uses his own case of having these passionate reading experiences that I think sometimes are most heartfelt perhaps in adolescence, you know, because you're not expecting to have such a sort of passionate love affair with a book. And he talks about, well he says, these writers of course they were repatriated, you know, Whitman, Cervantes—has a whole list—otherwise, what were they doing in my room? They were living with me under the blanket with a pillow. And he sort of challenges this notion of immigrant writing. He's saying, is there such a thing as an immigrant reader, and so—I think every reader knows, you know when you're having that experience of—you don't want your—you're savoring every word, and I think one hopes to do that for a reader as a writer, which is probably where for a lot of writers, the reader and the writer overlap a lot.

**Holdengräber:** You state in your book that when the pain is too great you go from writing to reading. Reading becomes a shield. Reading becomes a refuge.

**Danticat:** For me they've always been together in the sense that if you felt—there's a Maya Deren quote that's the epigraph for the book where the revelation of that first creation, I think for a lot of writers that is tied to reading, to this amazing experience of feeling that hammer and then taking it, perhaps full-heartedly or foolhardily to that next step and saying, "oh I want to do that," and realizing too that it's not as easy, but I think that if you have that great passion, the cherished passion for reading, you're always aiming to create for others that sensation, you know, that urgent sensation that you feel yourself when you're immersed in something you really love.

**Holdengräber:** Explain to me the subtitle of your book, which is "The Immigrant Artist at Work."

**Danticat:** Well, the other Camus piece that sort of overshadows this book is a short story *"Jonas, ou l'artiste au travail"* (Jonas, or the Artist at Work) and it's a fascinating short story. People often criticize Camus for being a great writer but not a good storyteller and that he sort of resolves conflicts too easily. But I think in the short stories, they tend to be so epic, and this one is about this painter, who suddenly starts having some success and then his house gets bigger, and everyone wants to have lunch with him and slowly the work gets, you know, it gets more pushed aside, but it's sort of a slow progression. He starts having more children and all this, and it's— and I thought if you can imagine it's an essayist's inclination maybe that he shows in actually subtitling this thing *l'artiste au travail*, showing this, so that's taken from that, *"Jonas, ou l'artiste au travail,"* and I've had since then a feeling that the subtitle is so wrong because it implies something bigger than it is, and it was meant to be maybe one immigrant artist at work, but there were so many, a few that I profiled, so the proper title, or subtitle might have been, "The Immigrant Artist, Maybe Haitian, Maybe Not Haitian, Sometimes at Works, Sometimes Not," but that was too long for the front of the book.

**Holdengräber:** When you say maybe Haitian, maybe not Haitian, what do you mean?

**Danticat:** Well, the immigrant artists I talk about, some are Haitian, some are not, particularly there's another fascinating artist for me, Michael Richards, who is a sculptor, who was sort of a sculptor of flight, you know, everything he did was flight-related. And he did these sculptures of his own body pierced by airplanes and people falling out of the sky, and he, it turns out, ends up dying on 9/11 in the World Trade Center—they used to do these offices for artists, you know, they had an empty space, they would give it to an artist, and he was there that day and his whole work when you look back on it almost seems prophetic, almost like, you know, you wonder if he was what you called double-sighted, like, was he clairvoyant, did he sort of have this sense that he was going to die, and so he's in there, and he's not Haitian. And James Baldwin is kind of there in that essay called "Another Country," which doesn't mention him, but that nod, it's sort of, you give a fiction writer this format and they just cram everything in, because we feel like we'll never have this chance again, so everybody's in this.

**Holdengräber:** Let's talk a little bit about the format, but then I want to talk to you about what you do when the world is on fire. The format interests me because so often it's the case that essayists aspire to the condition of novelists. A very good example, I think, might be Susan Sontag, who tried her hand with degrees of success that remain to be ascertained in the novelistic form. In your case, you have gone from the novelistic form to this essay form, and I'm wondering what you are flirting with here when you try your hand at the essay, what the essay affords you that you might not be able to do when you write novels or short stories.

**Danticat:** I have been writing over the years some essays while I was writing fiction, and it forced me in a way to be declarative if you will about certain things, even as I was forming my own feelings about things.

**Holdengräber:** Did that make you feel uncomfortable?

**Danticat:** Yeah, yeah. There's such a—fiction, too, but I felt that there were many ways—and this type of essay, it's even like the French *essai*, it's almost like you can be—

**Holdengräber:** An attempt.

**Danticat:** An attempt, exactly.

**Holdengräber:** And you know the word *essai* both means an attempt, a trial, but it also comes from the word *assay*, which means to weigh. So to—

**Danticat:** Exactly. Exactly. But—it gives this opportunity to sort of explore something that you're thinking in this way and to sort of play with this journalistic element, and there are truly things that I feel would be hard to do in fiction.

**Holdengräber:** Such as?

**Danticat:** Like, this piece about Daniel, like if you had this character who had this epiphany, it's too easy in fiction in a way, you know, and there's the thing too that in this essay "The Artist in His Time," which I've been calling "Create Dangerously," but this where Camus talks about this too, sort of the ambivalence of things, and just coming, just trying to find a subject in your own mind, and I prefer—that goes to this term of essay, this essay that's a kind of search, you know, and sort of trying, an attempt at trying to come to a conclusion, and knowing that it's not definitive, but it's saying, "this is what I see, this is how I see it," and not that you should see it the same way, but it's this moment, this moment, and there's so much to delve into from places—things to connect in a way that life helps you to and sometimes there's some marvelous connections that occur all by themselves that are amazing in nonfiction when they come together, they feel sort of like a revelation that you don't make happen as you do in fiction, but that the universe is collaborating on with you.

**Holdengräber:** I mentioned that I would get to this point, which is the title of an extraordinary novel by the Portuguese writer António Lobo Antunes, *What Do You Do When the World Is on Fire?* And in part you describe in your first chapter what the recourse of literature was when the world was on fire. Haitians would perform a play by Camus, again, called *Caligula*, and I'm wondering whether you could in some way explain or express what recourse literature offered in moments of extreme terror and pain.
**Danticat:** One of the things that I was also looking into that would ask family members in the place where I grew up in a neighborhood—

**Holdengräber:** Bel Air.
**Danticat:** Bel Air. And there was a *centre d'etude*, a center there where people went to study and my uncle talked for years about sort of the plays that the young people put on there and one of them was I believe *Caligula* based on how they described.

**Holdengräber:** You were not sure.
**Danticat:** I was not sure. I was not sure, and I didn't want to say I was sure and then somebody would come and say you lie like a rug on the floor, from what they were saying, by the time that I could belabor it they were gone, but another play that they put on was a Haitian-written version of *Antigone* by Félix Morisseau-Leroy. It was particularly poignant at this time and there was also Numa, Marcel Numa had a writer uncle, Nono Numa who had redone *Le Cid* in a Haitian setting, and they did this for example, *Antigone*, if you do *Antigone* at a time when people can't pick up dead bodies on the street it is—it seems so far removed, it goes back so far to the Greeks that it gives these—that was part of their creating dangerously, because it gave them a sort of veil of credible deniability, which a lot of Haitian political art has, a lot of the music, the protest music, at difficult times when people could say I'm singing about a leaf, or this is a play about somebody in a time that has nothing to do with us. But if you look at the *Caligula* of Camus, or if you look at the *Antigone* of Félix Morisseau-Leroy there are certainly parallels, and the people it's meant for recognized them but it was this other way of creating without completely risking your life.

**Holdengräber:** The book is dedicated, the first line is, "two hundred thousand and more."

**Danticat:** Well, I was there borrowing from Toni Morrison, who actually—the book comes as a result of a series of lectures that they do at Princeton in Toni Morrison's name and I had the honor of doing the second of the lectures, which was the first essay.

**Holdengräber:** She mentioned you on this stage with Angela Davis two weeks ago.

**Danticat:** Wow. I can die now. If not for my small children. She's actually shown extraordinary kindness.

**Holdengräber:** But just don't.

**Danticat:** I think in one of the epigraphs to *Beloved* is the sixty million, it was sort of a reference to that, but I had been working on the book before, the book started really in 2008 after I did the lecture, but we were about, was about to—we were really far along in it when the earthquake happened, and I thought it was a way of acknowledging that, but the strange thing was sort of the Maya Deren quote, which was part of the book long before, where she talks about remembering, you know, memory and memoriam and sort of resisting this idea of constant in memoriam, but also going along with that a kind of celebration and that's partly what I wanted this to be, like an elegy but also a celebration of what remains of all those wonderful things that we have left.

**Holdengräber:** I'm always struck in the English language by the strength of the word "remembering," because it really means literally to put the members back together, and one of the haunting images I think in your book which comes back as an obsession is our place of burial, and I think is it your aunt who passed away I think not very long ago but who was unwilling to move from her locale because she had built a mausoleum to her daughter and wanted to be buried there, and you describe the two- or three-day journey you took in the mountains to get to her. Why this obsession and one could say interest in the very place of burial, as you are indeed very interested in Numa and Drouin's place where they were shot?

**Danticat:** Well, I think because it's so—it's one of those things. I mean I think probably for a lot of families, you know, after the earthquake of all the sad things, one of the sad things was that for a lot of people there, that there is no particular place of burial. Where you're buried is so crucial. My aunt Ilyana was the one person in our family who never—she didn't go through those layers of migration that people go through first to the countryside then to the city, she just stayed where my father's ancestral village was, and to go see her, it's like a two-day trek and I remember just bathing in nostalgia when I got there. I said to her, I immediately declared, I want to be buried here, this is where I want to be buried. And, you know, she was a very funny woman, she looked at me and she said, "Did you not climb for two days, who's going to carry a corpse this long?" And I said, "okay," I said, "I'll shift the plan, I'll be cremated," and she said, "No, we have enough dust in Haiti, you don't need to act." She was still—we had—my great-grandparent's graves are there, and I was thrilled to see it, but she had built for her daughter who had died young a kind of mausoleum right behind the house, and that's where she wanted to be buried, and it's not very unusual to go in many places in the Haitian countryside where you see a very elaborate tombstone and a very modest house, and sometimes the burial place is much more beautifully painted, much fancier than the house, which gives you a sense of what it means to your place of burial. I often you know, stretch it maybe and go—I think sometimes—we're like the ancient Egyptians in a way, we're sort of this constant fascination with death, but not even fascination, but perhaps this understanding that death goes along with life.

**Holdengräber:** In other words it is not morbid.

**Danticat:** It is not—on a mass, catastrophic scale, of course, but in an individual sort of spiritual way it's this continuation, and what was fascinating to me is that when I was staying there in the mountains with my aunt, she would have conversations with her daughter—the night we were there she would say, you know, "Edwidge is here, she's Mira's daughter," and it was still like—

**Holdengräber:** She wasn't quite sure who you were, also, she didn't quite know if you were the writer.

**Danticat:** Yeah, she called me a *journaliste*, which is probably the highest kind of writer of her experience, and it was sort of an honorable title.

**Holdengräber:** Not everybody gets, though, a mausoleum or a tomb. In the last chapter, which appeared first in the pages of the *New Yorker*, you describe Maxo's death and finding his remains and finding his date of birth and death on a makeshift tomb. Is it still there that way?

**Danticat:** It still is there. My cousin Maxo who actually I wrote about in *Brother, I'm Dying*, a memoir that I'd written previously to this book, died in the earthquake. And the interesting thing was that he has a maternal cousin—he's my cousin on my father's side—who sort of stood vigil at the site and was able with cooperation from a lot of people in the neighborhood, to save Maxo's wife and three of his kids, but one perished with Maxo, and she kept saying, you know, before we could get there, she kept saying, "I want to make sure that when you guys, when you come back, that there will be a place to visit, that you will be able to pay your respects someplace," and it was very important to her and I had imagined because Maxo was sort of a freewheeling person, I'd imagine this not being as important to him as it was for this cousin, and finally when they did find him, and this happened with a lot of families, they couldn't—he wasn't taken out of that, so he was just basically where they dug a hole and he was buried there. But they went, which I found so extremely loving, which you see in all the also different manifestations all different places, is that they had cemented, and then they had put the date of his birth and the date of his death, and when you look at the date of his death to realize that your individual person shares this date of death with so many people, so that if you had a visible cemetery that all these lives were suspended on that one particular day, and that filled me the most standing there, in that you see the very singular date of his birth, and then you see this other date that is shared with so many people.

**Holdengräber:** You say in the book that someone, maybe you had made the comment that there were not plaques around everywhere, there can't be plaques around everywhere, because the whole cities would be covered with plaques of the dead.

**Danticat:** Well, actually, this was—when I would talk to a lot of people about Numa and Drouin, this execution, and as I would about other things, sort of memorial, and maybe it's from living here too long and going to a place like Washington, DC, where you turn around and everyplace is a memorial, and I would say—about a massacre of Haitian caneworkers in the Dominican Republic in 1937 and I would go to that river and I would say to myself, "well, why isn't there a plaque here?" And so I used to say this about the cemetery where Numa and Drouin had been executed and actually right before the earthquake, when Daniel was in Haiti, and I said to him, Daniel, before the book goes to press, take some pictures for me, I just want to make sure at that place that there is still no plaque before I say there is no plaque. And I was saying this to someone, not Daniel, another person, before the earthquake, and the person said, enough with your plaques, because if we were doing plaques there would be plaques all over the city, and then I had disengaged this notion of constant memorial, but this forces the situation where—and I felt it standing there over Maxo's grave—is that we are the plaques, it's like you have to kind of be the people who are family members, the friends, you have to be like the living memorial for these people, a lot of them who have no other—there is no possible that they're remembered except through this memory. And I had sensed this many, many years with Numa and Drouin before when I was thinking about this other kind of remembrance, and how do they live and this memory of how they transformed a young boy's life, and so now this is true for—in a much larger sense, and that we are all walking around, we're like sort of these—the mausoleums behind the house of these people—many of them have no trace.

**Holdengräber:** So writing is a form of haunting in some way.
**Danticat:** Among other things. I mean, it's—I sometimes feel privileged that I have this way of doing it—

**Holdengräber:** Do you sometimes feel that you have the burden of being a spokesperson for Haiti?
**Danticat:** Not a burden. I sometimes joke that I do PR for Haiti and it's a privilege and because I love to share this other part of Haiti that I know, this other—these writers, these creators, this art—I love to share that.

**Holdengräber:** That's the sunny part.
**Danticat:** That is the sunny part. The other part, there's no burden in it beyond the burden I think of any other artist with a story that you feel like is weaved into your soul.

**Holdengräber:** You know, Edwidge, and you encouraged me to say this tonight so I will. Haiti has been part of my life for as long as I remember. My parents—it's an unknown, a very unknown story, maybe someday I'll be able to write it. My parents fled Vienna in 1938 and '39 and spent the war years in Haiti. There were a hundred and seven Jewish families in Haiti. My father, who was a medical student, became a farmer in Haiti, growing vegetables that hadn't been grown before and which now still exist there, certain kinds of cauliflower, so that when we went to the markets of Kenscoff and Toujours and other places, he would show me these vegetables and say, this is my legacy.
**Danticat:** Broccoli.

**Holdengräber:** Yeah, broccoli. And so my father whose name is Kurt, some people still remember him, Monsieur Kurt, you know, he is now ninety-two years old, and just this morning when I was mentioning to him and to my mother that we were talking, they of course were sending you very warm regards and my mother said, it is such a different life, because we fled Vienna to find refuge in Haiti. And my mother started her love of literature by reading books that a man whose name I should mention, my mother and I'm wondering if this person, André Laraque, a man named André Laraque, whose I think brother became an ambassador would give my mother, she was thirteen years old, books to read, and so her discovery of literature happened on your island at the age when she arrived in Haiti, the age at which you left Haiti for America.

**Danticat:** Yeah, and how extraordinary—that—you know, do we ever think of Haiti as a place of refuge, how extraordinary is that? I feel like it's something wonderful to share. And Paul Laraque was an extraordinary poet, who I think was the brother of your mother's Laraque. It's phenomenal.

**Holdengräber:** The sunny side of Haiti, though, is something that you also try to bring forward by quoting and encouraging some of your readers to discover some of these writers who are fairly unknown in this country but who you discovered yourself by going to the Brooklyn Public Library, so when you were twelve or thirteen years old, you discovered a shelf at the Brooklyn Public Library. Tell us something about that discovery, particularly since we are here in another one of those libraries.

**Danticat:** In the library. You know, libraries have always felt like, almost like church to me and I would go to that particular branch—they just started having this section "*la vie haïtien.*" And I had not, I mean, it's ironic, I wasn't taught Haitian literature in Haiti. You were taught French literature, read excerpts, and so when I came here I was looking for things about Haiti to read and they had this little shelf of "*la vie haïtien,*" and most of the books were political-type books and a lot of poetry—we have a lot of poets. And then there were these two short books, the J. J. Dominique memoir, J. J. being the daughter of Jean Dominique the radio journalist, and the Jacques Roumain novel, which is much longer in French than it is in the Langston Hughes translation. And so I kept going back to that shelf, until thankfully it kept growing, but it was a kind of revelation that in all my efforts to share writers that I love—Haitian writers I love with other people, that I wish on others that sense of discovery, of just like "Oh! This person is like me, and I recognize this." Because I think, you know, when you read voraciously, sometimes you read to escape but sometimes you read, especially when you're thirteen, fourteen, you're looking for a kind of mirror of yourself and so that's what I found there in the library and I could never—it took me a very long time to get over the fact that you were allowed to go home with those books from the library. I was like, "Are you kidding me? I can have ten and I can take it and they trust me?"

**Holdengräber:** You have to return them.
**Danticat:** Oh!

**Holdengräber:** At some point.
**Danticat:** Oh, that's the catch?

**Holdengräber:** Yeah.
**Danticat:** I did return them. It still felt so—I mean I remember just reading through them so quickly because I just couldn't believe that I could walk away with them—that was one of the amazing things that there are very few lending libraries, if you will, in Haiti, but the ones that they do have, you see—I see that same eagerness in the kids who are there.

**Holdengräber:** You were talking—we once met, both of us, we found ourselves at a wonderful literary festival in Jamaica called Calabash, which is just one of the most tremendous moments I've had at any literary festival, interviewing a writer in this particular case, it was when you were there, it was Pico Iyer, the year after that was Wole Soyinka, with fifteen hundred people on the beach saying "yeah, man," every two minutes. I'd never felt an audience so present, and you were telling me earlier on that in Haiti, there is now a literary festival where hundreds, thousands of people come and that Dany Laferrière was signing books for—did you say eight or nine hours? How do you explain that in a country perhaps where reading is such a challenge?
**Danticat:** Well, it's Livres en Folie, they usually have it either in May or June, and it's just amazing, you know, just so packed and the hunger, the hunger to read and the reverence for these books—

**Holdengräber:** The written word.
**Danticat:** And sometimes the agony I think for some of us to see the price of the books, but they have a program now with the National Library where they do less-expensive editions of the books in translation that are

sometimes—première at this Livres en Folie. But it's just incredible. It gives you hope.

**Holdengräber:** Not to take away from that hope. The earthquake. How has it transformed writing? The writing that Haitian writers produce about their own island? And I think particularly of this new magnificent collection which has actually not even really come out now—Akashic Books, which is run by Johnny Temple, who is actually here in the audience—hello Johnny— in a wonderful series called *Haiti Noir—Boston Noir, Brooklyn Noir,* and here it's *Haiti Noir.* There is in this volume which is coming out officially in January, but we have a few copies here in advance, thanks to Johnny. There are a few stories already that are describing so soon thereafter, which is so rare, the earthquake.

**Danticat:** Is that Farai Chideya next to Johnny? Hi, Farai. Well, this was great. We were working on *Haiti Noir* before—a year before, and then the earthquake happened and we had so many stories, and I was really scared that suddenly they would become—you know, like everything had changed. That the stories that we had just wouldn't fit. And then this amazing thing happened—they fit, of course they fit, and then we started going back to some people we had contacted for stories and see if they had stories for the earthquake, and I think the challenge of writing fiction so soon after was that it's hard not to replicate the news, and so we would get stories—

**Holdengräber:** You do not want to be a *journaliste—*

**Danticat:** Well, and I think for fiction it's strange because people feel like, "Oh, I know this." And so it's interesting the approaches that some of the writers have, and a lot of it is sort of surreal, and I think it's interesting to see how it's turned out. The other thing too, a lot of—this was different during the earthquake, we hadn't had this before in that suddenly these writers could speak directly to us. And I think a lot of media sources did this well in that they went directly to Haitian writers, like Évelyne Trouillot, who is a novelist, had two pieces in the *New York Times* about what it was like to be in Haiti during the earthquake. And the cover—the drawing we have—was done by Pascal Monnin and was also a part, so there was this other thing we hadn't had before. People were speaking directly to the experience for themselves. And so that, but I've noticed since the earthquake, a lot of the—we used to—people who wrote nonfiction in Haiti were mostly politicians, it was sort of like the political thing. But now we have a lot of even the fiction writers like Dany Laferrière and others who are writing about what it was like to have been there during the earthquake.

**Holdengräber:** How has the earthquake changed Edwidge Danticat's writing?

**Danticat:** We'll have to see, I guess. It's certainly—I mean, I feel like I have to struggle even more with this idea that—because I've always had this, where it's like does it—it pales, you know this notion that what you're writing pales in comparison to what's actually happening and this thing I wrestle with myself all the time, like "Does it matter? Does it fit?" Of course, that is more now in the sense of, like, "what is the purpose, what is the purpose of this?" But, you know, we'll have to see. I think of it in the same way that, here after 9/11, for example, and how people started talking about how 9/11 changed the fiction that people were writing or the stuff that—their creation—and it's a process. We have seen for example the first cry that is nonfiction, this *essai* if you would, this desire to testify, this testimony. But how the rest of it evolves, we'll have to see.

**Holdengräber:** My father is always obsessed when he speaks about Haiti of the *deboisment*, the fact that so many trees have been cut down, which creates incredible problems with agriculture, and I'm wondering what you feel the biggest challenge is now with Haiti, and I know that cholera is such a huge problem.

**Danticat:** There are so many extraordinary challenges—the fact that you have so many people homeless, I mean it just—

**Holdengräber:** Nearly a million.

**Danticat:** Just exposed to—Something like a million and a half. And one of the worrisome things is that, you know, as you go it seems like it's lingering, like there's a lack of urgency in terms of even with this, even with hurricane season having been—people are so vulnerable. That's an extraordinary challenge and what will this new place look like? Where will all these people go? Will they always be there? And their vulnerability to everything, vulnerability to things like cholera and hunger and for women and girls, sexual violence, and it's heartbreaking on a certain level. And the fear that I have and the fear that—when I speak to a lot of my relatives have, is that this will become sort of the new Haiti, like a normal, like this sort of—you get the sense that this whole thing, this very difficult way that people are living is becoming permanent, and I think that's worrisome, because you feel like it would be—

**Holdengräber:** A permanent state of emergency in some way.
**Danticat:** But a permanent state of misery on some level, because . . .

**Holdengräber:** Better stated.
**Danticat:** Of course there are people who—because you don't see necessarily a path being offered to one of the half-million people who live in tents and under sheets and people often talk about the resilience of Haitian people, they are extraordinarily resilient, but one worries that that resilience—I think some people take that resilience to mean that we can suffer more than other people, and I think that's the danger.

**Holdengräber:** I wonder if you see shards of hope. I'm taken back to a line by Václav Havel where he says hope is definitely not the same thing as optimism; there is not the conviction that something will turn out well, but the certainty that something make sense regardless of how it turns out.
**Danticat:** What sort of quashes the hope here is that the people most affected are not even really part of the conversation of how it should turn out. I think that's sort of the missing link, and it's very hard to see that turning out well.

**Holdengräber:** Do you feel you had some kind of a goal in writing this book, something that you wanted to inspire the reader with, some form—did you want him or her to be a creatively dangerous reader, in some way seek something that he or she didn't know before, and if so what?
**Danticat:** Empathy, maybe. Reading—art in general forces you to step into another body, to step into other skins and—one of the things about Haiti and maybe the earthquake—I don't think the earthquake has changed that even though we're seeing people naked, at their worst, at their most painful, at their most vulnerable, but we're still often deprived of complexity and even—it's either you're super resilient or you're wretched, or perhaps it's something in between. And I want people to look for that in-between place. I am allowed more complexity if people know—

**Holdengräber:** The luxury, really a luxury—
**Danticat:** I am allowed that if people know that I come from this great culture, that there are people like Daniel, people like Dany Laferrière, people like Hector Hyppolite, in my culture and my background. And it sounds—you know, it's sort of a—it becomes a clichéd mantra, like in your family you become annoying if you're always citing those, but I think it's important. It

makes me a more complex human being that I'm connected to these other people. I want to send people down all these paths, to know more, and art on some level, I think, grants us that complexity, because you're looking at the thing, but you also have to, if you're a careful reader, if you're a careful viewer, you have to take the next step and go—but where does that come from? Who are these people who created that? That's what we think when we look at the pyramids and when we think of the ancient Egyptians, and so I want to claim that complexity for people who I think are sometimes simplistic—looked at in a very simplistic and pitying way.

**Holdengräber:** A middle ground.
**Danticat:** A middle ground where we're not demons or angels, either. And I think that's all—isn't that what art is, always that search, whether the extremes or the middle ground? It's a constant quest, I think.

**Holdengräber:** Edwidge Danticat. Thank you very much.
    We have a mike coming up here. I'll ask you to come to the mike and to ask good, short questions.
**Danticat:** I just want to say hi to Alix Delinois—we did a book together called *Eight Days* and Alix Delinois illustrated it. Can you stand up, Alix? And hi, Farai, because Farai is also one of these people who gives us great complexity, who tells our stories so well.

**Holdengräber:** Please.
**Q:** Hi. Thank you for this book. Every book is a gift to us, so thank you. Hearing you read chapter eleven, what struck me is what has struck me throughout the years reading most of your books, I think all of your books, is the way you describe profound violence in, I don't want to say a banal way, but in a poetic way. So my short question is—what is your relationship to violence that, unfortunately, is an everyday fact in many of our lives, not just in Haiti, and what is the process by which you reach the reader in a way that's deeply touching but also so troubling, I think, to see such poetry while describing horrific acts performed by people upon other people.
**Danticat:** Thank you, Taina. Taina Bien-Aimé is the executive director of Equality Now. They do wonderful work on behalf of women and girls around the world, and so Taina knows of what she speaks. Of course, I abhor violence. I think it's something that perhaps is in a way a part of so much of our history, even though when the country came to be through revolution, but there's an example, I think, in the language where torturers were called

*shouket laozi* in Haiti, I translated it as "dew breaker" but it means someone who sort of rattles the dew, who shakes the dew. And that's always been, you know, and just the way everyday language sometimes in Creole attempts to address violence and that's the cue that I follow in that—something that shows that we don't want to live with it, but the first thing in acknowledging it in a way is to name it and you constantly have this struggle to make sense of it. For example the way—someone was explaining to me that gang rape, more recently on women and girls, is called *béton*, and *béton* is like the concrete, like the sidewalk, and then you have to stop and think how that comes to be. So I think there is the struggle even in everyday language especially in Creole to try to address violence by naming.

**Q:** I work at the writing center at Hunter College, and I wanted to share with you that I get to read many essays of students who write about your books. And most frequently it's *Breath, Eyes, Memory*, and I also wanted to think about the fact that I work with students who are from Korea and Japanese and their take on the messages that you have to share. I mean, how do you feel about that?

**Danticat:** Well, it's funny—the books in a way travel their own journey. Sometimes when I'm being lazy and I'm in a high school, and if the students say, "Well, what does that mean?" I'll say, "Well, it's your book now, you paid for it, you tell me what it means." But just in my own reading experiences, and I know that when I read *The Joy Luck Club*, Amy Tan's book, for the first time, I was like, "Oh, that's my mother." And so there are all these common experiences that sometimes transcend particularities and sometimes the most singular thing is so universal. I'm glad when that happens, because it's kind of meant some bridging has been done.

**Q:** Hello, Edwidge. My name is Roland. I just came here to tell you your book is absolutely superb, great. I'm here to ask basically your advice, and your opinion. I'm currently working on a documentary about Jeune Haiti at this moment in time and I'm currently interviewing people from that generation, that time. In your opinion, why—I'm encountering a lot of resistance to tell the truth, and their side of the story. In the Haitian culture—do you think—how should I approach them and they have such fear of talking about an event, and I need your opinion or advice how to approach them to talk candidly about an event.

**Danticat:** Well, because Haiti is such a small place, your uncle had written to me, and we sort of discussed this a little bit. The thing about Jeune

Haiti, it's very interesting, because there were so many people—because there were thirteen of them who left Queens to go fight this battle. And then there were so many people who were almost like the fourteenth, and you often meet people like that. I think there is generally a kind of silence around that era anyway and it might be that there—it might be with Jeune Haiti that even when you read documents, internal documents, things that circulated between the men, they disagreed on sort of where their financing—so sometimes people will say they were CIA-sponsored. That's one of the reasons that people don't, they don't want to talk about it for that reason. There's a general silence around that—you know, the dictatorship, a couple of years ago in Haiti, Jean Dominique did a program where he had people come in and talk about the dictatorship, and that took a lot, it's hard for people to talk about that because they feel that they want to leave that behind. We can talk afterwards a little bit more about that but I find a lot of reluctance, too, of people who want to talk about that. I actually wanted to talk with some family members who are still in Miami of Louis Drouin's especially, but you also don't want to encroach, to just relive this for people, because it was a very painful time, even for a lot of people in Jeune Haiti, a lot of them were killed, had family members who were killed, but we can talk a little bit after.

**Holdengräber:** You were speaking earlier about your interest in silence.
**Danticat:** That's one thing—that's a very—you know, I'm amazed that Daniel was even so open about it.

**Q:** Hello, my name is Adolphe and I grew up in Haiti just like you and I don't know but whenever I read anything of yours, it makes me feel like how when I'm listening to music, someone like Michel Martelly, or some like Ali Farka Toure, or someone like Tracy Chapman, or something of the sort.
**Holdengräber:** Jay-Z.

**Q:** Not necessarily Jay-Z. But even me personally, and I would say that I would think that literature boils down to conversation, and even me when sometimes like I'm having a conversation with someone and the fact that I'm from Haiti. And sometimes they'll ask me all these questions and I don't necessarily want to talk about whoever, whatever happened to this person, whatever happened to that person, sometimes I just want to, I guess, talk about other things, you know, and because your writing reminds me so much of music, will your essay collection become like, instead of *Create*

*Dangerously*, like "Create Beautifully"? Will you ever write something about language or about the use of words, about things that are lost in translation, about even how one would say "I love you," in Jacques Roumain or something of the sort, and will it ever become that? Does that Edwidge Danticat exist, and are you working on that Edwidge Danticat?

**Holdengräber:** I would like to quickly say one thing before you actually answer the question. What you describe as a longing already exists in this book.

**Danticat:** In this book.

**Holdengräber:** But go ahead.

**Danticat:** Yeah, that's what I was going to say. I was going to say that a lot of that—you've described a lot of the chapters in the book, but what you're saying, though, is something that I encounter a lot, like at some point well would you like happy things about Haiti and maybe this sort of—my melancholy personality. So this is the first time I've purposely tried to do that but I do think—I think there is that in—

**Q:** I have one more question—it's not necessarily happy things. I remember one time I was in college, I was in this creative writing class. It was a story about this prostitute and a doctor who goes over to these prostitutes, to go see this prostitute, things of this sort. The first thing that I thought is my sister's in college now, whenever she speaks to me, and she calls me up, she's like a feminist, and all that, and I thought to myself, why did Edwidge Danticat destroy this, why didn't she say this and that, but another side of me goes, "but that was probably one of the more beautiful things I've ever read," and that's what I'm asking for in terms of create beautifully. I mean, will it ever become like, "this is how I felt walking down some street and looking at the street," even if it's not like melancholic, but closer to music, you know, closer to folk.

**Holdengräber:** Would you please do that?

**Danticat:** Create prescriptively.

**Q:** Which is why I said—I feel like that Edwidge Danticat does exist, I think personally because of the way that I felt when I read that story, but I was asking does that Edwidge Danticat exist in writing?

**Danticat:** Well, I think—I'm glad you said you were in creative writing. I think because the Edwidge Danticat you're talking about I think is you. I think you should write those stories. And I would read them.

**Holdengräber:** And when you do, you'll come up here and I'll talk.

**Danticat:** Yeah, I think you—Because that's the thing. You ask a lot of writers they'll say, why did you write a certain thing, they'll say, "I write what I want to read." And that's the seed of a lot of creation, you know, it's like you write what you want to read. Because I'll never be that Edwidge Danticat, I'm sorry. I'm already the one I am.

**Q:** First I want to say thank you especially for *The Farming of Bones*. I taught that to my class this semester after the event, after the earthquake, and it was a way of—I went to Haiti to report, after the earthquake, and your book *The Farming of Bones* was very helpful to me to kind of map out the emotions I was feeling, so I wanted to say thank you for that.

**Danticat:** Thank you.

**Q:** The question is, when the political disaster of Papa Doc and Baby Doc was happening for decades, there wasn't this kind of global or mass sympathy for Haiti. When the neoliberal economic disaster was devastating Haiti's agriculture and forcing people into sweatshops in Port-au-Prince, again, there wasn't that same kind of global and specifically American sympathy for Haiti, but when there's a natural disaster—and of course, how natural really was it?—but when there was a natural disaster, Haitians were allowed to be innocent and Americans could have sympathy, and I wanted to ask, why is that? In terms of narrative, what's happening in the consciousness and in the narrative, that people had to be innocent and then there's allowed to be sympathy, and does it have anything to do with the narratives of race that circle Haiti and seem to choke it, especially in the eyes of an American audience?

**Danticat:** Well, I think that particular sympathy that you're talking about, it's a momentary sympathy that's born out of any kind of tragedy. Because the only parallel I can immediately think is when we were all looking at Somalian—you know, for my generation, we were all looking at these starving Somalian people and how often after that have we given that same kind of thought to it? So I think that's something that in the moment and that even those of us who are trying to keep people from not forgetting Haiti without evoking those same particulars like ultra tragedy, and the next step is what you're saying, is to bring people's attention to the source of these disasters, and the underlying questions that are not going away when those tragic images leave the screen. But that sympathy, that thing you're talking about is a more long-term thing that perhaps most people don't have the same attention span for. And what is that sympathy anyway beyond just that moment when you're looking at something tragic, and then you go back and have your cereal, you know? But those people who stay with it, who are concerned in some way, who are interested, they will look into these deeper issues, but that's not particular to Haiti in that sense, in that in the face of tragedy, sometimes, it's just tragic no matter who is playing the role on the screen at that moment.

**Q:** Just to push you a little bit on the second part of the question—how has racism and the narratives of race affected how Haiti has been seen?

**Danticat:** Oh, I think it's, you know, when people talk about—I think, for example when people talk about—you had this narrative that some of these op-eds that Haiti is sort of unsavable, failed, and all that, that emerged after the earthquake, that's always part of the underlying—because I think part of the conversation is sometimes, "Well, why can't these black people get their act together, we've put all this money in?" And sometimes I think if people, you know, if you take race out of it, and you say, the United States and Haiti had to start at the same time. Imagine if this country had all the same amplified obstacles where you had a crippling debt, isolation, sort of an embargo by the rest of the world because there was slavery in other places and these slaves had formed this nation that we needed to isolate here and, you know, occupation upon occupation where other people control your finances. Put anybody in that situation and see how they bear out, but people never take race out of it, too, because they feel like, "Oh, Haiti's mired in this situation perhaps because these are these black people who have been trying to rule themselves for two hundred plus years."

**Holdengräber:** We'll take a few quick questions, but quick ones.

**Q:** I'll try to make it very quick. I just want to say I'm honored to see you and hear you. My name's Joshua. I'm a filmmaker. My question is, you know, as a storyteller, would you feel limited writing for the cinema? I mean, a book is so experiential and so powerful, I get all my inspiration really from literature, and you're one of my favorite writers. I'm just wondering if you've felt that pressure, if people from Hollywood approached you, you know, and what your take is on it?

**Danticat:** No, I've never felt that pressure, and actually I used to work with great filmmakers who have since become friends, but I see it—I got to see that whole process up close, and I feel sort of the luxury of just, you know, all it takes me, is just me and some paper and a pen. I don't have to gather a thousand people together to reconstruct this scene, I mean, it's a beautiful art, there's in the book also of the wonderful seventh art, but I don't feel pressured in that way at all.

**Holdengräber:** One of those filmmakers wanted to be here tonight. Jonathan Demme wanted very badly to come but couldn't.

**Q:** Would you consider your books being made to films?

**Danticat:** Oh, yeah, are you making me an offer?

**Holdengräber:** Speak afterwards.

**Danticat:** Then, yes, if you are making an offer.

**Q:** Hello, Edwidge.

**Danticat:** Hello.

**Q:** My question is whether you consider yourself a Haitian writer or an American writer—after all, language is such an important part of somebody's identity, yet you write in English. And my second question is whether in Haiti there has been interest in your books in perhaps translating them in French or Creole and whether that your stories are valid for Haitians in Haiti or are you just writing for a Haitian American audience and others?

**Danticat:** I guess we would have to ask the people in Haiti. I've gone to— I've had interactions with audiences in Haiti, a lot of young people. It's an exchange. It's seen as, you know, someone who left Haiti, who writes about Haiti but also the Haitian American experience, which is its own experience. I consider myself, when I consider myself at all, I consider myself a Haitian American. And yes, the books are translated, and I'm excited.

**Holdengräber:** On this note, I will end our evening, and the people who have questions come up to Edwidge afterwards. Thank you very much.

# Writing in Exile Helps Authors Connect to Home

## Jennifer Ludden / 2010

**Jennifer Ludden:** This is *Talk of the Nation*. I'm Jennifer Ludden, in Washington. Neal Conan is away.

When Iranian writer Azar Nafisi first lived in the US as a graduate student, she dreamed of going home to teach at the University of Tehran. But when Nafisi returned to the United States years later as an exile from Iran, she joined countless other writers who've been forced to leave their homelands, fleeing war, political persecution, or natural disaster.

While being forced to leave one's home can be a source of pain, even guilt, it can also be a source of creativity. Writing itself can be a way to stay connected to a life that seems increasingly distant. Azar Nafisi joins us in a moment. And we'll also talk with Zimbabwean author Chenjerai Hove and Haitian American writer Edwidge Danticat.

We'd also like to hear from writers and artists in our audience today. If you've had to leave your home country, how has that influenced your work? Tell us your story.

Azar Nafisi is the author of *Reading Lolita in Tehran: A Memoir in Books* and *Things I've Been Silent About.* Her forthcoming book is *That Other World: Nabokov and the Puzzle of Exile.* And she joins us here in Studio 3A. Welcome to *Talk of the Nation*.

**Azar Nafisi** (Author): Thank you very much, Jennifer.

**Ludden:** Azar Nafisi, you've said that literature is the best answer to the feelings that an exilee has of loss and absence. What do you mean by that?

**Nafisi:** Well, to begin with, as a writer, you always have to look at the world through the alternative eyes of imagination, because you cannot see reality as it is, but in terms of its essence. So you always come to the world as a stranger. [Unintelligible] used to call authors as pariahs. Salman Rushdie recently said, we're all international bastards. [Soundbite of laughter]

**Ludden:** No one has a home.

**Nafisi:** No one. And so you have to feel a little bit restless, a little bit not at home to begin with in order to be able to write. And then the feeling of exile and loss of home is all about loss and absence. And through memory, and through literature, you retrieve what you have lost. You make presence than absence and you create a portable world that neither tyrants nor nature can take away from you. And I think that, for me, that's the safest place to be.

**Ludden:** You called it the republic of imagination.

**Nafisi:** Yes. It's the name of a book that I am also writing. *Nabokov* is a translation of my book in Persian into English. And this other book, *Republic of the Imagination*, is all about this portable home.

**Ludden:** Do you think you see things in Iran, or details, or see things differently in a way that you would not have had you stayed there?

**Nafisi:** Definitely. I think you can never take away the pain and anguish of loss and of exile. But at the same time, you feel a little blessed because you can look at one world through the alternative eyes of the others. And always you look at it through the fresh eyes of a child, of a stranger, of a visitor.

And even in the home that you were born into, the language you speak, you find the details and marvels that you had not seen before. So in another sense, I am glad that both America and Iran have been my home, and I keeping seeing one through the other.

**Ludden:** You've talked about explaining one to the other.

**Nafisi:** Oh, definitely. One of the ironies, at least of my life, was that, as you mentioned, for decades I wanted to go back home. And as soon as I went home, I discovered that home is not home anymore. And one of the things that Nabokov writes about, in *Invitation to a Beheading* and *Bend Sinister*, is not feeling at home in your own home. And I think that is the most anguished form of exile, to be a stranger in your own home. People whom you expect to know you treat you as an alien and as a stranger, and that is how I first felt, like that.

**Ludden:** How did that happen?

**Nafisi:** Well, when I went back home, after the Islamic Republic, living in a totalitarian society, the first thing that society that—the regime, the state, not the society, does—is take away from its citizens their sense of individuality and identity.

So everything that I was as a woman, as a human being, a teacher, a writer, they said, this is not Iranian or Islamic. I felt quite orphaned. And the second thing that they do is rewrite history, so they confiscate both your past and your present. And if that is not an exile, I don't know what it is.

**Ludden:** How do you keep current—I mean, do you feel like anything you write about Iran has to be set in the time that you were there? Or can you continue writing about contemporary events even though you're not there?

**Nafisi:** Well, sometimes absence opens you to things that you routinely do not see or observe. So although I miss the physicality of Iran, it is always painful, and I miss a lot of things because of that. This is one time I can say thanks to Internet, you know? [Soundbite of laughter]

I'm very much technologically challenged, but I can say that thanks to that virtual world, I am in contact. But I also see and observe and hear things that I had not seen and observed and heard when I was there. When I was there, I was so involved in the life that I was leading, and sometimes I was so angry that I didn't see things. Now, I see them through a distance, and I think that sometimes I see better, and definitely sometimes I miss certain things.

**Ludden:** We're also going to bring in another writer now, Chenjerai Hove. He is an author and poet from Zimbabwe. Chenjerai left his home country nine years ago, after running afoul of the government of Robert Mugabe.

He's now a writer-in-residence for the City of Refuge Program at Miami Dade College. And this week, he's taking part in the 27th Miami Book Fair, which runs all this week. And he joins me now from member station WLRN. Thank you for being on *Talk of the Nation*.

**Chenjerai Hove** (Author): Thank you. Thank you very much.

**Ludden:** You have said that you felt also like an exile in your own country, even before fleeing. How did that happen? What made you feel that way?

**Hove:** I was writing for a newspaper every Sunday, had a column. And also, at home, I was organizing a lot of literary activities, using every possible space that I could find. And that didn't go down very well, and then I became quite isolated by people not even wanting to talk to me. You go and sit there alone, and people are afraid to be associated or be seen to be associating with you. And you walk in the street, and people are asking you whether you are still out. And when you say out of what? They say out of prison, you know. [Soundbite of laughter]

So it really became a kind of very painful, internal exile. I was inside my country. I was in my home, but I was like under house arrest, as it were.

**Ludden:** And you left—initially you went to France, is that right?
**Hove:** Initially, I went to France, yes, where I stayed for three years.

**Ludden:** And how did that, then, influence what you wrote about after you left?
**Hove:** Actually, I discovered that when I left—I had been traveling a lot throughout the world, but when you leave and you know that the possibility of coming back is not anywhere near, you have a different feeling from the feeling you would have if you were leaving for a few weeks and coming back. But a lot of things do change, as well. Of course, when one—especially the landscape, the language, the metaphors, the imagery that one uses in one's creativity. All those things go under some kind of intense transformation.

**Ludden:** What do you mean?
**Hove:** You are looking at a right—always looking at the country or to—its own motherland or fatherland from a distance. And then, like the lady was saying, there's certain things, when you're in the country which you actually take for granted. When you've left, you begin to hear even the sounds of birds, the rivers, and the wind. Everything becomes different and much more intense because you now have an element of longing with you. And that becomes part of the creativity, as well.

**Ludden:** Let's take a quick call here before our break. Louisa is in Norman, Oklahoma. Hi, Louisa. Are you there?
**Louisa** (Caller): Oh, yes. Hello. This is Louisa, calling from Norman. I'm from—originally from Guinea-Bissau and also been, you could say, in exile for three decades now. I've lived in Europe. I've lived in England, France, and I now live in the United States. I've been here for twenty years. And this

past summer, I went back home. And much like the writer from Iran has said, you know, you feel alien in your own country.

In our case, Guinea-Bissau went through a series of coups d'état and military takeovers that have turned the country into—it's now basically a narcotic state. The Colombian narco-traffic has moved into Guinea-Bissau, so, you know, the possibility of me going back is not there.

But what I've found coming back to the United States is that it hasn't half my creativity. I'm also a journalist, was a broadcaster for seventeen years myself. And I'm now working for RuMBA, which is a nonprofit to help people living in rural areas access the Internet. So I'm doing something that I think is very, very positive here in the United States.

But, you know, what I wanted to add to the discussion is that—what I've realized is that the world is but one country, and mankind its citizens. In fact, it was an Iranian prophet that coined that phrase, and I'm beginning to believe that we can make a home of the place we live in and we can all be very helpful to the . . .

**Ludden:** Oh, right. Louisa, we've got to leave it there, but thank you so much for calling and sharing that. We'd like to hear from other writers and artists in our audience. If you've left your home country, how has it influenced your work? [Soundbite of music]

This is *Talk of the Nation*, from NPR News. I'm Jennifer Ludden. We're talking with writers today about living and writing in exile and how that experience changes them and their work. The idea came from the Miami Book Fair. They'll host more than 350 authors from around the world this week in downtown Miami. Many of them will discuss their own stories of living in exile.

Our guests are Azar Nafisi, author of *Reading Lolita in Tehran*, and the forthcoming book *That Other World: Nabokov and the Puzzle of Exile*, and Chenjerai Hove, novelist from Zimbabwe and currently writer-in-residence for Miami Dade College's City of Refuge Program.

We have a tweet from Jeff Arquette(ph), who says: "It set my career back ten years. Otherwise, I'm much more aware than I used to be. Was it worth it? Some days, yes. Others, no." Chenjerai Hove, was it hard to get go—was there a period when you just felt like things had just fallen apart for you creatively after leaving Zimbabwe?

**Hove:** No, no. Not at all. Not at all. I actually was able to look at my country from a distance, and it gave me a lot of creative energy and a lot of thinking to do about certain things which I'd taken for granted about my country. That's actually when I began to realize how beautiful my country was.

**Ludden:** Huh. That's nice. Let's go to a caller, Sayeed(ph) in San Jose, California. Go right ahead.

**Sayeed** (Caller): Hi. Thank you for taking my call. I have a question to ask Miss Nafisi, and I understand that she has been going through a lot of the experiences that I had to go through as an immigrant who came to this country about thirty years ago, and have . . .

**Ludden:** And also from Iran, is that right?

**Sayeed:** Yes, from Iran. That's right. And I had to witness raising my kids in Americanized manner, but knowing that they're living here in a different culture. And I had to assimilate and adapt, as well. And so the question was always raised at dinnertime: Are you Iranian? The answer to which was yes, of course. Then what do we do here? And if we are Americans, how come we are different from the parents of our classmates?

Meanwhile, daughter and son—and Fabio my son, they both asked me. They were in—like six and ten years old then, and one of them was born here. And I really didn't know what to say, exactly, so I had to read some books then, which were—unfortunately, they couldn't understand. I had to read some really long stories in English to understand what happened.

And so that was one major problem I had here as an Iranian parent and [unintelligible] living here and trying to help our kids not to feel like they're being, you know, developed and raised in an unrealistic and hypocritical kind of a way. And our cultures being different, we could always be the best of both. So that's why I sat down and wrote this book. And I understand this now . . .

**Ludden:** So you've written your own book, Sayeed.

**Sayeed:** Yes. I wrote the history—seven thousand years of history in Iran in a concise form in English for—yeah.

**Ludden:** Wow.

**Sayeed:** And I [unintelligible] 123 books to myself to be able to start doing that. I don't call myself a historian, but I have to do it because there was no English version available that could be understandable in a short form for our youngsters, the young American generation here. And that book is now available. It's a compact history of Iran.

I'm glad that people like Miss Nafisi—by the way, my wife's name, who helped me write that book, is on there, as well. I'm happy to see ladies here, Iranian ladies, come here—and some of them are single parents. Single-handedly, they raise families, and they create a bridge between the past and the future. I'm proud of people like Miss Nafisi and other writers and other—honorable guests on your show, and I raise my hat to them.

I just wanted to ask Miss Nafisi if—does she particularly have a hope that experiences that she had gone through where people like me can anyway be introduced to the Iranian people, the younger people there who have no idea what an immigrant has to go through in any place, under any circumstances. And has she been doing anything in Iran in there, because I've been away from my country for three decades. I have no idea what's going on in there. Thank you very much for taking my call.

**Ludden:** Thank you, Sayeed. And we'll put that to you, Azar Nafisi.

**Nafisi:** Thank you very much, Saitwan(ph). I very much enjoyed hearing your voice and look forward to reading you. I do understand the dilemma that you're talking about. Of course, one good thing about living in this country is that you can carry your past with you. And I was very happy to know that I'm not just an American, but I am an Iranian American, and I think that that is a quality that once this country loses, it would lose its soul.

So as an Iranian American, your history of Iran will not only be useful to Iranians, but it will also be useful to the new—to the country you've adopted. But I wanted to tell you that one of the—I always think, whenever I feel homesick, of what the German thinker Theodor Adorno said, that the highest form of morality is not to feel at home in your own home. And when I was back in Iran, I was so much stripped of everything that I thought was me, my history, my religion.

The Islam that the regime talked about was not the Islam of my grandparents or the Islam of my parents. So I had to genuinely ask myself: Who is telling the truth? Am I really not Iranian? Was I not born in a Muslim family? And like you, then I had to excavate the past and investigate my own past, and through the past of my poetry and my history to connect to my own people.

And when I was there, whenever the regime talked about the US being decadent and imperialist, the country that I knew so much about and that had accepted me so well, I would connect to my own people again through Saul Bellow and Emily Dickinson and Zora Neale Hurston. So literature became a vehicle through which I could communicate both with people inside Iran. And now that I am outside, whenever I want to talk to people about Iran, I want them to know that Iran is not the Iran that Mr. Ahmadinejad is representing.

Iran is Iran of its great poets. It is of its great philosophers. It's of its great culture. And so I think wherever we go, the absence brings to us new challenges, and challenge is what keeps us alive.

**Ludden:** All right. We have another—one last writer we're going to bring into the conversation now. Edwidge Danticat was born in Haiti and came to the United States when she was twelve years old. She's the author of several books that draw heavily upon life in Haiti, including *Breath, Eyes, Memory* and the American Book Award–winning *The Farming of the Bones.* Her new book is *Create Dangerously: The Immigrant Artist at Work*, and she joins us now from member station WLRN in Miami—there for the Miami Book Fair, as well. Welcome to you.

**Edwidge Danticat** (Author): Thank you. Thank you for having me.

**Ludden:** Now, you consider yourself an immigrant, not an exile. What's the distinction for you?

**Danticat:** Well, I am probably the child of, you know, of that exile generation for my particular group of people, for the—for Haitian Americans. So I am what exiles perhaps eventually become or what their children become, as the gentleman was talking about earlier. And in exile, I'm able to go back to Haiti, and I have been able to for as long as I can remember. So I don't consider myself an exile. I'm probably closer to an immigrant than an exile.

**Ludden:** But you have written about artists creating art while exiled from their home countries, or at least severely separated from them when their homelands are experiencing a time of crisis. How did you find that this separation informs their work?

**Danticat:** Well, I think for, you know, a lot of us who, as I mentioned, come out of this generation, that before—my parents' generation, for example, considered themselves sort of in wait here. They came here during the Duvalier dictatorship in the seventies. And through the eighties, they perhaps envisioned this time when they would be able to go back and restart their lives. And then slowly, there's been this transition for people who are not artists, people who are artists, where they realize, well, maybe I'm here for a while. Maybe I'm—you know, because there are other things, besides political power—you know, natural disasters, economic problems—that are keeping us here.

And it's the same for the artist. And some of them—now, there's this possibility that some have to go back and forth. There's also this thing in this conversation about exile and immigration that's called transnational-ism, and that especially if you live in a place like Miami, I can be in Port-au-Prince quicker that I can be in New York City from Miami. So that also adds another dynamic to the conversation for—I think for both people who are creating artistically and feel like they need to go back and refresh, and other people who just going back to see relatives and so forth.

**Ludden:** And gives you, as we've been hearing, that unique outlook on both places.
**Danticat:** Yes. What I think of as a mixed gaze, because you are looking at the United States as a—with Haitian eyes and that you're looking at Haiti with American eyes. And so there's a kind of—something in between that's per-haps sometimes personally uncomfortable, but I think it's rich terrain for art.

**Ludden:** All right. Let's get another caller on the line. Sukomar(ph) is in Folsom, California. Hi, there.
**Sukomar** (Caller): Hi. Thank you taking my call. I just—very interesting dis-cussion. I just wanted to make one comment. I'm an engineer by profession, but I've been writing for a long time because my parents have. And I write in my native language from Kanada which is a very, very big language in south India. I've been in the United States for almost thirteen years now and have published poetry as well as short stories for several years.

The key point, though, is it's been so long since I've come here and I've kind of adjusted to life here. But even today, when I write either in Kanada or in English, what happens is I go back to my youth and my childhood, and every single poem or short story I write is from my past. However much I want to try and write today's stories of my neighborhood here, I somehow end up writing every single small story that I experienced in my youth and in my childhood.

**Ludden:** And do you think if you wrote in English, it might be different?
**Sukomar:** No. I actually am trying to write something different in English. But when I actually try to write in English, it just goes back to my stories from India of my teenage years and my childhood years. It's all different stories, but it's all from my past. So it's kind, you know, it's ingrained and it's really hard to change that.

**Ludden:** Huh. Well, thank you for sharing that with us.
**Sukomar:** Thank you so much for taking the call.

**Ludden:** Chenjerai Hove, do you feel that you left—it's been nine years since you left Zimbabwe. Are your stories still set in that time? Or could you write something in modern-day Zimbabwe, do you feel?

**Hove:** Oh, yes. I have just finished writing a novel called *Others*. It's about the violence which we have allowed to infiltrate our politics. And also, an anthology of poetry called *Love and Other Ghosts*. And the more I write, the more I actually am able to feel the coarseness or the smoothness and softness of the land of my birth. So it is really a way of going back all the time. And I think one also realizes the dynamic that no society can, no culture can be stagnant. It is to be moving all the time.

And one has to realize that as a writer, for me to write is always—even when I was in the country, sometime I was writing about my aspirations and I put characters in a future Zimbabwe somewhere and let them deal with certain issues in a certain way. So one is always looking for these possibilities being possibilities of the past and the future and the present, mixing all those and being able to search for another possibility because for me, literature is a journey of exploration.

**Ludden:** All right. Let me just mention, you're listening to *Talk of the Nation* from NPR News. And let's take another call. Mahnoz(ph) is in San Francisco, California. Go right ahead.

**Mahnoz** (Caller): Oh, hi. My name is Mahnoz Badician(ph) and I'm Iranian American like Azar Nafisi. And I just want to tell you that it is to be in exile and live in a country that you didn't grow up with is such a dramatic experience. You actually become two person. One person that—you belong to other, your original country, and then the second person in a host country.

And I also although I lived in this country more than half of my life, but still, always with my poetry, with my writing, I'm trying to bridge the gap between these two person inside me, or bridge the gap between the two cultures that I'm dealing with every day. And that's a very, very amazing experience that I, you know, I just try to prostrate in my poetry and my writing. And actually, I made a website that—it's for language, and the main goal is to bridge this gap between cultures.

**Ludden:** All right. Well, thank you so much and I appreciate your call. And let's take one more here. I'm going to get your name wrong. Rahja(ph) in Seattle, Washington.

**Rahja** (Caller): Yes, hello. Thank you very much for taking my call. Yes, my name is Rahja Harbie(ph). I reside in Seattle, Washington. I'm a published author and artist working out of Seattle. But I travel and I still work internationally as well and read internationally.

What I would like to add to the conversation is just the observation—I've been in the United States for well over twenty years, perhaps thirty-five. It is the fact that I, as a person, as an artist and a writer, I quite often come across a reaction to—not a reaction to my work, but I oftentimes finds that there are, including in some media outlets, there are some predetermined perimeters as to the topic, the themes that should be or are in my work, whether it's the visual arts or in the literary work, arts.

And I must admit that, for instance reviewers and critics have more difficulty sometimes writing review of my work in paintings than they do in poetry because, obviously, the word is more accessible. And I think it's because the there is an expectation which I think is really done at the detriment of cultural, individual cultural distinctiveness. And these predetermined parameters expect that we write about certain things . . .

**Ludden:** Because you have come from a different country, is that what you're saying?
**Harbie:** Well, they expect that you're going to—that your work is going to be informed mostly by, for instance, the experience of an exile caused by very visible political reasons, such as political . . .

**Ludden:** And we've just a few seconds left here until the break. But you're saying that's not necessarily so? Is that what you're saying?
**Harbie:** I'm saying it's more complex than that. There is—I think every biculturalism is very often just like in the—throughout the conversation that I'm listening to, biculturalism seems to be the focus. And I'm saying there is multiculturalism in each one individual artist. Our work is very often informed by love of cultures, and culture is something that's really dynamic.

**Ludden:** All right.
**Harbie:** I mean, there's so much in what we, I mean, we didn't use . . .

**Ludden:** Rahja, we've got to leave it there. But we thank you so very much for the call. We're talking about the literature of exiles. We're joined by Azar Nafisi, Chenjerai Hove, and Edwidge Danticat. And they'll be back with us in just a moment. [Soundbite of music]

We're wrapping up our conversation about writers in exile. Azar Nafisi is with us. She's author of a number of books, including *Reading Lolita in*

*Tehran.* Also, Edwidge Danticat, her new book is titled *Create Dangerously: The Immigrant Artist at Work.* And Chenjerai Hove is an author and poet originally from Zimbabwe.

Let's get one more call in. Jay is in Otterbach, Germany. Hello, there.

**Jay (Caller):** Yes. Hi. Can you hear me?

**Ludden:** Yes. Go right ahead.

**Jay:** Yeah. I'm in sort of a different situation. I'm actually recently retired from the air force. And I was a professor in English at the Air Force Academy. And I chose sort of to put myself in a year-long exile to write. And, cause I find that it's that distance that gives you kind of a perspective on some of the insanity [unintelligible] that's going on in our own world—but I should say the United States. But . . .

**Ludden:** So you've self-exiled yourself from the US to write about the US? [Soundbite of laughter]

**Jay:** Yes. I'm blogging also about war literature which is sort of my passion, but I'm also a fiction writer. And, you know, historically, getting perspective and sort of stepping back and hearing different voices around you, it's like being in your own imaginative bubble in a way. You hear all these voices that sort of work through you in a different way, I think, when you're out of your own place. And I'm also a pilot, so I'm fascinated with this notion of distance and how our imagination works differently with distance. And I'm interested in what your panel has to say about that.

**Ludden:** All right. Well, Jay, thanks so much for the call. Edwidge Danticat, do you think there are things you can say about Haiti that you just couldn't have had you stayed there?

**Danticat:** Well, I . . .

**Ludden:** And not just politically, but just things that you wouldn't have even thought the same way or looked at things the same way.

**Danticat:** Probably. I think there's the value of distance, as we've been talking about, even linguistic distance in my case because English is my third language. So there's a level of sort of social politeness or level of fear of offending that you benefit from. For example, I always say that I have a year, for example, between translations of my book. And I cherish that year because I get a year to, you know, not to worry about being in trouble until the translation comes out a year later. [Soundbite of laughter]

So there are certain—there's a certain level of freedom that, perhaps one allows oneself that one may not from inside the language or inside the culture. So that's something that I've always thought as possibly one of the consoling benefits of being in a situation where you're outside the place where you were born.

**Ludden:** Hmm. Chenjerai Hove, who do you write for? Are you writing for Zimbabweans at home or abroad like you, or for Westerners, or do you think about that?

**Hove:** I actually, to be honest, when I'm writing I just want to express myself sincerely about a subject. I cannot stand up and say I write for so and so, for Zimbabweans, because they didn't elect me to write. I write because I have my conscience which says I should write certain things, certain stories or poems, which if I don't, I will feel burdened the rest of my life.

But what I'm also doing is, by communicating with myself in my writing, I also, in the process, discover the other. I will resonate with the others, with the other people who would read. So in a situation also when, for example in my country, the economy is in rather bad shape, you cannot assume that people can afford to just walk into a bookstore and buy books. And publishers cannot even sometimes afford to publish the books because it's so expensive. So I really write in search of myself.

**Ludden:** Hmm.

**Hove:** And in the process, also search and find the other, who is the reader, whoever it is.

**Ludden:** Azar Nafisi, the same question to you. And I'm wondering also, though, if social media has changed this. We learned during some of the demonstrations last year in Iran that quite a few people are on Twitter and, you know, the Internet over there. Has that changed who you feel your audience is?

**Nafisi:** Oh, well, I, like Chenjerai, feel that my—I call the readers strangers who, through sharing the same passions and dreams, become intimate strangers with you. So my readers are—I don't know where they are. Because the only place where there are no boundaries of nationality or ethnicity or language, is the realm of imagination. And so that is the realm where I work.

But social media has changed means of one level, which is information. But still, to know—to put yourself in place of how someone feels in Zimbabwe or Haiti or New Orleans or Iran, you have to experience the story, you have to have the feel of it. And for that, you go to the land of imagination.

I just wanted to say one small thing. Up to now, we've been talking about how we can illuminate our past or the places where we came from. But I think some of the greatest writing has been also about writers like Conrad or Nabokov, who have illuminated and given us fresh views about the new countries they adopted. Nabokov's best work was about America, and it was written during his period of exile in this country and later in Switzerland. And I think he could see this America through the eyes of his Russia. And even Russian language glimmers through those amazingly light field scenes in *Lolita* or his other works.

So it is not just that other country that comes to us. This new country is also nourished because language is also a home. And when you change that home and come to a new thing, you'd love to play with it. And that's what I love about English, I can play with it.

**Ludden:** All right. And I think we have to leave things there. This has been fascinating. Azar Nafisi is the author of *Reading Lolita in Tehran: A Memoir of Books.* Her forthcoming book is *That Other World: Nabokov and the Puzzle of Exile.* She joined us here in Studio 3A. Thank you so much.
**Nafisi:** Thank you so much.

**Ludden:** We're also were joined by Edwidge Danticat, the author of *Breath, Eyes, Memory* and *The Farming of the Bones.* Her latest book is *Create Dangerously: The Immigrant Artist at Work.* And Chenjerai Hove, the author and poet originally from Zimbabwe. He's now a writer-in-residence for the City of Refuge Program at Miami Dade College. And they—you both joined me from Station WLRN in Miami. Thank you so much.
**Danticat:** Thank you for having us.
**Hove:** Thank you so much.

# We Are All Going to Die

## Nathalie Handal / 2011

From *Guernica*, January 15, 2011. Reprinted with permission by Nathalie Handal.

"Haitians are born surrealists," says Edwidge Danticat (quoting a friend). It's a surrealism found in *le quotidien*. In Haiti it's common to see a peasant sleeping in a tight space—the author and MacArthur Fellow explains—his toe on a poster of Brigitte Bardot's eyes. Or a one-room house with *Paris Match* collages all over its walls. Art is at the heart of the island's daily life and the most nuanced and powerful ambassador Haiti has, she tells us in her latest book, *Create Dangerously: The Immigrant Artist at Work*. But what can art solve in this country's present?

On January 12, 2010, a devastating earthquake followed by more than fifty aftershocks ravaged the island, leaving an estimated three million people affected—over two hundred thousand dead, three hundred thousand injured, and more than one-and-a-half million displaced or homeless. This dark and horrid day also killed Maxo, Danticat's cousin. The same Maxo who accompanied her uncle, alien 27041999, to the United States, and upon arrival was denied entry and accused of faking his illness. The next day, her uncle died in the custody of US officials. Her uncle's life story was poignantly captured in Danticat's 2007 memoir, *Brother, I'm Dying*, nominated for the National Book Award and winner of the National Book Critics Circle Award.

As Danticat and I spoke in November while she was visiting New York City, news of a cholera epidemic spreading in Haiti made headlines. This news was followed by accusations by Haitians that UN peacekeepers from Nepal were to blame. As the toll increased to one thousand dead, elections brought more instability. Riots broke out in the streets when preliminary voting was followed by rumors of fraud. Most candidates asked that the elections be discounted. There were nineteen candidates on the ballot; among the most popular were former First Lady Mirlande Manigat, who was in first place, and Michel "Sweet Micky" Martelly, who was eliminated by ruling-party candidate Jude Celestin by less than 1 percent. The Organization of American States asked Haitian President René Préval to delay the announcement of the election results until an international panel of experts could review the vote. This action was taken in hopes of ceasing violence in the streets and conflicts between supporters.

In light of all the upheaval and tragic circumstances that have haunted Haiti in 2010, what solution can art offer? Perhaps none; perhaps, as Danticat suggests in *Create Dangerously*, art gives voice, and takes the international community away from a one-dimensional and narrow view of Haiti. It eradicates the idea that the island is only about turmoil and unrest, holding the world close to its pulse—its art, literature, and music. Danticat reminds us how far images of Morgan Freeman and Queen Latifah dancing on television to the music of Haiti's Tabou Combo went.

Born in Haiti in 1969, Danticat came to the US at age twelve. She holds a degree in French literature from Barnard College and an MFA from Brown University. Author of numerous books, notably, *Breath, Eyes, Memory*, a 1994 Oprah Book Club selection, *Krik? Krak!*, nominated for the National Book Award, *The Farming of Bones*, winner of the 1999 American Book Award, and *The Dew Breaker*, winner of the PEN/Faulkner Award. *Create Dangerously* is her first book of essays, which was adapted, updated, and expanded from the Toni Morrison Lecture she gave in 2008 at Princeton University.

Haiti is her shadow, and shadows loom around her. She allows them. And in return, they save her. While writing *The Farming of Bones*, she watched horrible videos of death in order to understand how people died. "It's a lot of work to die," she concludes. She saw this more personally with her father who struggled with pulmonary fibrosis for nine months before dying. "I've always had this fascination with death," notes Danticat. "I don't know if it's something that was said to me in the neighborhood I grew up in. So I keep looking for it."

Like all of Danticat's books, *Create Dangerously* has her heartbeat—a steady movement, a wide cry, a constant echo, a soft breathing. She offers us glimpses of an island and culture she is passionate about—and her dedication to which never ceases. She has just finished a fiction anthology, *Haiti Noir*, that appears this month. Readers will discover new and unknown voices, as well as masters, such as Madison Smartt Bell, Yanick Lahens, and Évelyne Trouillot. As we prepare to part, I ask her what she thinks Toussaint L'Ouverture would say about Haiti today. What revolution would he lead? We look at each other. A blank stare. Maybe these daily surrealistic portraits are leading a revolution. They're insisting on existing and in so doing, resisting.

**Guernica:** In your new book, *Create Dangerously*, you speak of art in a time of trouble, how from the singular or the personal comes the collective story. What is the responsibility of artists?

**Edwidge Danticat:** The responsibility of artists is to create as freely and as openly as possible. There should be no restrictions whatsoever on any artist or art. No prescriptions, orders, commands given to artists. They should engage us, make us think, entertain us in whatever way they see fit. There are, however, moments when art becomes part of something bigger, where a singular expression becomes part of the collective. That's what the book is about.

**Guernica:** As an immigrant and a writer yourself—are you limited in any way?

**Danticat:** Not at all. If anything, I find it enriching because I am looking at two different cultures cross-eyed. I am looking at Haitian culture through American culture and American culture through Haitian culture. But also, I have a mixed gaze, and I am both an insider and outsider in both cultures, which might be an uncomfortable place personally. But it's an extraordinary place artistically because all these things that you are processing mesh. Nuance is important to art and being from different places offers nuance. A writer is like an actor, especially a fiction writer. You have to inhabit different bodies to write convincingly about them. So the more experiences you have, the more you are able to do that.

**Guernica:** But do you feel that your community would be accepting if you wanted to write about Paris when people are dying in Haiti?

**Danticat:** Well, some people would say, she sold us out. Other people would say, good riddance, she's exploited us enough . . . [laugh]. I would hope, however, that they would judge the work more than the subject. I would rather read a great book on a subject I care less about than a bad book on a subject I love. When a writer feels passionate about a subject, he or she writes better about it. I happen to feel passionate about Haiti and Haitians and Haitian Americans and out of that passion is born my subject. But writers are eternally curious and other subjects will come up and I am not going to deny myself the pleasure of writing about them just because I might risk offending or alienating some people.

**Guernica:** If a writer doesn't write about the country they are from, that doesn't mean they stop being from that place.

**Danticat:** Of course not. I recently read a collection of short stories called *The Boat*, by a young writer named Nam Le. It is a fictional meditation, in its execution, of the dilemma of the immigrant writer. The writer grew up in Australia of Vietnamese parents, I believe. The first story in the book is about a writer who is trying not to write about the immigrant experience in his Iowa workshop. He seems to have disdain for the immigrant writers who visit and he thinks they're famous because they're exotics. He vows to write worldly fiction, but then the book is framed with two stories about Vietnam. His point, the fictional writer's point, is, I think, that you can both write about your roots—maybe it is even that you don't only have to write about your roots—and other things as well.

**Guernica:** Felix Morisseau-Leroy wrote in Creole. Frankétienne, who also happens to have written a play about two people under the rubble that really echoed after the earthquake, wrote in French and Creole. How has Creole and French affected you as a storyteller?

**Danticat:** Creole, more than French, is always behind the English I am writing. My characters are speaking in Creole and in my mind I do a simultaneous translation as I am writing. Frankétienne and Felix Morisseau-Leroy are wonderful writers who gave Creole the respect it deserves by writing wonderful, innovative prose and poetry in it. Sometimes people will say you have to write in Creole, even if badly, to raise up the language. I'd rather have people writing in Creole who do it because they love it and are good at it and who think that it's the best tool for the story they are telling, rather than people who write badly in Creole, just to have things in Creole.

**Guernica:** Do we need a "Guernica" to produce art?

**Danticat:** You mean your publication [laughs]. Of course we don't need wars and massacres to produce art. What's wonderful about Haiti is that we have produced great art in spite of those things. Art—and by that I mean song, dance, painting, as well as literature—has been one of the many tools we have used for our survival.

**Guernica:** I remember being fascinated as a young girl in Port-au-Prince by what people in the streets would turn into art pieces—using a small stone, a *chacha* branch, whatever was available to them as canvas. Haitians truly have art in their soul.

**Danticat:** Yes, it shows you that art will not be denied. Think of the daily functions of art in Haiti. The lottery stands. The tap tap camions. It's all covered with beautiful art. My friend, the painter Ronald Mevs, used to say that Haitians are born surrealists. We are doing collage all the time, in daily life as well as in our art. So old oil drums become metal sculpture and old carnation milk cans become lamps, called *tèt gripads*, like bald-headed girls. Art is our communal dream.

**Guernica:** How has Haitian art changed people's perception of Haiti?
**Danticat:** People sometimes think they know Haiti through what they have seen in the news. When they see a piece of art that we've produced, listen to a song, or read a piece of literature that we've written, we become closer to them. We are now part of them when the art stays with them. They then come closer to meeting us, and closer to the different layers of who and what we are.

**Guernica:** *Create Dangerously* opens with the execution of Marcel Numa and Louis Drouin in 1964. You say that artists have stories that might be called "creation myths . . . that haunt and obsess them." And this story is one of yours. Can you elaborate on that?
**Danticat:** I have always been curious about these young men, Marcel Numa and Louis Drouin, who had left Haiti and were living in Queens and decided to return to Haiti to fight the dictatorship and ended up dead in the last openly state-sponsored public execution in Haiti. For me, and a lot of people I talked to, their deaths signaled a more brutal dictatorship and created a new reality that drove a lot of Haitians away from their homeland. That connection between this very brutal act and the further migrations it inspired has always intrigued me. Even though it happened five years before I was born, I have always felt that it is, in part, why I am here, why my parents and so many other people have left Haiti. That's why it's not only a very tragic story but a type of creation myth for me, in which a whole new generation of Haitian immigration emerged from that act. After the executions, people also tried to react with art, by reading and producing plays or reinterpreting Greek plays. I feel as though a new generation of artists also came out of that and I wanted to highlight some of that in the book.

**Guernica:** Do you think art always has to involve some kind of engagement—social or otherwise?
**Danticat:** Of course not. As I said before, I think artists should be as free as they want to be. It is up to the artist to decide what he or she wants to

do. But we should not "penalize," if you will, people with a certain political view. In "Create Dangerously," the Albert Camus essay that inspired the title of the book, Camus writes for the writers of his time something that is still true today. "The writers of today know this. If they speak up, they are criticized and attacked. If they become modest and keep silent, they are vociferously blamed for their silence."

**Guernica:** You say we create to fight forgetfulness and that when the news moves on, art keeps a nation alive, allows a people's stories and reality to stay present in the minds of the world. Can you give me examples that you have noticed in the last nine months?

**Danticat:** Less than a year after the earthquake, there have been dozens of books written by Haitians about it. Most are memoirs, rather than the novels that were the dominant literary genre before the earthquake. There have been collective anthologies by Haitian writers as well as personal narratives, such as Dany Laferrière's *Tout Bouge Autour de Moi* and Rodney Saint-Eloi's *Kenbe la.* There's been a lot of poetry published on paper and online. Visual artists like Frantz Zephirin and Pascale Monnin have created many pieces inspired by the earthquake. Art is one of the many ways people express their feelings about what happened to them. It's also a way for them to celebrate their survival, in pictures, in song, in dance, in words.

**Guernica:** In the essay "Walk Straight," you discussed being criticized when you wrote about a virginity test and that some Haitians accused you of exploiting your culture for money.

**Danticat:** I think criticism is necessary. It's all part of it. I usually try to learn from criticism, see if in some way the person criticizing me is really trying to teach me something. But you can't become obsessed with criticism. Same goes for praise. You listen, take a deep breath, and move on. Keep working. That's the most important thing, to keep going.

**Guernica:** The photographer Daniel Morel was present as a boy at Numa and Drouin's execution and this incident led him to become a photojournalist. In this book you wanted to look at how people come to their art. Can you tell us more about how you came to your art?

**Danticat:** I came to my writing by listening to stories my aunt and grandmothers told me. I used to make my own little books with folded paper, then I started writing for school papers when I moved to the United States. My first novel *Breath, Eyes, Memory* was my MFA thesis at Brown.

**Guernica:** Do you think you still would have been a writer if you never left Haiti?

**Danticat:** The publishing part of it might have been hard in Haiti. There are few publishing houses in Haiti, so most writers self-publish, and we didn't have the kind of money that would have made that possible. This makes me think how many powerful voices will never surface because of that.

**Guernica:** You speak about the great history of Haitian painting, how significant it is to Haitian culture and history. George Nader was the world's biggest Haitian art collector. Galerie Nader in Pétion-ville was destroyed by the earthquake—some twelve thousand works, an art collection with an estimated worth of $30 million to $100 million dollars, gone. Only about fifty pieces survived.

**Danticat:** And there were other art collections destroyed too, like the wonderful collection at the Centre d'art and those amazing murals at Saint Trinité.

**Guernica:** Like the National Library in Baghdad: so many books destroyed. How does a nation recuperate, heal, and deal with such a loss—historically and culturally. Even if more art is being produced. What do you do with that loss of memory?

**Danticat:** Fortunately, some of the art works, especially the work of the masters, had been photographed so there are records of some of them. There are also great collections of Haitian art outside of Haiti. Yet the works we have lost are irreplaceable. I think that is what inspires some of the painters to create new works, not just to replace but to honor what we have lost.

**Guernica:** You said something interesting about Haitian painting, that you see dreams in it, and it is also a way to ponder death. Can you expand?

**Danticat:** Art is about life as much as it is about death. Art is a way, I think, of acknowledging that we are alive, but also a way of leaving our imprints because we know that we will die one day and we hope that the work will outlive us. The novelist and essayist Susan Sontag has said that photography is an elegiac art. All art is in some way, I think, elegiac.

**Guernica:** In Haiti, music has always played an important role in politics—carnival, *rara*, Haitian Vodou music. Today you have groups like Ram that seem to have a political message. Can you speak about the role of these bands in Haiti?

**Danticat:** The *rasin* bands have always led the way in terms of offering a political message. That is in part because their music is drawn from *Vodou*, which has a spiritual message at its core, but also a message of survival, and when necessary rebellion. *Konpa* music can also offer that—and at carnival time more than any other time it does. These bands are as important to Haiti as they are to the outside. During the summer they travel all over the country to the *fèt champet*, the country festivals, and draw thousands of people.

**Guernica:** What is their impact in the international community?

**Danticat:** I can't speak for the international community, but I believe they offer yet another side of Haiti. After the earthquake when Wyclef Jean was on the NAACP Image Awards with Tabou Combo, a lot of foreigners called me and told me how they had no idea we had that kind of music in Haiti. To see Morgan Freeman and Queen Latifah dancing to Tabou Combo went a long way with a lot of people. Also, when the Rara, which can be as mournful as it is festive, came on during the Hope Haiti telethon, that lifted a lot of spirits.

**Guernica:** Your thoughts about the election?

**Danticat:** I hope [the new president] will wake up every single morning and remember that there are more than a million people homeless and jobless and that he or she needs to do something about it. I hope it will be someone who cares about hunger, food security, education, agriculture, jobs, jobs, jobs. And I hope that his or her hands won't be tied by the Parliament and/or the international community so that he or she can help make life better for the millions who are living in such indescribably horrible situations. There are people who think that elections should not be happening now. It's a great shame that so many parties were excluded, particularly the Lavalas party, the party of former President Jean-Bertrand Aristide. These are certainly not ideal conditions for elections. But it seems to me that the leadership now wants to turn it over and move on, so we should certainly not force them to stay. The specter of an "I am the only one who can do it, president for life" is always hanging over our heads. It seems like Haiti is always making Faustian bargains when it comes to elections. Damned if you do, damned if you don't.

**Guernica:** What do you say to those who criticize Haiti, say that it's poor, Haitians haven't done anything, and Haiti hasn't advanced?

**Danticat:** I say look at Haiti's history. When Haiti became independent in 1804, it was strapped with French debt and isolated by the world. It's suffered a long American occupation from which it inherited more debt and a brutal army. Yes, we've had some of our own homegrown dictators, but every time the Haitian people have shown some desire to lead themselves, they've been slapped down for some reason or another by some larger power. I'm not making excuses. But I think people should take in the entire picture before making a judgment like that. Haiti is much smaller, of course. But would the United States have prospered with Haiti's same obstacles? It's worth looking at because both nations became independent around the same time.

**Guernica:** Langston Hughes visited Jacques Roumain in 1932 in Haiti and translated Roumain's *Masters of the Dew* later on. What do you think Roumain and Hughes would say about Haiti today?
**Danticat:** The first line of *Gouverneurs de la Rosée*, which Langston Hughes translated as *Masters of the Dew*, is, "We are all going to die." And if you read the travel narratives of Langston Hughes in Haiti, his description of Haiti in the 1940s is eerily similar to the Haiti of today. Roumain didn't romanticize Haiti and neither did Hughes. I think they would both be shocked by how little has changed.

**Guernica:** This brings us to immigrants. They risk their lives for another world—like your uncle who died in US custody—and are too often rejected. What did you learn from that experience?
**Danticat:** I learned, or was reminded, how much people sacrifice to be here, to make it here. My uncle was one of hundreds who died seeking asylum, trying to find safety in the United States. We have a very nasty environment in this country now for immigrants. Because of the bad economic situation here, everyone wants to blame immigrants.

**Guernica:** Concerning immigration laws, what do you think of the temporary protected status granted after the earthquake? Can you comment on that and on the rumor that after Arizona, Miami is next.
**Danticat:** I was happy that temporary protected status was granted to Haitians after the earthquake. It meant that people who were already here could work to support their families. That was long in the making and a wonderful thing. Haitian activists had been asking for it for such a long time, after other disasters in Haiti. It's been granted to others and we were never

quite sure why it could not be granted to Haitians. There are a lot of people running for office in Florida, the Tea Party element especially, who would like to see Miami have an Arizona-like draconian immigration law. We've already seen the ugly days of home raids here in Florida, where families are torn apart and kids are left alone. We've already seen people taken off buses. We've already seen people die in custody. How much worse can it get?

**Guernica:** Do you think the law would pass with all those immigrants in Miami?

**Danticat:** The generally progressive multicultural melting pot that is Miami is only a tiny part of Florida, which is generally more conservative. Yes, I think if the economy gets bad enough, that and many other laws could pass. That's why we have to be vigilant. We have seen with the Patriot Act and other post–September 11, 2001 measures that in times of crisis, certain rights and freedoms can be considered dispensable.

**Guernica:** The Dominican Republic and Haiti historically have had a strained relationship. You wrote a foreword to the René Philoctète novel *Massacre River*, which speaks about a middle place in the border where people are neither one nor the other.

**Danticat:** After the earthquake, the Dominicans were the first on the ground. There was rapprochement during that time. Many Haitians ended up in Dominican hospitals. Now I think things are returning to the way they were before, especially since there are now more Haitian migrants in the DR. I hope there will be a continuation of that good feeling, on both sides that we saw after the earthquake. The Philoctète novel is a great surrealist-type novel about the 1937 massacre of Haitians in the Dominican Republic. In the book there is a middle ground, a mixed group of people who can potentially make peace. There are a lot of people like that, thankfully, both intellectuals and others, and I hope that one day they will outnumber the others.

**Guernica:** What is the role of the Haitian diaspora in rebuilding Haiti?

**Danticat:** The Haitian diaspora certainly wants to, and will, contribute in small and large ways to contribute to the rebuilding of Haiti. They have been doing it for years with grassroots NGOs, neighborhood associations, sponsorships of kids, etc. . . . That will continue. We only have contentions now because many diaspora business people are competing with the foreigners for big contracts. The efforts I most believe in, however, are the grassroots efforts by people in the diaspora who have been working in Haiti for years and continue to do it today.

**Guernica:** Race is one of those subjects people are careful not to address but it's still an issue. There are many debates on who is a Haitian and the issue of representation often comes up. Who should or shouldn't represent Haiti—and it's often in reference to black or white. On the other side of that is someone like Dany Laferrière who wrote the novel *Je suis un écrivain japonais*, or *I Am a Japanese Writer*, echoing Roland Barthes that "text's unity lies not in its origin but in its destination."

**Danticat:** Race, in my opinion, is not as much an issue as class. It's like the saying, "If you're black and rich, you're mulatto. And if you're white and poor, you're black." Not that I agree with it, but I've heard people say it. I think it's safe to say anyone can represent Haiti. Look at the faces in the elections and that should give you a clue. There are all kinds of people in that presidential race. Perhaps cultural representation is a more thorny issue, as in the Miss Haiti debate recently. But most people were just glad that someone from Haiti was in the contest. I don't know if it's experienced differently from the other side. If you don't look like the majority of the people. There are privileges, I suppose, and downsides that go with everything.

**Guernica:** You also just wrote your first children's book, *Eight Days: A Story of Haiti* (Scholastic), in a way to explain to your two daughters what happened on January 12, and read the story to the children in Haiti. Can you speak more about this experience?

**Danticat:** *Eight Days* is the story of a boy who is trapped in rubble after the earthquake in Haiti and dreams about his life, his friends, the games they used to play. I have read it for both kids in Haiti and here, and it gave them both a chance to discuss the earthquake in a safe and open way. The interesting thing is that the kids then open up to you about all sorts of things, when they feel like you've opened your heart to them.

**Guernica:** What's next for you?

**Danticat:** The earthquake in Haiti has shown me, and everyone else, I think, how precarious life can be. I hope that there is more fiction and more writing in the future for me. More time with my family in the United States and my family in Haiti.

# The Nuance of Noir: An Interview with Edwidge Danticat

## Carolyn Gan / 2011

From *Fiction Writers Review*, May 23, 2011. Reprinted with permission by Carolyn Gan.

Renowned for her stirring and insightful stories about Haitian life, Edwidge Danticat recently turned her eye to genre as the editor of *Haiti Noir*, part of Akashic Books' *noir* series. The book was published in December, following the 2010 earthquake in Haiti. Danticat discusses the disaster's impact on the book and the way that *noir* captures some of the mystery, darkness, and complexity of her homeland.

Danticat's novels, including *Breath, Eyes, Memory*; *The Farming of Bones*; and *The Dew Breaker*, are praised as much for their cultural specificity as for their poetic universality. Critics call her Haiti's literary voice, and *Granta* named her one of the Best Young American Novelists in 1996. She received a 2009 John D. and Catherine T. MacArthur Foundation "genius" grant, so one might even say that some have even called Danticat a genius. But no one would have pegged her for a noir writer until now.

Though not commonly associated with genre fiction, Danticat was a natural choice to edit *Haiti Noir*, the most recent volume in Akashic Books' groundbreaking series of original noir anthologies. The author speaks widely and often about Haiti, not only of the issues facing her countrymen abroad and at home, but also of her fellow Haitian writers. She includes many of these emerging and established authors in *Haiti Noir*. Moreover, it's hard not to think of Danticat as a noir writer after reading her story "Claire of the Sea Light," which is included in the anthology. Classic elements of noir—mystery, misfortune, even a graveyard—emerge masterfully from her powerful prose. "Claire of the Sea Light" is a remarkable story in a collection with many other extraordinarily nuanced tales.

Danticat was nearly done with editing the collection when, on January 12, 2010, Haiti suffered a devastating earthquake, an unimaginably destructive natural disaster that was followed by widespread suffering, flooding, and a cholera epidemic. At first, the editor worried that the stories would no longer seem relevant, but after adding three pieces about the earthquake, she found that *Haiti Noir* actually offered a unique portrait of the country before and after the disaster, snapshots of moments and places not often seen on the nightly news. What is more, the collection truly entertains; it is dark, surprising, and even funny. In the book's introduction, Danticat confesses: "I can honestly say that, in spite of the difficult circumstances in Haiti right now, I have never felt a greater sense of joy working on any collective project than I have on this book. . . . Each story is of course its own single treasure, but together they create a nuanced and complex view of Haiti and its neighborhoods and people."

The editor's joy will certainly be shared by her collection's readers.

In addition to being an acclaimed novelist and the editor of *Haiti Noir*, Edwidge Danticat is a prolific writer of short stories, published in more than twenty-five magazines and journals and collected in the National Book Award–nominated *Krik? Krak!* She received the American Book Award for her novel *The Farming of Bones*, and her many other awards include a grant from the Lila Wallace Reader's Digest Fund. Her moving memoir *Brother, I'm Dying* received the National Book Critics Circle Award. She has also written several books for children, including *Eight Days: A Story of Haiti*, which tells the story of a seven-year-old boy trapped in rubble after the 2010 earthquake. Her recent essay collection, *Create Dangerously: The Immigrant Artist at Work*, is an extraordinary manifesto that will be appreciated by both immigrant and nonimmigrant artists. Beyond her prolific work as a writer, Danticat has taught creative writing at both New York University and the University of Miami. She lives in Florida with her husband and children.

The following interview was conducted by email during May 2011.

**Carolyn Gan:** How did you come to edit *Haiti Noir*?

**Edwidge Danticat:** Johnny Temple from Akashic Books called me one day and asked me if I would edit *Haiti Noir* for the publisher's noir series. I was already a huge fan of the series, having read many of the books, so I jumped at the chance and said, *yes.*

**Gan:** *Haiti Noir* features new stories by well-known, emerging, and even a couple of unexpected writers, including Mark Kurlansky. How were the stories collected? Were there authors or particular perspectives you sought out, or did the submissions shape the collection?

**Danticat:** I'd like to think of the book as a kind of party. Most of the writers are Haitian and live in Haiti, but others are Haitian writers who live outside of Haiti, in Canada, Berlin, and the United States. We decided to also include two Haitiphile writers, Madison Smart Bell and Mark Kurlansky, who know Haiti well and have written about it extensively. The writers in the book range [in age] from early twenties to early seventies. There is a broad scope of experience represented. I did seek out some writers whose work I already know, and some other writers came to me via friends, particularly the younger writers. Marvin Victor, for example, was recommended by an older writer who had been his teacher. Now he has a hugely successful novel, *Corps Mélés*, that was published by a prestigious house in France. We got him just in time before he was huge, and he is going to be really huge among the next wave of Haitian writers.

**Gan:** You say in the collection's introduction that only a few of the included authors identify themselves as writers of noir. Your own work is not typically classified as such. Are you a reader of noir?

**Danticat:** I am a reader of noir . . . not an obsessed one, but if I see a name I recognize, I go at it. The beauty of this series is that it brings new writers to noir, so it's always fun to see what they come up with. I think people have said that my work is dark, which would be the literal definition of noir, but they might not call it noir. It was interesting to see, though, how much the writers wanted to jump in and try this. It was like having an assignment, coloring outside of the lines, for them.

**Gan:** Themes and images repeat throughout the collection. Unreliable electric generators, for example, buzz in the background and even appear as a plot point in Kelly Mars's story. Magic winds its way through many stories as well, especially Marie Lily Cerat's fantastic "Maloulou." Are there aspects of Haitian culture that are inherently noir? Or that can be understood more clearly through the lens of the genre?

**Danticat:** I guess there are aspects of Haitian culture that you might call noir or that lend themselves easily to the genre. The police investigations that are always ongoing and may never really be solved. The mystical elements of Haitian life, class difficulties, and conflicts. The writers, I think, made great use of those elements and more. In one of our earlier reviews, someone listed all the similar tropes, including *Comme Il Faut* cigarettes. It was interesting to see where many of the stories overlapped.

Unfortunately that's often true, especially in terms of solving crimes. In April 2000, one of Haiti's most famous radio journalists, Jean Dominique, was assassinated outside his radio station. At the time he was a friend of the president's, yet his murder still remains unsolved. I guess one other way to say it is that it is very easy to bury a mystery under even more mystery in Haiti.

**Gan:** You include your mesmerizing story "Claire of the Sea Light" in the book. Was it written especially for the collection?
**Danticat:** Thank you. It's part of a longer book I am writing about how a child's disappearance affects an entire small town in earth-shattering ways— earth-shattering in the sense that as the people of the town remember their last interaction with the child, they realize that they are all connected in more ways than they knew. It's one of those tricky books, and it has a different ending than the story, but that story is the first chapter of that book.

**Gan:** "Claire of the Sea Light" is structured in reverse chronological order, which adds so much suspense. What inspired that choice?
**Danticat:** I love playing with time in fiction. That's somewhat noir inspired. Noir *film* inspired. I wanted to go back and forth in time but focus on one day, this girl's birthday. Because her birthday started out so tragic—her mother dies in childbirth—she is never allowed to be happy. The entire plot of the book also happens in one day, in one night, really.

**Gan:** Do you always write fiction in English? How have your first two languages, Creole and French, affected your writing?
**Danticat:** I moved to the United States when I was twelve. I speak French and Creole and write both, but I have always written creatively in English. It's not even a commercial choice as people sometimes think. It's just that when I got here and started writing, I started writing in English. If my family had moved to Spain around the same time, I would probably be writing in Spanish as one Haitian writer, Micheline Dusseck, does. Maybe English also offers a veil, some kind of distance that makes me bolder, but that's just the way it's always been. Always behind my English, though, are Creole and French certainly. I sometimes think I am doing simultaneous interpretation while writing: the characters are speaking Creole, and I am interpreting for them.

**Gan:** I've always admired that you never hinder the flow of your narrative with awkward translations. Somehow your translations enhance the rhythm. When do you know that a line in Creole or French is necessary?

**Danticat:** When I use Creole and French it is easy, I think, to understand contextually. If you read carefully you should get what it means. However, I try not to do literal translations because I know a lot of people are reading the book who speak both languages, so I try to add a bit of extra nuance for them.

**Gan:** There is a heartbreaking moment in "Claire of the Sea Light" when the little girl sees a child's tombstone near her mother's and ponders "who the child was that her mother was now looking after in death." It reminded me of Anne in your novel *The Dew Breaker*, who holds her breath when passing cemeteries because she imagines her drowned brother searching for his grave. Can you talk a bit about that intimate relationship between the living and the dead in your work?

**Danticat:** It's a morbid fascination for me, this fine line between the living and the dead. When I was little, my uncle was a minister and presided over a lot of funerals, so I often heard that death is not the end, and that there is something else, and that the dead are always with us. I believed this deeply and grew less afraid of the dead and less afraid of death. I was just telling a friend the other day—who is obsessed with past lives' experiences—that my childhood made me totally unafraid of death because of all the post-death possibilities it provided. I only became afraid of death again, I think, when I had children. My only fear is of leaving them. Writing a story like "Claire of the Sea Light" is almost like getting those fears out of yourself, placing in someone else's life a moment that personally terrifies you and then taking it out of your nightmares and putting it on the page.

**Gan:** You mention the idea of "leaving them"—that is, death as separation from your children. Of the father in "Claire of the Sea Light," you write: "It took watching another child die in her mother's arms to make him realize how very much he'd miss Claire when he finally gave her away for good." Is separation just another kind of death?

**Danticat:** Separation when you're a little kid, I think, can feel like death, which is also something you are struggling to understand. In Haiti when people say someone is *lòt bò dlo*, they can mean that the person has died or that he or she has migrated, has gone to live in another country. After my first book was published, I met a woman who was five when her mother left Haiti for New York. She was asleep when her mother left, and no one had prepared her, so when she woke up and was told her that her mother was *lòt* *bò dlo*, she thought her mother had died. She was twelve when her mother sent for her. When she got to New York, her mother had changed, and she had changed, and she told me at nineteen years old that she never quite believed that her mother was really her mother. In her mind, her mother is dead, and she was tricked into an adoption of some kind. This is an extreme case, but it feeds my nightmares about parental separations when they are badly handled. Some families can be severed by that kind of separation forever, even when they are physically reunited.

**Gan:** In your recent essay collection *Create Dangerously: The Immigrant Artist at Work*, you wrote that "All artists, writers among them, have several stories—one might call them creation myths—that haunt and obsess them. [The historic public execution of revolutionaries Marcel Numa and Louis Drouin] is one of mine." What are some of your other creation myths?
**Danticat:** There are some new ones now, which I talk about in *Brother, I'm Dying*. My father's death. That was and still is so painful. My uncle's death, the death of my minister uncle who raised me. The birth of my daughters. Slowly I think your foundation myths change as your foundations shift under your feet.

**Gan:** You also write in *Create Dangerously* that "I used to fear [my parents and uncle] reading my books, worried about disappointing them." When did you stop worrying about disappointing them? Did that worry extend to your larger Haitian audience?
**Danticat:** Thankfully I worry after the writing is done, and the book is about to be published. While I am writing I give myself free rein. Yes, I used to worry about a larger Haitian or Haitian American audience that they would recognize nothing of themselves in my work. But then I know, too, that we all have the stories we have, and those are the stories we tell by various means. It's foolish to try to accommodate your story to any audience's taste. The most important thing I can do as a writer is tell the truest story I know with the most love and passion and respect I possess. The rest will just have to take care of itself.

**Gan:** You've spoken and written widely about the situation in Haiti since the January 12, 2010, earthquake, including conversations with NPR and articles for the *New Yorker*. Do your Haitian readers approach you to share their own stories?
**Danticat:** They often do, but not forcefully. When I am in Haiti, I just observe. I don't badger people for their stories. They go through enough of

that. I just observe and live the moment I am living because, especially with family members, there are so few of them.

**Gan:** Could you talk a bit about your last visit to Haiti?

**Danticat:** It was a private visit. Most of my visits are. There was still a lot of devastation. A lot of people without homes as another hurricane season is approaching. The visit before that I went with a group of women activists from an organization called We Advance that was cofounded by the actress Maria Bello. We visited one of the first women's clinics in Cité Soleil, where they do rape recovery and counseling. Rape has become a very big problem in post-earthquake Haiti. We also met and broke bread with and sang and cried with some extraordinary women who had run for parliament at great risk to their lives. These women were just exceptional, some of the most amazing women I have ever met in my entire life.

**Gan:** Part of the profits from *Haiti Noir* will be donated to the Lambi Fund, a nonprofit organization. Could you talk a bit about their work and why you selected Lambi?

**Danticat:** The Lambi Fund works in the rural sector in Haiti, and they work with women, which was very appealing given as we often say that Haitian women are the *poto mitan*, the middle pillars of our society.

**Gan:** *Haiti Noir* was almost complete before the earthquake struck in January 2010. How did you select the three stories in the collection that reference the earthquake?

**Danticat:** I thought we had to represent the earthquake somehow in the book so I asked a few folks if they had written some stories since the earthquake, and we got the three wonderful stories in the book. I think it's really hard to write fiction so soon after a tragedy, but our writers did an amazing job, and I am really glad we made that choice.

**Gan:** Was the completion of the project part of your own healing process after the tragedy?

**Danticat:** Those stories, as disturbing as they are, were indeed healing. I think a year, ten years from now, this is a book that you will be able to read and appreciate in terms of how it's represented Haitian fiction in general and the post-earthquake moment in which the book was published.

**Gan:** Thank you so much for your work and for your time.

# *Create Dangerously*: A Conversation with Edwidge Danticat

## Kimberly Nagy and Lauren McConnell / 2012

From *Wild River Review*, January 2012. Reprinted with permission by Kimberly Nagy and *Wild River Review*: www.wilddriverreview.com.

On a September day in 2009, Haitian American writer Edwidge Danticat sat before her computer in her Miami home holding her nine-month-old daughter, Leila, when she heard the phone ring.

After the caller advised her to put her baby down, Danticat learned that she had been selected for the MacArthur Foundation Fellowship, a five-hundred-thousand-dollar no-strings-attached grant awarded to "enable recipients to exercise their own creative instincts for the benefit of human society."

No one could have foreseen just how much the 2009 MacArthur award would benefit not only Danticat's work and her family but also the country of her birth. In January 12, 2010, a 7.0 earthquake killed approximately 316,000 people, injured 300,000 and left 1,000,000 homeless in her native country.

"The fact that the award came just a few months before the massive earthquake in Haiti meant a great deal," remembers Danticat. "That money touched so many people's lives."

Danticat came to the United States at the age of twelve, during the oppressive Duvalier regime in Haiti. Like many immigrants, she left behind beloved aunts, uncles, and cousins. But she took her country's traditions with her. "My best writing teachers were my aunts and uncles, who were all storytellers," recalls Danticat during an interview at the 2011 Langston Hughes Festival. "Storytelling and oral tradition, was, when I was growing up, a strong part of how things were passed on. That's what made me want to tell stories. It was a kind of gift. A moment where children and adults could interact in a free way."

Part memoir, part manifesto, Edwidge Danticat's book of nonfiction, *Create Dangerously: The Immigrant Artist at Work* (Princeton University Press, 2010) sheds light into the lives, stories, and creative works of immigrant artists from Haiti—artists who created (and consumed) censored works "despite, or because of, the horrors that drove them from their homelands and that continue to haunt them." Danticat writes about those who inspired her own path, from beloved aunts to the Haitian novelists she first discovered and voraciously consumed at the Brooklyn Public Library as a girl.

*Create Dangerously* emerged from a Princeton University Second Annual Toni Morrison Lecture Series. Danticat took her title from Albert Camus's last public lecture, "Create Dangerously," in which Camus declared, "For the person with creative potential there is no wholeness except in using it."

The book was selected as one of the best books of 2010 by the *Miami Herald* and *Mosaic Magazine*, named a 2010 *New York Times Book Review* Editor's Choice, and in 2011 went on to win the OCM Bocas Prize for Caribbean Literature in the nonfiction category. It was recently selected for the One Book, One Philadelphia reading program.

*Create Dangerously* continues to play an important part in keeping the Haitian earthquake crisis in the forefront of people's minds. "Part of my role is to try to keep people's awareness up," Danticat says in a feature in Brown University's *Alumni Magazine*. "Just because you don't see this in the news anymore, it doesn't mean that it's gone. The world might have moved on to the next catastrophe, but it still goes on."

Edwidge Danticat is the recipient of the 2011 Langston Hughes Medal from City College of New York, winner of the Harold Washington Literary Award (2011), and recipient of the 2009 MacArthur Foundation Fellowship among other awards. She has written eight books, including *Breath, Eyes, Memory*; *Krik? Krak!*; *The Dew Breaker*; *The Farming of Bones*; and *Brother, I'm Dying*. Danticat is currently working on the final chapters of her new book, *Claire of the Sea Light*.

**Wild River Review:** You were holding your nine-month old baby when you learned that you had received the MacArthur "Genius" Award. What did winning the award mean to you, your family, and your work?

**Danticat:** In addition to the usual wonderful things that come with this fellowship—the financial support you receive for five years and the prestige it bestows in the eyes of some—the fact that it came just a few months before the massive earthquake in Haiti on January 10, 2010, meant a great deal to my family. That money came in handy and touched a lot of people's lives during the months afterwards and even now. With my immigrant work ethic, I still feel I have to prove that I deserve it, so I work even harder every day to do that, venturing off my usual path so that at the end of these five years I will feel as though this great investment in my life and in my work has paid off somehow.

**WRR:** Turkish novelist Elif Shafak has talked about her challenges in balancing her role as a mother and writer (in her book *Black Milk*). What do you see as unique challenges for female writers? What is your advice for young female writers?

**Danticat:** I read that book. It has an incredible author's photo and of course the subject matter appealed to me, having had many black milk days myself. I don't ever want my daughters to read these interviews in the future and feel as though they robbed me of anything. So when I answer this question I often think of them as women reading these interviews, perhaps long after I'm gone. That being said, there are days when I am so thrilled to be a mother that I could burst with joy. There are other days when it has brought me to tears.

I think it's important that we do not overidealize motherhood. It's important to tell the truth about it to younger women. I went to a wonderful women's college, the great Barnard College, and recently I was back there and one of my mentors, Professor Quandra Prettyman, said this and it rang so true for me. We don't often talk openly to young women about balance. A woman writer who is a mother has to balance a lot more perhaps than a male writer or a writer with no children.

I chose to be a mother and all that comes with it. I now write around it. I have more to write about, but less time in which to do it. The bright side is that I often feel that my children save me from a lot of drivel. I probably would be writing more if I didn't have them, but I don't think it would have as much depth. What I would tell young female writers is that the key is balance, which is I think the conclusion that Elif comes to. You have to know how to ask for help. You must realize that it can't be all about work. I think my life would be lame without my children. There would be this void that I would feel without them.

You have to find some way to keep all your balls in the air, which is a bit more challenging because writing requires a lot of quiet time, but many have done it before and many more will. Look at the great Toni Morrison. She was a single mother of two boys and having met her children, I think she did a great job on both the home and writing fronts. I always come back to this one thing she said in an interview—that in the end she narrowed things down to two things she had to do that no one else could do for her: mother her children and write her books. I think that's kind of where I am now, most of the time.

**WRR:** In describing your visit with your Tante Ilyana in the mountains of Beauséjour, you coin a great phrase: "memory elixirs"—that is, "Elixirs against fading memories, a panacea to evoke images of spaces lost to us, to instantly return us home." For example, your Tante Ilyana gives you coffee to bring back for your father and she says to you, "When he has a taste of this coffee, it will bring him home." Can you share a couple of your favorite memory elixirs from Haiti and what they make you think of, smell, taste, feel?
**Danticat:** Coffee is certainly one of them, along with good Haitian food like diri djon djon, rice and beans with dark mushrooms. Also hearing Creole being spoken. Smelling the earth after the rain always reminds me of my summers in the countryside in Haiti. Reading a good book about Haiti, particularly fiction. Feeling loved by my family. Those are all memory elixirs.

**WRR:** You coin a beautiful term—fake-lore. How do you define that and can you give our readers some examples in your writing?
**Danticat:** I have actually heard others say this term before. It's invented folklore, I suppose personally invented folklore. I think that's what all fiction writing is. You're inventing people, places, time, space: you're inventing fake-lore.

Sometimes people also do that with their lives. They invent folklore about themselves, their families, or convince themselves of things that become fake-lore.

**WRR:** In your first book, *Breath, Eyes, Memory,* you tell a multi-generational story of women, a mother who moves to New York and sends money back to her sister and daughter in Haiti—and the daughter who after growing up in New York returns to Haiti. In an early scene Sophie aches to give her aunt a Mother's Day card (which her aunt refuses and insists she will save for Sophie's birth mother). The scene is so difficult and touching. In one way, that scene demonstrates how art can take readers directly into a complex and deeply emotional family division not uncommon to the experience of immigrants. What inspired that scene for you?

**Danticat:** It was inspired by an actual thing that happened to me. Every year on Haitian Mother's Day, which is the last Sunday of the month of May in Haiti, I used to give a Mother's Day card to my aunt, Denise, who had raised me. The year before I was supposed to leave Haiti, I gave one to her and she didn't take it. I knew I had a mother in New York and that Tante Denise was my "symbolic" mother, if you will, but when she turned down the card and told me to send it to my actual mother, I felt really heartbroken and rejected. That scene has always stuck so strongly in my mind, which is why it is the scene that opens the book.

**WRR:** In *Breath, Eyes, Memory*, you wrote a letter to Sophie, the main character. After you wrote it, you were criticized for including a scene in which Sophie's virginity was tested by her mother (a practice which you point out has gone on in all different locations of the world for centuries).

You write: "I guess I have always felt, writing about you [Sophie], that I was in the presence of family, a family full of kindness as well as harshness, a family full of love as well as grief, a family deeply rooted in the past yet struggling to confront an unpredictable future. I felt blessed to have encountered this family of yours, the Cacos, named after a bird whose wings look like flames. I feel blessed to have shared your secrets."

We get a deep sense of your intimate relationship with the character Sophie in this tender letter. Can creating dangerously sometimes mean creating intimately?

**Danticat:** Of course it can. I think intimacy is crucial to any kind of creation. I spend so much time with my characters that I ultimately grow to love all of them, even the despicable ones. You have to become intimate with your characters in order to get them.

I also think of writing as an intimate conversation between two people, one writer and one reader. That's how it works: one person at a time holding one book, so the whole process is full of intimacy, someone opening up his or her heart to another person through some words that as you read them—in the best of all possible worlds—feel as though they were written just for you.

**WRR:** In your chapter "Daughters of Memory," you point to Haitian novelist Marie Vieux-Chauvet, born in 1916 during the first year of the US occupation. She has one of her characters write in her journal, "There is hunger of the body and that of the soul. And the hunger of the mind and the hunger of the senses. All sufferings are equal." What hunger moves you most in your writing?

**Danticat:** The hunger for nuance, to understand things a lot better. Writing is a constant journey towards exploration for me. I learn the most about the world, about myself, about others when I'm writing, in whatever genre, whether fiction or nonfiction.

**WRR:** Can you elaborate on your answer? In our view, the concept of nuance, and where it can lead us, is hugely important to writers and readers all over the world.

**Danticat:** We live in a world where things can seem so black and white. Now or later. Good and evil. You're perfect or you suck. What art, good writing, music, and other forms of art offer I think is nuance. Good writing digs deeper and looks for those gray areas. That's what interests me most in what I read. I want a writer to make me see something I have never seen before, even in a situation I think I know well. I want to see that onion peeled to its core. I want deeper. That's what I am aiming for myself and when I read it I know it, and though I don't always reach it, I am always aiming for it.

**WRR:** And as Vieux-Chauvet asks, are all sufferings equal?

**Danticat:** The wonderful Elie Wiesel says that we should never compare tragedies. All suffering, to the sufferer especially, is individual and unique.

**WRR:** In *Create Dangerously,* you devote a chapter to Alèrte Bélance, casualty of the 1991 military coup d'état, who went on to become a very vocal "face of the junta's atrocities in Haiti." A supporter of Aristide, she was macheted and left for dead and has an amazing survival story. As you were working on the documentary featuring her, *Courage and Pain,* there is a scene where her son asks to speak about his experience . . . and as he talks and weeps you say it is as though a knot is loosening inside of him.

After such atrocity and violence, how can telling stories not only serve as an agent for change and greater social awareness, but help us move through terrible grief and reinforce our notion of human dignity?

**Danticat:** Alèrte Bélance is proof that when we speak out, it makes a difference. She could have kept her suffering to herself, but she used it as a way to galvanize and inspire others, to speak for their pain. She is so incredibly brave, an amazing woman, who in her own view, survived to testify.

**WRR:** In the first chapter of *Create Dangerously*, you write: "My stories do not hold a candle to having lived under a dictatorship for most of your life, to having your neighbors disappear and not being able even to acknowledge it, to being forced to act as though these neighbors had never existed at all." In your view, what difference can writers truly make in the face of pervasive violence?

**Danticat:** The only thing writers can do in those types of situation is, if they choose, to add their voices to those of others who bear witness to that type of violence, those types of crimes, that kind of injustice.

**WRR:** What project are you working on right now?

**Danticat:** I am working on the final chapters of my new book, *Claire of the Sea Light*. It's fiction. I just finished a picture book with Leslie Staub, the illustrator. It's called *Bedtime for Sara*. I am also writing a short script for a film which will be produced by Martha Adams and directed by Richard Robbins, who made the award-winning documentary *Operation Homecoming*. The film will be written by ten women writers from ten different countries, including Haiti, and will be based on the work of a great organization called 10x10, which works on girls' education worldwide. I also just wrapped up a film called *Stones in the Sun*, which was partly shot in Haiti and written and directed by my friend Patricia Benoit. I have a small part in that film. I wrote a song with a wonderful Haitian American Jazz musician named Pauline Jean.

This is all part of expanding my horizons in my forties. A positive midlife crisis. I would love, and I mean LOVE, to do a graphic novel à la Marjane Satrapi, whose work I absolutely adore. I have a graphic novel script, but if anyone is interested in collaborating, please call.

Once I'm done with *Claire of the Sea Light*, I'll take a deep breath then plunge into a young adult novel I have under contract for Scholastic. I'm not saying all this to brag. You caught me at a good time at the beginning of the year, where I am taking stock. I'm just reminding myself how much work I need to do.

**WRR:** In the chapter you write about the 2010 Haitian earthquake, you say that words often failed you when you were asked to write about the event. And so you did what you always did when you felt unable to write: you read as much as possible. What would you recommend as a must-read for *Wild River* readers about the 2010 earthquake?

**Danticat:** I would recommend *Tectonic Shifts: Haiti Since the Earthquake,* which was edited by Mark Schuller and Pablo Morales, *Haiti: The Aftershocks of History* by Laurent Dubois, *Haiti Rising: Haitian History, Culture and the Earthquake* by Martin Munro, Paul Farmer's *Haiti After the Earthquake,* to which I contributed a chapter. I would also recommend that people read these other pre-earthquake books, written by Haitian writers or Haitian writers in the Dyaspora. Some of them are translations and translations always need our support.

1. Jacques Stephen Alexis, *In the Flicker of an Eyelid* and *General Sun, My Brother*
2. René Depestre, *Festival of the Greasy Pole*
3. Jan J. Dominique, *Memoir of an Amnesiac*
4. Dany Laferrière, *Heading South, Dining with the Dictator, The Aroma of Coffee, How to Make Love to a Negro,* and *Why Must a Black Writer Write about Sex*
5. René Philoctète, *Massacre River*
6. Jacques Roumain, *Masters of the Dew*
7. Lyonel Trouillot, *Street of Lost Footsteps*
8. Myriam Chancy, *The Serpent's Claw* and *The Loneliness of Angels*
9. Yanick Lahens, *Aunt Rezia and Other Stories*
10. Marie Vieux Chauvet, *Love, Anger, Madness*
11. Paulette Poujol Oriol, *Vale of Tears*
12. Philippe Thoby-Marcelin, *The Beast of the Haitian Hills*
13. Jaira Placide, *Fresh Girl*
14. Joanne Hyppolite, *Seth and Samona* and *Ola Shakes It Up*
15. M. Sindy Felin, *Touching Snow*
16. Marilene Ketterel-Phipps, *In the Company of Heaven* and *Crossroads and Unholy Water*
17. Jean Robert Cadet, *Restavèk*
18. Félix Morisseau-Leroy, *Haitiad and Oddities*
19. Danielle Georges, *Maroon*
20. Patrick Sylvain, *Love, Lust and Loss*

# Edwidge Danticat: The Interview

## Kreyolicious / 2012

From Kreyolicious.com, February 2012. Reprinted with permission by Kreyolicious.

One of the most acclaimed writers of this century and last, and arguably the most prominent Haitian American writer in the United States, you'd think that Edwidge Danticat would put her pen away, and rest on her laurels which include a National Book Award Nomination, and a win, the National Book Critics Circle Award, the International Flaiano Prize, and the Langston Hughes Medal, and others, if [we] were to list them all we'd risk getting typist cramp.

Non, non. The lady scribe hasn't put away her blood for ink, nor her parchment paper. Instead, she chose to release her latest literary opus *Creating Dangerously: The Immigrant Artist at Work*, to explore the creative journeys of immigrants. She opens her collection of introspective essays with a written remembrance of Louis Drouin and Marcel Numa, two artist-students who in 1964 were mercilessly executed, as one of the thirteen members of Jeune Haiti, a revolutionary group that attempted an invasion of the country during the presidency of Francois Duvalier. From there, she explores her journey and that of other artistic greats, who often had to create at the risk of their own lives, and that of their families. A decade and half after she made her literary debut with *Breath, Eyes, Memory*, Danticat approaches her craft with as much enthusiasm as when she was the young writer blushing over acclaim from critics. Get into the circle and listen to our conversation.

**Q:** Will there ever be a sequel to *Breath, Eyes, Memory*?
**A:** It's probably wise to never say never, but I don't think there will be a sequel to *Breath, Eyes, Memory* anytime soon. I have a lot of other stories I want to write. I'm not sure I'm ready to revisit those characters again in the very near future, but I am always extremely moved by the way that this

book has touched some people. I would have never imagined what it would mean to a lot of young women, for example, which is why I am hesitant to touch it. *Breath, Eyes, Memory* is like a first child. You try everything on your first child and make all your mistakes and hope and pray it still turns out okay. Maybe at some point I might revisit Sophie, the main character, as a grandmother—maybe when I am a grandmother myself—see how she has done in America late in life. Who knows? But I'm not thinking of writing a sequel right now.

**Q:** You came to the United States as a little girl of twelve. Did you, in your wildest dreams, think that you would become the writer of world renown that you are now?

**A:** Well, you know how they say that God can dream a bigger dream for you than you can dream for yourself. This is certainly the case. I would not have been able to dream any of this, and by "this" I mean having the great blessing of doing something I absolutely love, as my work, every single day of my life. That to me is the definition of success, doing something you love and are passionate about and having good health and most days having relative peace of mind.

**Q:** Out of all the books you've written, which one do you think would lend itself the most to a film adaptation?

**A:** I used to work in film and I still try to work as much as possible in documentary for example, because it is a medium I love, but I am probably the worst person to make that determination. I think they would all make good films in the right hands. I have to tell you that in the last couple of years, I have had many promising conversations with so many wonderful young Haitian and Haitian American filmmakers, some in film school, some out on their own, that I am very optimistic about our having some wonderful films made within this community over all. I want to take the opportunity to incidentally plug Jacmel's Cine Institute, Haiti's only film school. They are doing great things in film. Also this short film was made by Rachel Benjamin from one of the stories in *Krik? Krak!* called "The Missing Peace."

**Q:** Which of your books has been the hardest to write?

**A:** Hands down, it has to be *Brother, I'm Dying*, my memoir about the death of my uncle and father. In one way of visiting with both my father and uncle after they died, but in another way, they were slipping away from me. It was the fastest book I had ever written, but also the hardest, emotionally, to write.

**Q:** Do you imagine ever sitting in front of your computer or with your notebook in hand, and not having one word come out?

**A:** No, because on that day, I would write, "Why I am sitting in front of my computer with my notebook in hand and no word is coming out? OH GOD WHHHHHHY?" And that would be something, right? Seriously, it has happened sometimes, but when it does, I read or do something else or try to go about living my life and not pressure myself too much until the words come back.

**Q:** Is a room with a view an absolute necessity for a writer?

**A:** I don't think so. Sometimes a great view can be distracting and make you want to go outside and play. I write at night mostly, exactly for that reason, to have as few distractions as possible.

**Q:** Your father and uncle are unarguably two of your life's biggest heroes. What is the best advice they've given to you?

**A:** Both my father and uncle were not the type to give me direct advice really, beyond the strong "recommendations" and suggestions, which are not really suggestions that we all get when we are young. But I learned a lot of things by example from them. My uncle was a minster so his sermons were filled with *konsey* ["advice"] to his congregation. One I remember clearly is about humility. *Sel pa bezwen di l sale*, he used to say. "Salt doesn't have to say it's salty." Beginning with the time I was a teenager, on my birthday, my dad always bought me flowers and chocolates. The first time he did that he said, "I want to be the first man to give you these things so that you don't lose your head the first time someone gives them to you, so that it feels normal to you, so that you know you deserve them." After that he always sent me flowers and chocolates on my birthday every year until he died. Wherever I was, I would always get flowers and chocolates from my dad on my birthday. And it was always a great reminder to me that I was loved unconditionally, which is something I miss so much from him, which is one of the reasons I still miss my daddy very very much. That and the fact that my girls and my brothers' children won't know either of these men are still heartbreaking to me.

**Q:** Of all the accolades that you've gotten which one means the most to you?

**A:** Every award is a gift, something encouraging you to continue and go on. That's really how I see them, as encouragement to try harder and do more and do better and hang in there. The MacArthur Fellowship was a most tremendous gift, of course. The Hurston/Wright nominations as well as the Langston Hughes medal which was very kindly given to me last November 18 meant a great deal to me, because I have always loved the work of Zora Neale Hurston and Langston Hughes, especially the work on Haiti. So it meant a lot to me to have this full circle connection between them and me and Haiti.

Recently though I participated in an event for the two-year commemoration of the January 12 earthquake organized by Dickson Guillaume and the Haitian Mass Choir in Brooklyn, and three young Haitian American women from the organization Beltifi presented me with a painting painted by the founder's mother. And right before giving it to me, the young women read a few words, and one of the young women said something like, "Thank you, because after reading you, we have no fear," and I was a total mess after she said that. I was at a total loss for words.

I kept seeing myself at fifteen and imagining also feeling momentarily fearless because of some book I had just read, and I knew exactly what she meant, and this was such a full circle moment for me and I was so moved and was so choked up that I was not even able to give the speech I came to give. I looked at those young women and I kept thinking of our journey as immigrants in this country, and I kept looking back and looking forward at what words, our parents' dreams and courage, their love, fears, pride, prayers, support, and these types of things can do, and what reading and art can do and what these things might mean one day to my daughters and other young girls and women like them, and I got really really choked up.

**Q:** You have two daughters. How has motherhood been for you?
**A:** Motherhood has been greatly sweetened by the fact that I have a most wonderful husband. My girls have been blessed with a great father who enjoys their company and carries a lot of the load. I often tell people that motherhood is a family project, from my mother and my mother-in-law to the great friends who love my daughters and sometimes care for them like their own, this all makes motherhood easier and my ability to do other things possible, so it bears saying, because we don't say it enough, that at its best motherhood is a communal project. It takes a village, sometimes several villages, indeed.

**Q:** With do-it-yourself book technology, do you think that one day, there will be no need for publishers and books, especially printed books?

**A:** I am not sure where it's all going. I think we're all a bit nervous, truthfully, about what all the technology will mean to writers, readers, publishers, booksellers, and books. Which part of the chain will be wiped out first, we wonder? Bookstores? Publishers? Writers? Who knows? All I know is that people have been telling stories since the dawn of time and they will continue to find some way to tell them and even if there is some day enough technology to tattoo a book behind my eyelids, I think I will always want to hold something in my hand and turn a page anyway.

# Haitian Youth Illuminated in *Claire of the Sea Light*

## Rachel Martin / 2013

**Rachel Martin:** On her seventh birthday, a little girl named Claire disappears in a seaside Haitian village. Her mother died during childbirth and her father is a poor fisherman struggling to make ends meet. Just moments before disappearing, Claire's father agreed to let a local woman adopt her in hopes of giving his daughter a better life. Word of Claire's disappearance spreads through the village. And from there, the reader is taken on a journey through time, connecting lives together in unexpected ways. Edwidge Danticat is the author of several award-winning works of fiction. She's also a 2009 MacArthur Fellow. Her latest book, *Claire of the Sea Light*, is her first new work of fiction since winning that prestigious award. She joins us from member station WLRN in Miami. Welcome to the program.
**Edwidge Danticat:** Thank you. Thank you for having me.

**Martin:** I'd love if we could just start off by having you introduce us to this young girl.
**Danticat:** Well, Claire—her Creole name would be Claire Limye Lanme—is a little girl who is born when her mother dies in childbirth. And her father feels as though he won't be able to take care of her the way he would like to. So, he makes this really difficult choice to give her to Madame Gaelle, who is a well-to-do woman in town. And Claire is luminous—as luminous as her name—and a lucky and unlucky little girl at the same time.

**Martin:** To give us a sense of this place, this village, and this young woman, would you mind reading a bit from the book? Near the end, there's a scene where Claire's walking through a market.

**Danticat:** Yes. [Reading] "Salt was life, she would often hear the adults say. Some of the fishermen's wives would throw a pinch of crushed salt in the air for good luck before the men left for the sea. Some would also refuse to eat or wash or comb their hair until their men came back. When zombies ate salt, it brought them back to life, or so she had always heard. Maybe if she ate enough salt, she would finally understand why her father wouldn't let her wander, *flannen*. She would always try, though. Sometimes while her father was at sea, she would walk through the open market and pretend that she was one of those children sent to buy provisions to bring home to her mother. And she would pick up things at the market and put them down, raising then crushing the hopes of the vendors who would mumble under their breath as she walked away. Every now and again, one of the vendors would shout: Just like her mother. And she would ask herself what else she might do to make them say even more often that she was just like her mother, besides dying, that is."

**Martin:** There are a lot of victims in this story, not just this young girl, who has lost her mom. But there are several characters throughout this narrative, who, through no doing of their own, are made to suffer from some grief. I wonder if you could talk about how that sense of loss or longing connects all these people and brings this story to life.

**Danticat:** I don't think of them as victims. I think of them more as survivors. And the way that they survive is by the sense of community that this town offers. One of the things that Claire's mother liked to say was we must all look after each other. Because their town is so small, and they're sort of precariously always on the verge of instability, the healing comes through their coming together as a community.

**Martin:** There is a real sense of place in this book. It is a small village, and you bring to life the people who make up the town, characters who might be familiar to a lot of us: shopkeeper, he schoolmaster, the undertaker, who also happens to be the mayor. There's a radio host. Are these people who are familiar to you in your own life?

**Danticat:** Well, the town itself, Ville Rose, is modeled after the town where my mother was born. And it was a town that was very devastating after the earthquake and I still have some family members there. But I wanted to have that sense of familiarity in the community so that you meet people there that you might find in any other town but they're singular in their individual issues and their problems in the way they interact with the rest of the town.

**Martin:** If I understand, you yourself were separated from your own parents when you were growing up. Do you mind sharing circumstances of that separation?

**Danticat:** Well, my father left when I was two and my mother when I was four. They went to Brooklyn. We were not a family of means, and my parents, I think, had the difficult choice that a lot of parents have. I stayed behind with my uncle and his wife, and we grew up in a house that was full of children like us, cousins whose parents were in Canada, in the Dominican Republic. We had also grown up with this notion—and I think this is something I wanted to show in the book—that family is not always just mother, father. I didn't feel abandoned, you know. Even at that young age, I understood that it was something that my parents were trying to do to offer us a better opportunity.

**Martin:** There is one point in the book, one of the characters talks about how feeling abandoned by a parent is the most profound kind of loss. And . . .

**Danticat:** And another one says feeling abandoned by a child is the second-most, yeah. It's sort of a volley of loss, of separations that one doesn't choose.

**Martin:** You say that you understood your parents' reasons for leaving when you were young, but was there a point when you did feel that they had left you inexplicably?

**Danticat:** This is why I understood it very young. Because I realize that I was able to go to a particular kind of school because my parents were abroad, and every month this money would come that enabled us to do certain things; get our uniforms on time, get our shoes made, which you could do at that time, and I had a crooked foot so I had to have a special boot. You know, and I used to write letters to my parents and I used to go to the calling center once a week with my brother and my uncle and aunt to talk to them.

**Martin:** Can you describe another character in this book, and that is the sea, which literally kind of pushes and pulls this narrative along. How did that come to you as a part of this story?

**Danticat:** I just fell in love with the idea of writing about the sea, and there are many proverbs about the sea in Haitian Creole. You know, one is *lanme pa kenbe kras*, the sea doesn't hide dirt, and proverbs about, you know, my back is as large as the sea, which is something you say if people start talking badly about you. So, of course, for a lot of people in terms of migration, the sea is also the way out. So, you have an island and you have the sea, and it's extraordinarily fascinating to me.

**Martin:** You are able to draw us into these characters' lives, sometimes very quickly. And I found myself at the end of the book wanting to know more, wanting to stay with them longer. I wonder if you feel that way inevitably. Do you build out the next chapter in their lives in your imagination? Have you thought about Claire and what kind of young woman she would become?

**Danticat:** Oh. When I was done with the book, I kept having this talk with my editor because up until we had the return of Claire, it was still so open-ended. And she kept asking me where does Claire go, where does Claire go? And I realized that I didn't want to let her go. Someone said, you know, a good story is like a painting. You know, you might wonder what comes before and what comes after but you're just mesmerized by what you're seeing.

**Martin:** Edwidge Danticat. Her latest novel is called *Claire of the Sea Light*. Thank you so much for talking with us, Edwidge.

**Danticat:** Thank you very much for having me.

# The Art of Not Belonging

## Dwyer Murphy / 2013

From *Guernica Magazine*, September 2013. Reprinted with permission by Dwyer Murphy. "The Art of Not Belonging" appears as is originally printed in *Guernica*.

Almost a decade has passed since Edwidge Danticat's last work of book-length fiction, *The Dew Breaker*. In the meantime, she's written a memoir (*Brother, I'm Dying*—National Book Critics Circle Award winner, National Book Award nominee), received a MacArthur "genius" grant, edited the *Best American Essays* and *Haiti Noir* collections, delivered a Toni Morrison Lectures series that was turned into a celebrated book (*Create Dangerously*), and, in successive years, received honorary degrees from Smith and Yale. She's been so busy it's almost easy to forget what a homecoming her new book is. After the long wait, *Claire of the Sea Light* has just been released by Knopf.

At the book's center is its title character, Claire Limyè Lanmè, a young girl whose father is trying to give her away, so that she can be raised as another's daughter. This tragedy, born of an act of love, radiates out and we come to meet the local citizenry through their respective tales. As the stories progress, the individuals begin to recede slightly, allowing the town itself, Ville Rose, to come to the fore. Danticat has always portrayed Haiti with a careful lushness, but in *Claire of the Sea Light* she seems to have a new fervor. It is her first novel since the 2010 earthquake, which destroyed so much of the country. (Danticat spoke to *Guernica* on the one-year anniversary of the earthquake, discussing the devastation it wrought.) The stories are set in a near, undefined past, but there's a distinct sense that most of what Danticat is describing is now gone. There are no omens or soothsayers, and the richness of the place—the tropical vegetation, the precise placement of shops and homes, the biblical presence and span of family trees—is often a source of joy. But it's difficult not to imagine a grieving Danticat cataloging these as the losses she and other Haitians have suffered. As she explained in our conversation, "When I'm writing anything set in Haiti now, whether fiction or nonfiction, always in the back of my mind is how people, including some of my own family members, have been affected not just by history and by the present but also by the earthquake."

I met with Danticat on the campus of Brooklyn College. She arrived with a stranger in tow, someone who'd recognized her on the street and had been telling her stories about his family. It was a sunny afternoon and a Friday, but I'd have to be cynical not to believe that this sort of thing happens often to Danticat. She has an exceedingly warm, inviting manner. We found a bench beside a turtle pond and spoke about the delicate job of mining family history for fiction, translating her characters' Creole, Wikipedia's struggle to categorize her, and the tricky ending to her new novel. There's a slight lilt to Danticat's voice, and she often seemed amused at the things that hadn't quite been said.

**Guernica:** We get a host of characters and voices in this book, but there seems to be a special affection reserved for Claire, the title character. How did you first find her?

**Edwidge Danticat:** Claire came like a vision, really. It was the year after *The Dew Breaker* came out. This was a painful time for me. My father was dying from pulmonary fibrosis. My uncle Joseph had just died in the custody of the Department of Homeland Security while seeking asylum in the US. My oldest daughter Mira was born soon after that. I started writing a memoir about all these deaths and a birth, a book called *Brother, I'm Dying*. And right about that time I saw a documentary about orphans in Haiti. Or rather, not quite about orphans. It was about kids who have parents, but their parents bring them to an orphanage so they can have a better life. One of the aid workers in the documentary said that the parents do this because these people are not that attached to their kids.

My own parents left Haiti to work in New York while I stayed behind. I didn't grow up in an orphanage, but I grew up in my uncle's house with a lot of kids like me, whose parents were abroad, working. So after I saw this program, a new character came to me, almost the way someone appears in a dream. Claire Limyè Lanmè. Claire of the Sea Light, a child that a beloved parent would rather rip his heart out of his chest than to leave, but has no other choice but to try to give her to someone else to raise because he does not have the means to do it himself.

**Guernica:** The story began to fill in around Claire?

**Danticat:** I started writing about Claire and her father, and then it became too about the town where they live and how some of the town people are linked in some way, large or small, to this little girl. The story is told from different points of view. At first you get the story from her father, then from the woman to whom she's being given, then from Claire herself. I broke those stories up, as the three pillars of the book, and I always knew that Claire's story would come last. Because one of the pressing questions of the book is where is this girl going. Even I wasn't sure for a long time. My editor, Robin Desser, was asking me until the last moment what would happen to Claire. Is she alive? Is she going to stay with her father? Will she go with the woman he wants to give her to? I have written many different endings. The last thing I did, just before the galleys went through, was decide what happens to Claire.

**Guernica:** You're coming back to this fictional town, Ville Rose, where you've set stories in the past. Did you have any tricks for getting yourself oriented in the old space? Maps? Telephone directories?

**Danticat:** No maps or telephone directories. Ville Rose itself is a hybrid of a town, a mix of several coastal towns I have been to or have spent time in while in Haiti. For a long time, I just had fifty pages of material that I had already written and kept reading over and over again to keep re-immersing myself in the town. But the best moment in writing any book is when you just can't wait to get back to the writing, when you can't wait to re-enter that fictional place, when your fictional town feels even more real than the town where you actually live.

**Guernica:** When you're writing in English about characters that live in Haiti and speak Haitian Creole, how are their stories coming to you?

**Danticat:** All of it basically comes to me in Creole, with mental SimulTrans.

**Guernica:** Like your work at the UN?

**Danticat:** Yes, except it's implanted in my brain. It's just automatic. Part of it has to do with the bilingualism/trilingualism of my life. The characters are speaking Creole in my mind. I can hear just what they're saying, and I'm the translator. Some things I leave in Creole, for readers who are bilingual and who may have another interpretation. The term "dew breaker," for example, was "choukèt laroze." That could be translated as "dew shaker" or "dew smasher." But "dew breaker" is much more poetic, so that's how I translated it. It all happens quickly. I feel like I'm there watching or listening to the characters. I remember an early review of *Claire* that called it "a love letter to her homeland." And for a tiny split second, I was surprised while reading this, because to me that implied that I wasn't there in my "homeland"—in Haiti. I thought "What? I'm not?" When I'm writing, it feels like I'm very much there.

**Guernica:** Would these be very different stories if you didn't translate? If you took them down in Creole?

**Danticat:** Oh, definitely. I had that experience with *Krik? Krak!* I made some of the stories into radio plays in Creole and they become totally different. More alive in some way. More immediate. In the epigraph to *Drown*, Junot Diaz uses a quote from a Cuban poet, Gustavo Pérez Firmat—"The fact that I am writing to you in English already falsifies what I wanted to tell you." This is the dilemma of the immigrant writer. If I'd lived in Haiti my whole life, I'd be writing these things in Creole. But these stories I am writing now are coming through me as a person who, though I travel to Haiti often, has lived in the US for more than three decades now.

Often when you're an immigrant writing in English, people think it's primarily a commercial choice. But for many of us, it's a choice that rises out of the circumstances of our lives. These are the tools I have at my disposal, based on my experiences. It's a constant debate, not just in my community but in other communities as well. Where do you belong? You're kind of one of us, but you now write in a different language. You're told you don't belong to American literature or you're told you don't belong to Haitian literature. Maybe there's a place on the hyphen, as Julia Alvarez so brilliantly wrote in one of her essays. That middle generation, the people whose parents brought them to other countries as small children, or even people who were born to immigrant parents, maybe they can have their own literature, too.

**Guernica:** Jonathan Lee recently interviewed your agent, Nicole Aragi, for *Guernica*, and she was talking about the insanity of a recent controversy on Wikipedia, in which you and other authors were moved out of the "American novelists" category, onto other lists. You were put in the "Haitian Women Novelists" category, I think. So apparently Wikipedia editors are part of that crowd that's fretting over how to categorize you.

**Danticat:** Isn't that something? The funniest reaction to all of this came from someone who was shocked that, with a name like Edwidge, I am even a woman. But I agree with Nicole that the whole thing is pretty outrageous.

And also, what's the point? I don't see any reason to keep microcategorizing women writers, setting them more and more apart, except to marginalize them. I'm happy that someone brought it out in the light before the categories could keep getting more and more narrow. Soon I might be [categorized by Wikipedia] in "Haitian novelists under five feet five tall."

**Guernica:** Talking about how these categories are used to marginalize women in the writing industry, it still seems to be the case that the literary press skews white and male, and that books by women are reviewed less often. Have you noticed any particular slant to the attention your work gets?
**Danticat:** There is definitely some imbalance. Sometimes you'll see a formidable book come out by an extraordinary woman writer go nearly unnoticed. Jesmyn Ward's *Salvage the Bones*, for example, was mostly reviewed in the big publications after she won the National Book Award. You also wish that there were more parity to the press that the book is getting. Last year when Jamaica Kincaid's book *See Now Then* came out, the press was so one-toned. It wouldn't have been that way for a male writer. It's not a matter of whether the reviews are good or bad, it's about being taken seriously, both as a woman writer and as a writer of color. Also, it worries me when people point to a couple of women writers or writers of color who get some attention—and I am sometimes pulled into that category—to prove that others are getting a fair shot. It's like those people who keep saying that racism no longer exists in this country because Barack Obama is President of the United States.

**Guernica:** You've talked about a certain pressure you feel from the Haitian community, which sometimes takes offence at the way you're portraying Haiti. How do you deal with those encounters?
**Danticat:** For better or worse, we all have a tendency to overgeneralize our individual experiences. After I've published something, I'll meet someone who says, "I'm Haitian, and I don't know this, so it must not be true." Even if we're talking about a work of fiction. I understand very well the desire to protect and defend Haiti. I've gotten very angry myself reading many things about Haiti. So my own personal barometer is this: Am I telling a nuanced and complex story? Am I telling my version of the truth, which I know may not be somebody else's. We're not a monolithic group; no group is. Also, it's important to keep in mind the genre in which we are writing. Fiction is full of invented stories about exceptional people in exceptional situations. Those situations are not always cheery or celebratory. Also, fiction is not

journalism or sociology or anthropology. Every story is singular. The way we get depth is by putting a bunch of singular stories together to tell larger more complex and sometimes even contradictory stories. This is why I love editing and why it's been such a pleasure to edit both *Haiti Noir* and *Haiti Noir 2*, which will be published next January. In those books for example, you have eighteen writers' versions of Haiti. You get sadness. You get joy. You get lyricism. You get darkness. You get light. And yes, you get the danger too. But what you don't get is, as Chimamanda Ngozi Adichie put it in her great TED talk, a single story.

**Guernica:** Many of your stories seem to arise out of painful episodes in your family's history. Do you find some catharsis in turning them into fiction? Does your family, once they've read them?

**Danticat:** I get some catharsis from it, yes, but I don't think my family always feels like what I'm doing is cathartic for them. Even with the fiction, they feel exposed. With the first book, you learn all your lessons. It was difficult for my parents at first. When people at their church started reading my first book, *Breath, Eyes, Memory*, it was uncomfortable for my parents because people immediately assumed that I was writing about myself and about them. After that book came out, my mother told me, "You know, people are going to think you're not a good girl." My parents also spent most of their adult lives under a dictatorship. To them being out there in the world talking about things was not safe. But as we all got older, there was a transition. They became happy that I was also telling people good things about Haiti. They saw it as a kind of service to the country and all was forgiven.

**Guernica:** In an essay in the collection *Create Dangerously*, you describe returning home to Haiti with the body of your cousin, Marius, and your aunt asking you not to write about it. Do you usually comply with those requests?

**Danticat:** Sometimes family members will ask to be kept out of certain things that I'm writing, and I try to respect that. I'd much rather have relatives than a book. With my aunt, when I ended up writing about that incident we came to a kind of compromise. I changed the names. If it would have totally wrecked my relationship with my aunt, I would have used it in fiction, maybe, but I wouldn't have written about it in an essay. This is something I had to balance carefully when I was writing the memoir. I've written essays where I mention things that I thought were very benign and those were the things that upset some family members. And sometimes the things you're expecting to upset them don't. When I was done with the memoir, I emailed the manuscript to my brothers and told them I'd take out anything they objected to. One of them said, "We don't like the way so much of it is about you." Even though it was more about my dad and uncle, I could see why he would think that. We'd all gone through these terrible things together and I was the only one telling the public story.

**Guernica:** Did you change things based on your brothers' notes?
**Danticat:** I did adjust some things. But one of the greatest compliments I ever got came from my youngest brother when he read the finished book. He said, "It's all there. Just like it happened."

**Guernica:** You're a mother of young children now. Will your kids be off-limits, like with the White House Press Corps?
**Danticat:** I think you mean the Little Haiti Press Corps. [*Chuckles.*] Some people get annoyed at women writers who even mention their children. Or there are all these theories about how many you can have, etc. I mention my children, first, because people often ask about the motherhood/writing balance thing and I also mention them because I can't tell you how much it meant to me when I was starting out to read about Toni Morrison and her two sons. It was very comforting to me that she was a mother of two and working full time and writing novels too. It made many things seem within my reach. So I'm not going be putting my children on full blast all the time, but every once in a while they are called to participate in the family project that are these books. My oldest happens to be on the cover of *Claire of the Sea Light*. She's very proud of it. She won't know what a remainder table is though because now I feel like I'll have to buy every leftover copy of the book I ever see.

**Guernica:** And you'll be okay with her reading it, too?
**Danticat:** I can't wait for both my daughters to be old enough to read all my books. I loved it every time I saw my parents acting like more than just my parents. And I'm looking forward to that with my daughters too. I am looking forward to having them discover me as someone completely other than their mother.

**Guernica:** Do you consider *Claire of the Sea Light* a novel, or a story collection?
**Danticat:** I think of it as something in between. A kind of hybrid. Notice, we didn't write "A Novel" on the cover. I don't want people to think I'm trying

to pass this off as something it's not. Many wonderful works of fiction have been written this way. Jean Toomer's *Cane* is one of my favorites. Sherwood Anderson's *Winesburg, Ohio*. Thornton Wilder's *The Bridge of San Luis Rey*, Elizabeth Strout's *Olive Kitteridge*, among others.

**Guernica:** This is the first book of fiction you've published since the earthquake—has your writing about Haiti changed since then?

**Danticat:** The landscape has changed so much, the physical spaces. There is this split between the Haiti of before the earthquake and the Haiti of after the earthquake. So when I'm writing anything set in Haiti now, whether fiction or nonfiction, always in the back of my mind is how people, including some of my own family members, have been affected not just by history and by the present but also by the earthquake.

**Guernica:** *Claire of the Sea Light* is set pre-earthquake, but certain passages about the town and the country feel elegiac.

**Danticat:** I started working on half the book before the earthquake and half of it after the earthquake. But at some point in the writing, even before the earthquake happened, this place I was writing about became a town on the verge of disaster. For a while, I had the year in the book explicitly. 2009. But eventually I took that out. I didn't want it to be some big revelation, a dramatic ta-da moment of the year before the earthquake.

**Guernica:** One of the aphorisms that Claire repeats seems particularly evocative of this seaside town: "Salt is life." Is that something you heard growing up in Haiti or something you invented for the story?

**Danticat:** I might have heard it. But salt is a powerful symbol in Haiti, as elsewhere. Salt of the earth, for example, is an American phrase isn't it? In Haiti, myth and legend has it that if you are turned into a zombie, if someone gives you a taste of salt, then you can come back to life. And in the life of the fishermen, there are so many little things about salt that I wanted to incorporate. The salt in the air. The crackling of salt in the fire. There's all this damage, this peeling of the fishing boats from the sea salt. But there is also healing from it, sea baths that are supposed to heal all kinds of aches and wounds.

**Guernica:** This might be a bit forward for our first meeting, but do you know where you're going to be buried? Your characters often have very definite ideas about that. It occurred to me that it might be a personal preoccupation of yours.

**Danticat:** It's always been something of an obsession of mine but has become more so since my eighty-one-year-old uncle died here in the United States, after never wanting to leave Haiti, except for short periods of time. When my uncle died, his body could not be returned to Haiti so he was buried in Queens, New York. He was always so sure that he was going to be buried in our family mausoleum in Port-au-Prince. He had also taken this very strong stand against leaving Haiti permanently. Someone has to stay, he always said. And he ended up being buried in Queens next to my father, who had been the one who left. Ultimately, we don't always get a say, but I'd like to be cremated, so that I can rest in many places. A little in Haiti. A little here.

**Guernica:** Gang violence seems to increasingly crop up in your work. It creates an important plot point in *Claire of the Sea Light.* Is it something you've set out to explore?

**Danticat:** I wrote about gang violence in *Brother, I'm Dying* because it is in part what drove my uncle to leave Haiti and the neighborhood he had been living in for fifty years and to request asylum in the United States, something that led to his death. A group from the United Nations force, which is still in Haiti now, had basically invaded my uncle's house and occupied the roof and had shot at people from my uncle's roof, and when they retreated some of the people from the neighborhood wanted to kill my uncle because they thought he had willingly participated in the operation.

Living in a poor area, you are easily criminalized. The UN people might have just as easily killed my uncle too, the way they had killed innocent people who become their collateral damage in other operations in other poor neighborhoods in Port-au-Prince. But I wanted to write about the gang violence in both the memoir and in this book because even with all that had happened I couldn't totally demonize the young people who ended up joining the gangs, because some of them I had known since they were young. Many have since been killed in later operations like the one that happened from the top of my uncle's roof that day, but they were not ghosts but people to me. My uncle had hired some of them who had been deported from the United States as English tutors or computer teachers for some of the kids in the school he had in the neighborhood. Some of these same young men who had threatened my uncle's life had been at my aunt's funeral not long before that. Some of their parents were parishioners in my uncle's church. I would see them during different visits. I can't tell you what they were doing elsewhere, but my uncle knew them as neighbors and tried to coexist with them because—and maybe this was because he was a minister—he never stopped believing in redemption. He believed that no matter what people were calling these guys, there was goodness in them. So this part of it, the more intimate and less sensational part of gang life, from my limited exposure and from a bit of my uncle's perspective, is something I wanted to try explore in fiction, after writing about it in the memoir.

Sometimes fiction allows you to explore these types of complicated spaces more deeply. I didn't want to redeem the face of violence, but it is important for me to show that it is not always coming from one side. In *Claire*, Tiye and his people, for example, are not the only gangsters in the book. A lot of other seemingly good people also have a lot of blood on their hands.

**Guernica:** Since your uncle died seeking asylum, in the custody of Homeland Security, you've been very vocal about immigration reform and about asylum detention in particular. Are you feeling frustrated that President Obama, of whom you were an early supporter, hasn't been able to make more progress on these issues?

**Danticat:** Yes, the fact that immigration reform has been so stalled is rather disappointing. On the one hand, you have the stalled reform and on the other hand all this draconian "show me your papers" legislation cropping up all over the country and some deplorable things happening in detention centers, where asylum seekers are still being treated deplorably and many of them are still dying the same way my uncle did. Last February, according to a group I am involved with called Americans for Immigrant Justice, several of their now clients, women who were seeking asylum, were taken into custody in Texas and placed in something called the icebox. They were put in cells with more than twenty-five people, cells with no chairs or beds, just a toilet. The lights were kept on twenty-four hours a day and the temperature was kept really low. It seems like in some quarters they want to make life so miserable for immigrants and asylum seekers that they will "self-deport" or think twice about coming to this country before whatever version of immigrant reform passes.

**Guernica:** Do you wish that other writers were as willing to get involved in politics?

**Danticat:** Albert Camus in his December 1957 lecture *"L'artiste et son temps,"* which was translated as "Create Dangerously," says, "The writers of today know this. If they speak up, they are criticized and attacked. If they become modest and keep silent, they are vociferously blamed for their silence." I think everyone should just do what they're comfortable doing. I wouldn't want to diminish the fact that writing itself, whatever it is, can be a way of being involved. And I would never want to presume to tell others what to do.

**Guernica:** Relative to other "literary" writers, your books enjoy quite a bit of popular success. Do you attribute it to anything in particular?

**Danticat:** Oprah! Everything changed when Oprah chose *Breath, Eyes, Memory* for her book club in the spring of 1998. I had published two books when she picked my first, and that fall when I went on tour for my third— *The Farming of Bones*—I could already see the difference in terms of a wider interest in my work. She introduced my work to people who might have never read me and a lot of those readers are still with me today.

**Guernica:** Are you working on something new now, while *Claire of the Sea Light* is launching?

**Danticat:** The best advice I ever got as a writer was from my first editor at Soho Press, Laura Hruska. Rest her soul. This was when *Breath, Eyes, Memory* was in galleys. We had just gotten a paperback deal with Vintage, thanks to two wonderful editors there, Dawn Davis and Robin Desser, my current editor at Knopf. I was working as an assistant at Jonathan Demme's film production company then, Clinica Estetico, which was just down the street from Soho Press. Laura came over and sat next to me in my little cubicle, and looked me straight in the eye and said, "Edwidge, you're now going to have to start thinking about a writing career."

Frankly, I hadn't been fully thinking that way. I thought I'd write a couple of books, then go on to do something else. Maybe work on films, which I have also been lucky enough to do. So Laura Hruska told me that I needed to start on something new right away, before the book came out, so that whether it got a really good or a really bad or an indifferent reception, at least I'd have another writing project already in the works to return to. I've always tried to follow that advice. So right now, I'm about a hundred pages into my new book. I will have that to return to once Claire has begun to make her way into the world.

# Maneuvering Myself around a Scene: A Conversation with Edwidge Danticat

## Brendan Dowling / 2013

From Public Libraries On-line, October 2013. Reprinted with permission by Brendan Dowling.

Edwidge Danticat's extraordinary new novel, *Claire of the Sea Light*, introduces the reader to the fictional Haitian town of Ville Rose. Centered around the resilient Claire, the novel takes place over the course of her seventh birthday, when her widower father asks a local businesswoman to adopt his beloved daughter in the hopes of her having a more financially secure life. From that wrenching decision, the novel spins out to the other members of the community, from the local principal and his visiting son, to the host of a popular radio show, to the gang members on the outskirts of town. Danticat's career has been incredibly prolific, ranging from her National Book Award–nominated novel *Krik? Krak!* to her National Book Critic's Circle Award–winning memoir *Brother, I'm Dying*. Her latest book has been equally praised. The *New York Times* observed that "the images in *Claire of the Sea Light* have the hard precision and richly saturated colors of a woodblock print or folk art painting" while the *Pittsburgh Post-Gazette* proclaimed that "the beautiful prose, captivating story and intricate narrative structure are to be savored." Danticat spoke to Brendan Dowling via email on October 14, 2013.

**Public Libraries:** All of the characters—whether they seem good or bad at first glance—have such rich interior lives, and many have huge secrets that are revealed as the novel progresses. Do the characters arrive fully formed as you begin the writing process or do these layers appear through subsequent drafts?

**Edwidge Danticat:** Some characters arrive fully formed, but that is rare. Most of my characters offer me a glimpse of themselves, then I have to dig deeper and think about them and even start writing about them before I fully understand who they are. I see the creation of characters as being a lot like getting to know actual people in real life. Some people you just meet and feel as though you've known them all your life. Others take a little longer or a lot longer to reveal themselves to you.

**PL:** The novel has a distinctive lyrical tone and you've talked in other interviews how the plot is structured on the wonn songs that Claire and her friends sing on the beach. Can you explain what wonn songs are for our readers who might not be familiar with them and how they worked their way into the book?
**ED:** Wonn is a children's game that is a lot like "Ring around the Rosie." Kids, often little girls, get together, hold hands, make a circle, and run clockwise, or counter-clockwise while singing. One child is in the middle while the others are singing and they switch places during different moments in the song. This game mirrors the structure of the book in that the book moves back and forth through time and circles back to different characters. The main action takes place in one night. I imagine the reader joining that circle, if you will, as he or she tries to understand what is happening in the town at that moment. Though the book is named after Claire, it is really the story of this entire town, Ville Rose, which is a fictional town based on the place where my mother grew up. The structure of the book also mirrors the waves of the sea, pulling back and forth towards the people on the beach, sometimes with tragic circumstances.

**PL:** All the parents in the novel go to incredible lengths to protect their children or provide them with a better life. How did your own role as a daughter and mother inform these parent-child relationships?
**ED:** My parents moved to the United States for work when I was very young, leaving me in the wonderful care of my aunt and uncle. I grew up in a house full of children like me, children whose parents were away in different countries working. It is a great act of sacrifice to leave your child. I understand that fully now from the perspective of both a child and now a parent, who can fully understand how much love and strength it would take to move to a new country and leave my child behind, which mothers and fathers all over the world are forced to do all the time. This is something I tried to show in the book, the difficulties of that choice from three points of view, that of Claire, her father who has to give her away, and the woman who might eventually take her.

**PL:** In your interview with *Guernica*, you talked about how when you adapted some of the stories from *Krik? Krak!* into radio plays, the essence of the stories changed when they were told in Creole. What about these stories changed when their characters were speaking their native Creole?

**ED:** The stories were more "oral." Part of that was Creole, which is a language I heard stories in when I was a child. But also because they were meant for the radio. They were meant to be spoken so there was more dialogue and the characters were speaking directly to an audience that understood everything they were saying, every reference, every word.

**PL:** You've served as editor for the anthologies *Haiti Noir* and the upcoming *Haiti Noir 2*. What do you enjoy about editing and what draws you back to it again and again?

**ED:** I love that conversation with other writers and their work. You read very closely and also have to see how things fit together to make a whole book which includes many voices but is not repetitive or inconsistent. It's also a lot easier than writing. Someone has already done all the hard work.

**PL:** You were working for Jonathan Demme's production company when *Breath, Eyes, Memory* came out. Has your work in film and love of cinema had any effect on your writing style?

**ED:** I have grown to love storyboarding for example, a crucial element in imagining a scene in movie making. Sometimes I will do story board now, with stick figure images as I can't draw to save my life. I will make a story board if I have trouble visualizing or maneuvering myself around a scene. I have also learned a lot from the way films are edited. A lot of writers linger too long on transitional scenes that don't add much to the plot. In films and on TV, those scenes are just cut and you jump to the next one that matters, so there is more narrative drive to the story.

**PL:** This year you worked with Emeline Michel on her album *Quintessence* and provided vocals for her song "Dawn." How did that partnership come about? Are you interested in exploring the music world more?

**ED:** Emeline is a friend and someone I admire very much. We have been meaning to work together for a long time. When she asked me to write a song for her new album, I was very happy. I would love to do more songwriting in the future. It would be amazing to write a libretto for example.

**PL:** And, finally, what role have libraries played in your life?

**ED:** Where do I begin? I have written entire essays on this. Libraries have saved me. When I first moved to New York from Haiti, I was very shy. I did not speak any English. I would go into the Brooklyn Public Library and find books in French, books by Haitian writers and other Francophone writers and those books made me feel as though I was back home. I would always borrow the maximum amount of books and devour them in a week. My parents didn't have enough money to buy that many books so I would not have had access to them if not for the public library. I am grateful, deeply grateful, for public libraries. I think if you interview a hundred writers, especially those of us who grew up in poor urban centers, you'll find that the shadow of a public library looms rather large in our formation and in our psyche.

# A Conversation with Edwidge Danticat

## Kima Jones / 2014

From *The Rumpus*, January 1, 2014. Reprinted with permission by Kima Jones.

Edwidge Danticat returned to fiction this year with her novel, *Claire of the Sea Light*. Set in the fictional town of Ville Rose, Danticat expertly takes us back through time on the rich story legs of this community. On our journey we meet a mute woman who has just lost her husband, a circle of girls playing ring games, a father desperately trying to make sense of his economic situation and his daughter's life. Claire disappears for most of the novel, and her tragic story is actually the bookend of so many other heartbreaking tales. As always, Danticat mixes fable and lore, myth and virtue to tell a book deeply shaped by communal suffering and love and want.

Edwidge and I discussed resistance. We talked about the little voice inside of us that puts fires out. We talked about the kind of resistance needed to learn to read and write in the face of execution. We talked about resisting the noise of the crowd long enough to tell a story that is uniquely your own. We talked about what resistance means for hundreds of thousands of displaced Haitian people in the Dominican Republic. We talked about resisting the urge to write the truth down and then finally giving into it as if our lives depend on it. As if resistance is the only thing that makes life worth the telling.

**The Rumpus:** I first want to talk a little bit about the formatting of *Claire of the Sea Light* because you are known for your short stories. I've seen this book referred to as a short story collection, novel-in-story, vignettes, a novel—what is the distinction for you?

**Edwidge Danticat:** I'm not sure what the distinction is, but I'll tell you what my intention was. I'm a huge fan of Jean Toomer's *Cane*. I love it because it's such a free, unruly book. It takes genre and form and bends it and forces it into the narrative he wants it to be. I love how that kind of freedom in narration echoes back to the old traditions of storytelling, through songs, to poetry, to shooting the dozens. In Kreyol we have *odyans*, which is storytelling but about real people. I love that mixture of things. I was thinking about writing a book like a radio show and each chapter would be like an episode, so, to me, they were always stories. That hybrid between the short story and the novel, that thing in between that some people call the story circle or the novel-in-story, is a form of its own that's been done before, from Toomer's *Cane*, to *Olive Kitteridge*, to *The Dubliners*.

**Rumpus:** Alice Munro won the Nobel Prize this year for short stories. Some called it a resurgence of the form, a resuscitation of a fairly unpopular genre. Can you talk about the magic of the short story and why it's your first form?
**Danticat:** The short story is like an exquisite painting and you might, when looking at this painting, be wondering what came before or after, but you are fully absorbed in what you're seeing. Your gaze is fixed, and you are fully engaged. That's the beauty of the short story. Some stories are really, really short, like Lydia Davis's brilliant prose. You capture the world in this really economical way. I was very happy to see Alice win because I think it does validate the form, but I don't know that it was ever unpopular. George Saunders, Junot Díaz, Jhumpa Lahiri are all examples of an interest in the short story. Alice Munro's career has proven that yes, one can make a career writing short stories. I don't know if one can make a living, though.

**Rumpus:** *Claire of the Sea Light* is set in the fictional seaside town of Ville Rose, a town shaped by its beauty—hence its namesake—but also the mountains above it, the sea at its border, the buzz of its single radio program, and the corruption of its civil servants. Talk to me about building this world. Specifically, I'm interested in how you break up and bring together social classes using topography.
**Danticat:** When my first book, *Breath, Eyes, Memory*, came out, I wrote about many real Haitian towns and a lot of people who were from those towns would say "you got this wrong" and "got that wrong," so I decided to write about my own town by borrowing elements of different places. If you are inventing a town, you have all freedom. I added the lighthouse. Langston Hughes has a children's book called *Popo and Fifina*, set in Haiti during the US occupation because he used to travel to Haiti quite a bit. And I remembered that the story has a lighthouse in it, so I reread it and thought, *I want a lighthouse*, and the lighthouse went in. I could visually see the town and see myself walking around in it, but that takes many, many layers of writing. Sometimes in writing

you have to live with things before you inhabit them, and that takes a very long time for it to stop feeling constructed and to start feeling like something real.

**Rumpus:** Communal belief suggests that Claire is a *revenan*, a spirit echo, because of the way she was born. How do you decide on the mythology of the people you're writing about?

**Danticat:** Well, a lot of the mythology I create on my own. I'm really into folklore, and that's one of the many reasons why I love Zora Neale Hurston: because she made such great use of mythology and folklore in her anthropological work and fiction. What people were calling magical realism was so much incorporated into people's daily lives. People create their own mythologies for their lives.

A *revenan* is also a resting place, a vessel, one who returns. I wanted this to be the "fakelore" in this family—that people believed this girl was somehow mystical. For example, in our own folklore, we have so many stories about missing mothers and stepmothers, and I think a lot of that has to do with maternal mortality. There are a lot of stories about children who grow up without mothers and often that's a child who suffers. I think the community often creates stories to protect our psyche, to comfort us, to give us some control back.

**Rumpus:** I'm absolutely a huge fan of Zora Neale Hurston and she has informed my work in so many ways. What do you think of her work around zombies in Haiti?

**Danticat:** Many Haitians have trouble with that. . . . There was a Haitian president whose goat died, and he had a full Catholic mass for the goat— very similar to the scene in *Their Eyes Were Watching God*, with the horse. Her other observations, her travels to the countryside, are so important, because had she not been around and gone there, some details would not have been recorded because society was changing so much both in Haiti and Jamaica. So much would have been lost. The outside eye can also be a sympathetic eye and that's powerful.

**Rumpus:** I'm really intrigued by the notions of "twinning" and "resurrection" in this book. For example, a pregnant Gaelle swallows a dead frog for life. Louise believes Claire may carry her otherworldly birthmarks. The rain births and kills frogs. Lasiren protects and swallows fishermen. Can you discuss these mirror reflections in terms of Claire's twinning—when we see her at the beginning and end of the novel?

**Danticat:** It is tied to the notion of the *revenan* and the dual notion of coming and going. For me, the closest my life came to a big theme in literature was when I was pregnant with my first daughter and my father was dying. I was in the middle of the cycle of life. If I were a poet, I think I would have written a grand poem about it, to capture what felt to me like a slip into the cycle of universal truth: a life was coming and my father was going. I felt like I was living a story that was beyond me. My father kept saying, "I want to meet the first child of my first child." And sure enough my daughter was born and we spent a month with him and then he died. Everyone said he held on to meet her. We call her Mira, and his name was Maracin.

Maybe the book reflects this a bit too much, but I've been sort of looking into these notions of twinning. This sort of idea of looking for the other half, and looking for your place in the world. Because Claire was born out of this tragedy, she is looking for that. Many of the characters in the book are looking for their place in the world.

**Rumpus:** The radio is its own character in this novel—almost that of the Greek chorus. Its listeners are speakers and jury and judge. Why did you make the radio such a major part of this book?

**Danticat:** I grew up listening to the radio, and it's a very powerful medium in Haiti. It's a medium of justice, of entertainment, but also it's where things are aired and talked about where they wouldn't be otherwise. I imagined the entire book would be like the radio. In a way, the book is the book Louise is writing. The radio is probably the most democratic form of justice where people can be heard. I think of the book as part of Louise's show and her narration of the town.

**Rumpus:** I want to talk about the heart of this book without giving away its secrets. I was dispirited by the narrative around same-gender-loving people. There are already so many tragically gay characters in literature; what was new for you in the story between these two men?

**Danticat:** If you are writing about same-gender-loving people in an environment that is hostile to their relationship, I think the dilemma is, do you reflect that reality? For those two characters, their class issue would actually trump their homosexuality within their community. Class is the first strike and the issue of their love is second. To portray their situation honestly, the overwhelming odds against them has to be written in. I tried very hard to validate them, and I imagined them as everyday love relationships. In reality, they would be Romeo and Juliet times two. Everyone in the book suffers for their love, but I agree with you about tragic portrayals. I agree with you, and I'll try to do better.

**Rumpus:** Maxim's decisions work for the plot but not toward self-actualization. Why don't we ever see the lovers together in the way that we see their straight counterparts? I want to juxtapose this question in relation to a quote from your novel, *The Dew Breaker*: "Life was neither something you defended by hiding nor surrendered calmly on other people's terms, but something you lived bravely, out in the open, and that if you had to lose it, you should lose it on your own terms."

**Danticat:** Really, they were hiding. They don't live in a place where either one of them feels like they can be fully who they are. Their entire struggle was to try to be together, but in this town, based on where my mother grew up, the only type of homosexuality that people would be willing to see unhidden is a caricature: a cross-dresser at Carnivale that everyone can laugh at. But the more honest, loving, everyday homosexual love, they would have to hide much more.

**Rumpus:** I want to switch gears and discuss the Dominican Republic's decision to revoke the citizenship of Dominicans of Haitian ancestry. You've written extensively on Dominican-Haitian relations on your own accord, but also with Junot Díaz. Can you talk about the social justice work that needs to be done, the work ahead, future collaborations between you and Junot?

**Danticat:** This has been an ongoing concern for a very long time, because Haitian cane workers and other workers have been going to the Dominican Republic for a long time. Also, little is known that there is a reverse migration for Dominican workers who come to Haiti with contracts to build roads, et cetera. Haiti is the number two, if not the number one trading partner of the Dominican Republic. It's one of the few places in the world where you have one island that occupies two very, very different countries. Haiti has become a kind of scapegoat for Dominican problems, but there have been moments of unity. For example, after the earthquake, the Dominican Republic was one of the first places to respond.

There are extraordinary human rights groups in the Dominican Republic that disagree with and are protesting the decision. On September 23, when the decision came down, Julia Alvarez and Junot Díaz immediately wrote me to ask, *What do we do? What can we do?* I thought it was brave and courageous to recognize a wrong just because it is a wrong. People have called Julia and Junot traitors. Ultimately we share this island and we share humanity. This is wrong, and it is unprecedented. It's not even creating an underclass or second citizenship—it is saying that you are stateless and you have no place to go.

I remember reading something by Toni Cade Bambara where she says that writing is the way she participates in the struggle. And it's not the only way, you need boots on the ground, but writing is most at our disposal. Junot and I first wrote about this fourteen years ago, when we wrote the op-ed for the *New York Times*, and now it has gotten worse. I want to encourage people to vote with their economic choices and actions. Do you want to go on a vacation to a place like this? To a place that treats people like this? Jacques Roumain, one of Haiti's great novelists, has a book called *Masters of the Dew*. In it, he says, "Cooperation is the friendship of the poor." It's been wonderful to not have to respond on my own, to have Julia and Junot's voice.

**Rumpus:** In the novel, Gaelle observes the struggles of documented and undocumented countrymen abroad. She fears that if she leaves Ville Rose, she will be buried with strangers rather than her ancestors. There is the fear of not being able to return but also the fear of being forced to return. Can you elaborate?

**Danticat:** Recently we've had an increase in the number of boats that we've seen coming from Haiti. Just a few weeks ago, four people died in a boat that was capsized right off the shore. I went to the funeral of a young woman, twenty-four, who had gotten on a boat and died getting here. People die and others are returned. My own uncle died in immigration custody. He came on a plane with a valid visa—he had been coming for thirty years—but he came at a time when the UN was shooting in his town and he requested asylum. At eighty-one years old, he was arrested, put in jail, his medication was taken away, and he died five days later. From the people who are coming across the border in containers in trucks, to the people who die at sea, it is a very complex matter of life and death. When people get here, certainly in terms of Haitian migration, there is unequal treatment in part to do with race and in part that we come from a poor country. You can talk about it ideologically, but when you are looking down at a young girl in a coffin who made that journey and realize that had she lived, she would have been turned back anyway, it becomes a very urgent problem.

**Rumpus:** *Create Dangerously: The Immigrant Artist at Work* is the most important book for me in terms of understanding the artist's life and the trials in truth-telling. The idea of being haunted by personal creation myths—those stories that have shaped and informed us and haunt our work—completely changed my understanding of my work and how I approach my writing. This framework of accepting the haunting and inviting the spirits in: when and how did you discover it?

**Danticat:** It comes slowly. I read Toni Morrison's *Sula* a lot. I read it for time. I read it for setting. I read it for every book I write. I read it for language and I read it for how much she squeezes in that little book without leaving anything out. It is the godmother of every one of my books.

When I was writing *Create Dangerously*, I had so much resistance, from myself and my family. *What are you going to do with your life? When are you going to get married?* I used to feel like if I had enough for groceries and a roof over my head and I could write my stories, I would be happy. Then I started looking into the lives of people who had it worse, who had greater struggles but still came into their art. A guiding essay for me is Alice Walker's "In Search of Our Mother's Gardens." I read it a lot.

*Create Dangerously* was about giving myself permission. There are people who come into writing emboldened and formed. I wasn't like that. I had to give myself permission. People asked me, "Well, what do you know of Haiti? What do you know of America?" I learned to give myself permission, that this is a worthwhile endeavor, that I would fail sometimes, it would work sometimes, but like Maya Angelou says, that place had been earned for me. All I had to do was claim it.

**Rumpus:** Create dangerously, for people who read dangerously. This is what I've always thought it meant to be a writer. Writing, knowing in part that no matter how trivial your words may seem, someday, somewhere, someone may risk his or her life to read them. Do you still stand by these words?

**Danticat:** I do. I know families who had to bury their libraries in their backyard. I know people who have gotten through impossible moments because of a book. I know the power of words. I am an accident of literacy, and in a way, we all are. When Nikky Finney accepted the National Book Award, she immediately cited that. For a lot of us, it goes back generations. If you come from a place where literacy is a luxury and not everyone gets to go to school, and not everyone gets to read, it makes it an even more powerful notion. I've seen the power of words in action. I saw Nikky Finney's ancestors in that glorious moment delivering that speech. I saw them smuggling words against death and censorship.

For aspiring writers, seek your truth and tell it. We live in a moment where it's so easy to see what everyone else is doing and to compare yourself to that. Seek your truth and tell it. Just seek your truth. It is a harder thing to sit in the stillness. You're the best person to tell your own story. Trust that.

# The Dominican Republic and Haiti: A Shared View from the Diaspora

## Richard André / 2014

From *Americas Quarterly*, Summer 2014. Reprinted with permission by *Americas Quarterly* and Edwidge Danticat.

In a landmark ruling, the Dominican Republic's Constitutional Court last September stripped an estimated 210,000 individuals—most of whom are Dominicans born to Haitian sugar cane workers—of their citizenship, effectively leaving them stateless. The ensuing outcry from the international community has included Junot Díaz and Edwidge Danticat—two of the best-known contemporary authors from the island of Hispaniola. Friends for over twenty years, Danticat (from Haiti) and Díaz (from the DR) have been relentless in their condemnation of the ruling. In a written exchange moderated by *Americas Quarterly* production editor and Haitian American Richard André, Díaz and Danticat discuss the roots and legacies of racism and conflict in the neighboring nations, the impact of the court's ruling, and the responsibility of the diaspora to build bridges between Dominicans and Haitians and defend human rights at home and abroad.

**Q:** What do you think most Haitians/Dominicans don't understand about the other side?
**Junot Díaz:** Depends on who you're asking. Some folks on the DR side know a lot more about their neighbor than others. Some Dominicans are in fact descended from said neighbor and might know a thing or two because of it.

Yet there is no question that there's not enough real contact, and that the anti-Haitian derangements of certain sectors in the Dominican Republic have helped to widen the gulf between the two nations, and have made it harder for our communities to be in fruitful communion except through the most reductive, divisive, and—on the Dominican side—sensationally racist generalizations about one another. But if I have to answer you most specifically: [neither side understands] we're sisters and brothers, that we share a poor, fragile island, and that without true solidarity we won't make it.

**Edwidge Danticat:** I agree that it has a lot to do with who you're asking, and also where you are. There are many mixed families, of course; and in many places on the island, people who grow up in close proximity to one another are practically indistinguishable physically. There are also a lot of people who understand that we share a common struggle, and especially that poor people on both sides of the island are battling similar types of detention and immigration policies in the diaspora. Perhaps we need to hear more about these people. Often in the dialogue we bring up our historical scars, but not our historical bridges. Because our neighbors are solely defined by what they did to us, rather than what we can do together.

That being said, I think some—certainly not all—Dominicans have a very limited, almost stereotypical idea of what a Haitian person looks and acts like. And it often has to do with the people some are most prejudiced against: the people who work in the *bateys* [sugar plantation towns]. When I used to travel to the DR, I would have to spend the first fifteen minutes of a lot of conversations going back and forth with someone trying to convince me that I'm not really Haitian because they feel they know what a Haitian is supposed to be. I know many people who never left Haiti and who've also had that experience. It is grounded in a kind of inflexibility of sorts; an inability on the part of some to see us in a variety of ways: as neighbors, friends, allies, and as brothers and sisters in both a looser and broader sense.

**Q:** What role, in your opinion, does history play in the way the two nations interact?

**Díaz:** Quite a lot. But for me to say simply that "history plays a role" without at least trying to examine the hard facts of what actually happened would only serve to obfuscate both the complexity of the situation and also the profound culpability that the European and North American powers bear in Haiti's immiseration and in the conflict between Haiti and the Dominican Republic.

History indeed plays a role in what you're seeing today. But it's a complex, multivalenced history that involves former dictator Rafael Trujillo and genocide [against Haitians and Dominicans of Haitian descent]—a history over which looms the predations of Europe and the US and Haitian elites and, yes, the Dominican Republic.

There's no question that many Dominican elites have historically deployed a metaphysics of Haiti-hating to curry favor with the colonial powers and also as a way to modulate all manners of internal contradictions within the Dominican state (and as a way of consolidating power through nationalist practices). But the Dominican Republic's tortured history with Haiti can never be understood in isolation from the larger histories of the colonial powers that helped initiate the DR into the metaphysics of Haiti-hating in the first place.

**Danticat:** History plays a huge role of course. Not just the history we can't avoid but speak out about—the time when the leaders of our side of the island were also on your side of the island. Or Trujillo's massacre in 1937. One thing that is not mentioned as often is that early in the twentieth century (1915 to 1934 for Haiti, and 1916 to 1924 for the DR), the entire island was occupied by the United States. Then again, in the DR in the 1960s, Trujillo—who not only organized a massacre, but wiped out several generations of Dominican families—was trained during the occupation by US Marines and put in power when they pulled out. Same with the Haitian army that terrorized Haitians for generations. It is not a matter of blame but a matter of historical record.

The US sugar interests grew more and more powerful during that first occupation, and the US even had a hand in deciding where the two countries' borders should be. So we have had our own internal problems, but there has also been this very powerful historical meddling to make sure that we stay divided—for our resources to be pilfered more easily, as in the case of sugar production; or to serve as a wall against communism. When people talk about colorism in the Dominican Republic—and I am sure this is not the only source of it—you can imagine these Marines from the southern US who came during the US occupations and set up their clubs and their hierarchies, just as they did in Haiti, rewarding any kind of proximity to whiteness, pushing us beyond colorism to a version of the US Jim Crow system.

**Q:** What can be done to heal those historical scars?
**Danticat:** We have to keep talking to each other and air the different layers of truth. We have to be willing to listen to the other side and accept being questioned as we, too, question others. Not just here where it's easier, but on the island, too. Often, when you talk healing, people think you mean

cultural occupation. We have to find ways to have difficult conversations about how we got here.

I know those conversations are being held. I know a lot of activists are having them, and students and friends. But people who speak the loudest speak with the laws they create, or with the notion that there is a whole nationalistic machine behind them.

We must keep dialoguing, and not just in the way that heads of governments employ to give the appearance that "they got this," while we wait for them to come up with some kind of solution that will probably mean more money in the pockets of the people at the top who want license and our silence so they can go forward with their trade and tourism projects, etc.

But we must keep talking to each other without dismissing the other side altogether. It is always a very painful thing to me to remember that very few Haitian leaders have shown much care or concern about the people working in the cane fields in the Dominican Republic. During the [Francois and Jean-Claude] Duvalier dictatorship, people were picked up by the *Tonton Macoutes* [Duvalier's militia] and practically sold across the border. As a child, I knew many people this happened to. After the 1937 massacre, outsiders had to urge our then-president to give a damn. The Haitian government was totally silent for weeks after the recent Constitutional Court ruling. The reaction reminded us—as if we needed to be reminded—that our governments, regardless of which side of the island they're on, discriminate against the poor.

But to cite someone I know you like, Oscar Wilde, in *The Picture of Dorian Gray*, writes, "The curves of your lips rewrite history." So let's all keep talking.

**Díaz:** All of us who want to see a better future for our nations need to fight the toxicologies of the past by practicing the simple revolutionary techniques of contact, compassion, and critical solidarity. And we really do have to find a way to get our elites out from between us. They have done more to promote the circulation of hate and suspicion than anyone else. I keep imagining what might be possible if our elites weren't constantly shouting in our ears.

**Q:** What role, in your opinion, does race and class play in the conflicts—past and present—between Haitians and Dominicans?
**Díaz:** Anti-Haitianism is a racist ideology, whether it's practiced by France, the US, the Dominican Republic, or Haitian elites. So race is clearly at the core. It is a racism born of colonialism, whose foundational tenet is that

people of color are not human. It's not only white folks who avail themselves of its bestial logic. If only white people were implicated in white supremacy it would have been a lot easier to extirpate, but, alas, the hydra has planted a hissing head in all of us.

**Danticat:** We also have a situation, I think, on both sides of the island—or maybe all over the world really, but it might seem more pronounced in these two poor countries—where light skin color is a kind of currency, where skin color can be perceived as a kind of class of its own. Even in the world's first black republic, we are still not exempt from that.

**Q:** Where do you think Haitians and Dominicans can find common ground?
**Díaz:** Are we not one African diasporic people, survivors of this world's greatest act of sustained inhumanity, sharing one beautiful island? Are not all of us being slowly destroyed by the same forces that colonialism put into play? Doesn't the fact that our elites spend so much energy keeping us apart suggest that our ultimate liberation begins with us coming together?

Many of us already work together both at home and in the diaspora. One day, we will become the majority, and I suspect that in the revolutionary eschatology of the future, this will be the first seal whose opening signals our liberation.

**Danticat:** I don't want to be "kumbaya"-esque about this, but we share a common vulnerability—an environmental vulnerability. Certainly we share some nasty fault lines. Our people often end up in the same boats in the same oceans. Haitians spend millions of dollars on Dominican products, so we are trade partners, formally and informally. Some people share blood-lines, a common history.

Two novelists are not going to solve this problem. It will require some real give and take to get to some point of balance in the exchange, and maybe the basic understanding that Haitians are not trying to destroy the Dominican Republic any more than Dominicans are trying to destroy the United States when they come here. And the "kumbaya" part, of course, is that we are always stronger together than torn apart.

**Q:** What was your first thought when you heard about the ruling?
**Díaz:** That the political leadership in the DR is both mad and cruel beyond measure. And also that when it comes to destroying immigrant lives, ex-President Leonel Fernández and current President Danilo Medina have learned well at the feet of the United States. What's going on in the DR is a nightmare in its own right, but has to be understood as part of a larger

global movement to demonize and marginalize immigrants—and as part of the US's post-9/11 push to "strengthen borders"—which is really to militarize them. The US helped the DR militarize its border, helped the DR create its very own border patrol based on a US model. The world is slowly dying and our elites are draining it to the lees, and yet this is what our idiot politicians want us to focus on.

**Danticat:** I remember feeling very sad. There is always this sense of ultra-vulnerability when you are an immigrant or the child of immigrants. But it's something you hope goes away with the generations. Or diminishes. I remember thinking, "What are all these people going to do now?" especially when I heard that the ruling was irreversible. But soon after, I was heartened by how many people spoke up: ordinary people as well as international organizations. . . . Dominicans who are not of Haitian descent speaking up for their brothers and sisters.

I spent time with two amazing women activists in Miami, Ana María Belique Delba and Noemi Mendez, who are part of an organization called Reconocido (Recognized). They are so unified in this struggle. That was also very inspiring. I also remember missing Sonia Pierre, the founder of the Movimiento de Mujeres Dominico-Haitiana (Movement for Dominican Women of Haitian Descent—MUDHA). I kept thinking, "She is going to have a lot of work to do." Then I remembered that she died of a heart attack at forty-eight, two years ago. This citizenship struggle, which was sealed but did not begin with this ruling, has been going on for decades. And it had broken her heart.

**Q:** Where do you see things going next?

**Díaz:** Fortunately, the mobilization against the *sentencia* has been strong and the international reaction unanimously negative. (Though it's worth noting that the [Barack] Obama administration, no friend of immigrant rights, has been pretty muted in its condemnation.) I am very sad to say that the politicians who masterminded this vast human rights violation clearly weren't expecting this kind of backlash. But we'll see how it goes. Right now, the party in power, the Partido de la Liberación Dominicana (Dominican Liberation Party—PLD), is trying to save face by making it seem as though they never intended this as an assault against our citizens of Haitian descent—just an attempt to "regularize" a broken system, which clearly is just a bold-faced lie. Like I said, we'll see. We'll keep fighting, of course. But it goes to show you that it takes more than helping out during an earthquake for a country to unlearn the metaphysics of Haiti-hating.

**Danticat:** I think it will probably go the way of individual action. People will start asking themselves if they can spend their money in a place where people can be treated this way in a legal fashion, which then of course gives license to others to act on what this ruling says or take it even further. I wish the commercial interests, the tourist boards etc., would jump into the conversation and become more vocal, because ultimately it comes down to money. Where pocketbooks are concerned, people are nudged into action.

**Q:** Why should the world—and especially citizens of the Americas—be paying attention to what's going on in the Dominican Republic? Given that you are both children of the island of Hispaniola living in the US, why is this issue important to you?

**Díaz:** First, the world should always be concerned whenever a vast human rights violation occurs anywhere on the planet. There's a reason it's called human rights: a blow to one is a blow to all. Injustices have a way of birthing horrors if left unchecked, and right now we have enough horrors in the world.

And why is it important for me? Because that island is my birthplace and one of my two homes; and if people like me don't fight its injustices, don't fight for the better future we deserve, who will? As a Dominican living in the US, it matters to me a whole hell of a lot that political elites in the DR are inflaming ethnic-racial hatred against Haitians to divide the *pueblo* and keep it from organizing against its real enemies—the elites themselves.

Supporters of the *sentencia* defend it with a lot of high-flying gibberish about bureaucratic necessity, etc., but the reality is that the ruling is all about creating a permanent group of second-class citizens in the Dominican Republic. As for the human cost, all one has to do is travel to the DR and you will see the terrible damage this kind of politics has caused and continues to cause. At a structural level, I know people who have had their papers taken away and others who are unable to secure documentation to travel or even to be educated. But on a more basic level, the anti-Haitian mood has reached a level I've never experienced before. It's a disaster. This is the type of deforming political sorcery that's going to take a lot of work and good faith to undo.

**Danticat:** Both Junot and I—correct me here if I am wrong, Junot—grew up in relative poverty on our respective sides of the island. . . .

**Díaz:** Oh yes, poverty aplenty.

**Danticat:** In both our lives, even when we were living on the island, we were also aware of our relative privilege when we traveled to see the relatives or spent time in the *campo* or the *pwovens* [rural provinces]. That makes you extraordinarily aware of what opportunity means. And it makes you hypersensitive to seeing not just a few but a slew of rights and opportunities being taken away in one swoop. You hope you would always speak up. Even when the issue is not as clear as this. You hope you would speak up if someone is sleeping on the floor in an immigration cell in Texas, or if people are being tortured in Guantánamo, no matter what their nationality. People's lives are being affected here in a way that touches their children and their children's children.

Even in the name of self-interest, the people in power in the Dominican Republic should see that they are creating an even greater problem here. They are trying to kick a Sisyphean boulder down the road for political gain or as a bargaining chip for trade. Maybe they are hoping that several generations of their citizens will "self deport" to Haiti if you take their identity away. But what they're doing is creating a tier of people who cannot contribute, beyond perhaps their limited physical strength, to a growing society. You take away their ability to learn, to work, and you also take away their ability to continue to build a society that they've helped sustain for many generations now.

**Q:** What should be the domestic and international response by individuals and policymakers? What role can you play in advocating on this issue?
**Danticat:** Recently, members of the Dominican senate and lower house approved a citizenship bill. But, at least at this point, it looks like people who were never able to get their birth certificates in the first place will still have a hard time using the channels offered by the bill.

When the lower house unanimously voted in favor of the bill, Juliana Deguis Pierre, who was the plaintiff in the Constitutional Court case that was central to the ruling, told journalists, "I hope to God they give [my citizenship] back to me because of everything I've been through and everything I've suffered." Just for those who doubt that the ruling has real consequences, Deguis was not able to travel to the US because, with as much attention as she'd gotten given her involvement in a landmark case, she did not have the papers to travel.

Imagine what it's like for someone who is much less visible living on a *batey.*

A Haiti/DR bilateral commission has met a few times, and as of the time that we're talking now, in mid-May, it has not produced conclusive results. The initial international interest in this has cooled a bit. News cycles are short and people move on quickly, but it's important to remain vigilant. There might have initially been a perception that this ruling would go undetected. But the little progress we've had, that the Dominican (and even the Haitian) government has been forced to take some action at all, has a lot to do with the fact that people have spoken out all over the world, that there have been calls for boycotts, that people have written letters and taken to the airwaves—and that some groups have canceled their conferences and taken their dollars elsewhere.

All this has helped and will continue to help. We must continue to listen closely to the leaders on the ground, to the people who are taking the heat every day. I am sure they are not ready to rest any time soon. And neither can we. Struggles like this are long and hard, and people have to keep their eyes on the prize. And when you have a just outcome, it not only improves the specific situation we're talking about; it is also a step forward for oppressed people everywhere. This is why we can still learn lessons from the US civil rights movement and the anti-apartheid struggle in South Africa. The right outcome in situations like this can eventually make the world itself a better place.

**Díaz:** We need to throw everything we can at the Dominican government to stop this travesty. We need protests and letters and emails. People are talking about a boycott against the country until the *sentencia* is dropped. Fortunately, there are plenty of organizations and individuals fighting this. One could always reach out to them. On my side of the island, there's Comité de Solidaridad con Personas Desnacionalizadas (Committee of Solidarity with Stateless People) and Reconocido. There's Dominicanos Por Derecho (Dominicans for Rights) and Sonia Pierre's MUDHA. As for myself, I do what I can. I fight these idiots with all my strength. But if you're like me, you always feel you can do more.

**Danticat:** And more, and more, and more. . . .

# A Conversation with Edwidge Danticat

## Josephine "Jo" Reed / 2015

Conducted June 2015. Reprinted with permission by the National Endowment for the Arts.

**Jo Reed:** Edwidge, your memoir *Brother, I'm Dying* has been chosen as this year's Big Read selection. Just take us back to where you were born and where you were raised, just the early part of your life.

**Edwidge Danticat:** I was born in Haiti in 1969 during the Duvalier dictatorship, a family dictatorship that would last thirty years. And I grew up in Port-au-Prince, spent the first twelve years of my life there. My mother and father left Haiti before I did, my father, when I was two, my mother when I was four, and I grew up with my uncle Joseph and his wife Tante Denise in a neighborhood in Haiti called Bel Air. Back then, a very lower-middle-class neighborhood but one that had grown increasingly poor over the years. My uncle Joseph got cancer in the throat when I was young and came to the United States for treatment and then moved back to Haiti and started speaking and preaching with a voice box. When I was twelve, my parents were finally able to send for me. I hadn't been able to join them sooner because they had moved to the United States as tourists and had overstayed tourist visa. So they were undocumented. Once their status was changed, they were able to send for my brother, Bob, and me. Once my parents were able to send for me then I moved to the US to Brooklyn, where they were living, at twelve years old.

**Reed:** That must have been quite a rupture.

**Danticat:** It was quite difficult because I feel as though I had made a place for myself, an attachment for myself, with my uncle, especially. He would take me with him to banks, to mean, to the countryside, to a lot of places where people might not understand him after he had the surgery on his throat. So I became a kind of interpreter for my uncle who I loved very, very much. It was very difficult to leave him and there was a great deal of uncertainty about what my life would be like in the States because I had not really lived with my parents before that I could remember. I was very young when they left and my brothers—I had two brothers who were born in the United States—who did not, I realize, even know about my brother Bob and me until we got to New York. They came to Haiti when they were very, very little but they didn't remember us and I don't think my parents discussed us very much with them. So it was a shock for everyone.

**Reed:** What was it like living with your uncle and your aunt in Haiti? You said that you were an interpreter for him. He was a minister.

**Danticat:** My uncle was a minister. He had a church in Bel Air, the neighborhood where I grew up. He also had a sort of clinic, a personal clinic, and a school. He was a prominent person in the neighborhood, a very beloved person, kind of a father figure to the congregation but also to different people in the neighborhood, different young people. So we grew up—I grew up, my brother and I—in this house where a lot of the children were the children of people who had left to work elsewhere. There were no strangers in our house. They were family. Everyone was family. Everyone was related in some way but most of the children in the house had parents who were working elsewhere, whether it was like my parents in the United States or—I had one cousin whose father was in the Dominican Republic and others who were in Canada. So there was a little group of us, of children with parents abroad, who had been entrusted in the care of my uncle and his wife in this beautiful pink house in Bel Air.

**Reed:** That is really not so unusual worldwide. I think, often, we in the United States don't realize how many parents leave their children behind and come to the US to work to be able to support their children and eventually bring them to this country, or to go back and go back with means so they can take care of them.

**Danticat:** It is not unusual at all, in my experience, for parents to leave their children and go work in other countries because, for a lot of parents the choice is to stay with your child and have a lot of problems in terms of finding work, in terms of being able to feed them and send them to school, or going elsewhere and leaving them with a family member and then sending money and making sure that they're better fed, that they go to a decent school. And also, it makes perfect sense because childcare then becomes a very important issue in the new country and if you're sure and certain about where your child is and don't have to worry about childcare, you can work a whole lot more. And many people work very odd hours, very difficult jobs, and having your child safely in the care of people you know and trust takes a big load off of the mind.

**Reed:** You describe Bel Air briefly, but say more about it because there was a way I felt as though Bel Air was another character in your book.

**Danticat:** Bel Air is an extraordinary neighborhood. It remains an extraordinary neighborhood and now it's an extraordinarily poor and politically volatile neighborhood. But it's, as the name would imply, "good air." Bel Air is on top of a hill and growing up there, from the roof of my uncle's house, we could see the port. We could see downtown. You had a very beautiful view of the horizons, of the city all around you. It was, as my uncle described it when he first moved there, it was a very leafy and beautiful neighborhood. And then, over time during the dictatorship, you had a kind of forced migration when François Duvalier, who was called "Papa Doc," would send for busloads of people from the countryside to come to these public events. And then the people had like one-way bus fares and some of them never went back and then there was so much decentralization that everything has to happen in the city. People have to go to school. You get to a certain point in certain parts of the country you can't go further in school. You have to come to the city. So then the population of the city went from something like 200,000 to over 2 million like it is now. So that led to a lot of [what they would call] in Haiti culture the *bidonvilles*, these shanty towns, and Bel Air slowly became a neighborhood like that. My uncle lived there when he moved from the countryside to the city. That was the first place they moved to and he lived there fifty years and it had changed a great deal in the time that he was living there.

**Reed:** And when you were living there, telephone calls were extremely expensive. Your parents would communicate via letter.

**Danticat:** We had one telephone call a week. We'd have to go downtown to the telephone company, the Teleco, just a few brief minutes in a booth and talk to our parents. We had no telephone at home. Very few people in our income bracket, if you will, did. We wrote a lot of letters. My father would write these types of formulaic letters, which would accompany the money that he would send us every month. It was sort of like, "Hello, how are you? I hope you're well. We are well." Kind of just basic. And my uncle would then host, if you will, a kind of reading of the letter because there would be listed in the letter the amount that my parents had sent and he wanted everybody to hear it. And then my brother and I would have to write back and I would write these letters that weren't too familiar too but would try to sneak in requests for things I wanted like dolls and once I wanted a typewriter. And they always had to be—I think, on both sides, they had to be rather cheery because I didn't want to depress my parents and they didn't want to depress us. So we never really talked about deep things that were happening like if we were having trouble in school. We would enclose our report cards. We would put some pictures in and just write a few words.

**Reed:** Your uncle's home is also a home that was culturally rich. There was a great tradition, ironically enough considering he lost his voice box, but a great tradition of storytelling in that house.

**Danticat:** There was a very powerful tradition of storytelling that, looking back now, I realize we all took for granted because my uncle's wife, Aunt Denise's mother lived with us, Grandma Melina who was very old but Grandma Melina was a very wonderful storyteller and she would tell us stories during blackouts, during power outages, of which there were quite a few. And sometimes—she had a very long grey hair and she would put coins in it. We would fight to comb her hair and, while we were combing her hair, she would tell us stories.

**Reed:** You were twelve, when your parents sent for you and your brother. What time of year was it?

**Danticat:** It was March when my brother and I first arrived in New York. It was still cold, cold to us. It felt cold to us. It was March 21 around 1981. I remember because it was the day before one of my brothers' birthdays and we got to the airport and I just remember being just awestruck by the vastness of the city. And an odd thought to me was—I was like, "Oh, there's so many lights on and they never turn off." I was really dazzled by the lights of Brooklyn, which I thought was just this incredible country. I thought, "Brooklyn is a great country." It was so, so vast.

**Reed:** Did you have English as a language?

**Danticat:** I spoke no English. My uncle had this morning ritual where he would play this Berlitz record while he was doing his stretches, so exercising in the morning. And he would practice phrases because part of my uncle's work was often greeting missionaries who came to Haiti to visit the church and he always wanted us to know a few words and to greet them, to understand if they said a few words to us. So I knew, from my uncle's lessons. I knew "Good morning. How are you?" and just a few phrases but I was far from fluent.

**Reed:** Did you have to start school right away or could you wait until September? What happened?

**Danticat:** We started school right away. There was briefly some debate in my house between my parents about whether we should wait, because it was already March, to start in the fall. But my dad said "no." We went to school the following Monday after our arrival because he wanted us to start on a Monday. And he said, "Well, these couple of weeks, then you can pick up a few things and then go to summer school." So I started school right away.

**Reed:** How long did it take you to know what was going on in your classroom?

**Danticat:** Well, I started in the ESL class, in an English as a second language class. And my teacher, Mr. Lemond Ducek, was an exile from Haiti. He had escaped the dictatorship. So it was an easier transition than it might've otherwise been because Mr. Ducek taught us every subject in Creole. And then he taught us life skills, sort of what you do if the kids start teasing you and things of that nature. But it was a very difficult year for Haitian kids at that school. It was the year that people started talking about AIDS. They called it GRID back then and there was the list, the high-risk groups, the four H(s) and—homosexuals, hemophiliacs, heroin addicts, and Haitians. And we were the only people on that list identified by nationality. And every night you would watch the news, there would be sort of two headlining things that referred to us. There was this AIDS announcements, and they would always go over the list, and then there were these images of people arriving by boat in Florida and a lot of pictures of bloated bodies on the beaches. So at school kids would call us boat people, AIDS people, and I remember there was a school trip, that we were not even allowed to go to, to the Statue of Liberty. Our class wasn't allowed to go, not so much because people— they believed we had AIDS but because the other kids were beating up the Haitian kids so much and they thought they would have a kind of beat down on the bus. So our class didn't go. So there were things like that that were beyond having to adjust with the family, getting to know my brothers, my parents again. There were things like that to adjust to at school.

**Reed:** What about reading. Were you reading in French?

**Danticat:** After the year was over, when I started school again, they started to transition me through sort of mainstreaming. So I would have half classes with Mr. Ducek and then start to have some classes with other kids. So I started having an English class with an English teacher where English was spoken throughout the whole class. So, slowly, gradually I transitioned—they didn't expect to keep you in the English as a second language class for more than a year. So you had to transition. So I had—I got to transition before I went through high school at Clara Barton High School.

**Reed:** And you were going to be a nurse?

**Danticat:** I was going to be a nurse and, actually, I didn't initially get accepted to Clara Barton High School. I was sent to my zone school because I hadn't done the application process where you select a special school. So I was just assigned to my zone school, which was strangely enough right across from Clara Barton High School Prospect Heights. And so my dad had heard good things about Clara Barton High School and my parents really wanted me to be a doctor but if I wasn't so much into a doctor, they were willing to settle for me being a nurse. So my dad went to the school and told the principal, Mr. Reznick, he said, "Well, my daughter got sent to her zone school and it's a very violent school," which at that time it was. And he says, "I don't think she'll survive there. I want her to go to this school." And Mr. Reznick was so moved by my father's initiative, I guess, that they put me in the honors program, which was called the Peak Program, and it was the best of everything. You started out with AP classes. And I was two years out of Haiti and suddenly in this honors program and spent really four years with the same group of kids who were wonderful kids who were very dedicated to the sciences and because so much faith had been placed in me that I just had to do my best to follow along. And I think, even though I didn't eventually become a nurse, I was able to get a top-notch education because my father had decided to go to Mr. Reznick and plead a case for me to go to that school.

**Reed:** What was your father doing for a living?

**Danticat:** My father, when I was still in Haiti, used to have two jobs. He said when he was alone in New York, before my mother joined, he had two jobs. He used to work in a factory where they made handbags and things like that and then had a second job where he worked in a carwash. And he always said that he had one job for—to sustain his life in New York and one job, another job, to send money to Haiti. When my mother came, they both started working in the same factory. And then my father often told the stories that the day we were coming, my brother and me, he had to pick us up at the airport and he asked his boss if he could leave early and the boss said "no." And, of course, he had to get us so he quit and from that day on, he decided he wouldn't work for anybody else. And so he started driving a cab, what they then called a gypsy cab, where people used—basically had a private car that they put a partition in and rode as a cab, a private cab. So we were always in my father's cab, wherever we were going. And, when he was working, he was in the car. When he wasn't working, he was in the car. So from that day that we came to the day he became sick and could no longer work again, he was driving that gypsy cab.

**Reed:** You open your book *Brother, I'm Dying*, with your father's illness. It was quite a monumental day for you. Tell us what happened.

**Danticat:** Well, I open the book with the day that I find out that I am pregnant with my daughter and the day that I also find out that my father is dying. I had gotten married and moved to Miami, Florida, and I wasn't seeing my father every day like I had in the past and he was looking more and more frail with each visit. He had a terrible cough that, over the years, we had called a smoker's cough but that just got more and more aggravating to him, and he had been seeing many different doctors, had many tests done. And that day I had left Miami and flown to New York to see a lung specialist and the lung specialist waited until my father was out of the room and told me that he had pulmonary fibrosis and that he was in a very late stage of it and that there was no hope for him. So I got that news and then I hadn't been feeling quite well and I had cramps and my dad was a very strong believer in herbal medicine. So he had been recommending this woman herbalist. So, after I got this news, we also went to this herbalist who then took hair samples and all of that. But she basically looked at me and said, "You're pregnant," and then I had a test done and sure enough it was true, and I found out both things on the same day.

**Reed:** You know one thing I found among the many things I found so moving about your book was the great love your father and your uncle had for one another, despite fate keeping them apart for most of their lives.

**Danticat:** My uncle and father's relationship was extraordinarily moving for me to witness as well, when I got an opportunity to see it, because they were both not very sentimental or emotional men. They were not those kinds of people. My uncle would sort of tease kids. He sort of shadowbox with you and things like that and, pinch cheeks and everything and he was a little bit more relaxed and laid back. I think having to be in a pulpit and having to be engaging made him more of a people person than my father. My father was a very sweet man and maybe it was also my age. I didn't see him and my mother hug, for example. It was sort of an event when they—if they kissed each other publicly at their twenty-fifth anniversary or something. So it was really sweet to see how brotherly he and my uncle were to each other and really how, I'm jumping ahead. When my uncle was in immigration custody and how much he was so concerned about him finding out and being so worried that it would kill him because he was very—my father was very sick at that point. And they were so worried about each other, but also in the quiet moments when my father was sick and my uncle would sit with him or would pray with him. I thought it was very sweet because they had spent really thirty years living apart and only seeing each other occasionally. And they never talked much about their childhood, sort of what they did together as boys, so it was very sweet to see their interactions. There were the subtle gestures and the things they said to each other and the way they talked to one another.

**Reed:** Your uncle resisted leaving Haiti, even though many people in his family, including your father, encouraged him to go. Why was he urged to go? What was happening?

**Danticat:** Well, my uncle always said that not everybody can leave the country. He said, "There has to be someone here to receive you all when you come back." And he had his church. He had his school. He had the clinic. Haiti was his passion and the ministry, the things he was doing, were very important to him and he had overcome so many obstacles to continue. He had lost his voice and was using a voice box. So he never imagined that he would ever leave Haiti. He really was prepared to stay forever and be buried, when he died, next to his wife in Port-au-Prince. But in 2004, the bicentennial of Haitian independence. And that September was also the anniversary of a coup against the first democratically elected president of Haiti, Jean-Bertrand Aristide, and Bel Air was very politically active at that point and people there were very attached to President Aristide. And there were some demonstrations and the UN force that was, and is still, in Haiti at that time came into the neighborhood and they climbed on top of my uncle's church and started shooting at some people in the neighborhood, at demonstrators. And people thought that my uncle had a choice in this, but it's as if an army is running through your garden and you try to say "stop." I mean, he could not stop them. And soon after they retreated and they left, the UN force had killed a couple of people and they thought that my uncle had called them and had caused all that. And people in the neighborhood that he had known for a very long time, many of them, especially some young men in the neighborhood, turned on him and they tried to storm the house, and somehow a neighbor hid him and he took him to another house, but in the meantime the house was ransacked. The church and everything was taken and he could not return to the house. So my uncle had a trip planned to come to the United States previously and just a few days after that happened, and so he decided to proceed with the trip and to come to Florida. He had been coming to the US for more than thirty years, had a visa that was to expire a couple of years from the time that he got on the plane that October. When he got to immigration and customs, he was asked how long he would be staying and knowing that everything he had or ever had was now destroyed, he said he might be staying longer than the thirty days that the visa required and asked if he could temporarily have asylum, not understanding the full implications, and so he was taken into custody by the immigration and customs enforcement. He was brought to a place in Florida called Krome. He was detained and as part of his processing his medication was taken away, and he died a few days later in the prison ward of the local hospital chained to his bed.

**Reed:** And meanwhile, you're hearing about this on the phone. You're expecting your uncle in Miami airport?

**Danticat:** I get a phone call the Saturday that he arrives. I was expecting my uncle to come in the afternoon and I always go by and I call the people in Haiti and they assure me that he actually got on the plane. They knew that he got on the plane and the plane when we checked seemed to have arrived and we wait, we wait, nothing happens, and then around late in the evening we get a call from immigration people at the airport saying that they have him in custody and he would be sent to Krome and we were very shocked because my uncle was eighty-one years old and spoke with a voice box, was a minister and so forth. So I thought there would be some mercy for him, but he was detained.

**Reed:** Your father, of course, is sick. You're pregnant. That whole triangulation, it's just so tragic, I mean, that's the only word for it. It's so tragic.

**Danticat:** It was—when one is living a situation like that all you try to do is just, you try to go from the moment to the moment. So immediately I started making phone calls and tried to get a lawyer, but it was the weekend and the lawyer couldn't get in there until Monday and my uncle called me whenever he had an opportunity from inside the jail and we spoke a little bit. My uncle's son, my cousin, Maxo, was traveling with my uncle and was also detained, and we spoke a couple of times during that period over the weekend before the lawyer could reach my uncle, and he was reassuring me. He was asking about my dad and he told me that he had brought my father some herbal medicine from Haiti that was also taken away from him and it was incredible. I was so terrified for him. I was so worried about him, but he was very calm and he was very reassuring and I imagined him, probably . . . something he was trying to frame a type of sermon around that he would one day give.

**Reed:** And it turns out that after he died he could remain in the United States.
**Danticat:** Yes. My uncle is now buried in Queens, New York, which would have shocked him because he had everything planned for his own burial, but the irony is that he ends up being buried next to my father and they spent all these many years apart and now they're both buried together in Queens, New York, something that neither one of them could've possibly imagined.

**Reed:** Your father lived long enough to see the birth of your child.
**Danticat:** Father, I think, waited for my daughter Mira to be born. The whole time he was sick, he would say, "I want to see the first born of my first born," and I really think he kept himself going to see that moment. I have a very sweet picture of my dad very skeletal with an oxygen mask holding my daughter Mira who is named after him, and I remember him holding her and he couldn't for very long because he was so skinny that eight pounds was such a massive weight for him at that point, but he held her for a little while and we took a picture and he said, "the two Miras," and he died a couple of weeks after Mira was born. And we spent some of those weeks together with him in New York with Mira and me and him, and then finally we had to go back to Florida, and forty-eight hours after I left with Mira, my father died.

**Reed:** When your uncle was buried at the grave site in Queens, your father said, "He shouldn't be there," that none of you should be there. You should all be in Haiti. Do you think he felt like an exile or do you think he felt like an immigrant?
**Danticat:** I think the way my uncle died made my father feel like an exile. I think he felt downright American before that. He had the passport. He voted. Every election my father voted. He voted in the school board elections. So

he felt very American and, you know, he had two US-born kids and with my mother. They'd been able to buy a house and I think he felt very American. But I think the way my uncle died, the fact that our being American, if you will, did not prevent that from happening to him. He was not entrusted in any of our care even though I was living fifteen minutes away from where he was. I think that made my father feel humiliated. He felt, I think, humiliated for all of us as a family and I think that made him feel again like he had just arrived in the US, I think, and there was a feeling as he was dying—because of what had happened to my uncle, I think he felt he had not accomplished much because he could not even save his brother and that's something that I shared too. I have to say that I couldn't believe that I wasn't able to do more for my uncle. I did everything I could, but there's a sense that because I'm a writer, I'm a public person that should have helped and so we all felt a little bit sort of diminished, and you feel you've been given a big kick out of a club where you starting to feel like you belonged.

**Reed:** When did you begin writing?

**Danticat:** I started writing when I was about nine, that's the first thing I remember writing, a little book with my brother and my cousin. The first book I ever got when I was a kid was from my uncle was the *Madeline*, the first one in the house in Paris that was covered with vines. It was in French, of course, and I wanted to write one. For a long time, I want to write one of those books because I really felt our house was like that house. My uncle and aunt were like the nun because there were little kids like that. We weren't all girls. I had the great sense of identification with that book, but my brother and my cousin were big readers of comics like Tintin and Asterix, these westerns that came as comics. So we all got together and tried to write one of those, and I didn't know how one goes about being a writer. I loved the stories I was told. I loved the stories that I eventually ended up reading and I didn't know how one would write one, but I knew, I said, "I want to do what that book does for me, what the *Madeline* book does for me." I didn't know how to put into words, I knew from very, very early in my life that I wanted to tell stories in some way.

**Reed:** How did you begin doing it when you got older?

**Danticat:** Well, it started actually at Jackie Robinson Intermediate 320. I had this English teacher at Thanksgiving one year who asked us all to write a story about Thanksgiving, and Thanksgiving in my house was basically like fried turkey chopped up. My mother never roasted a turkey, but I was trying to make it sound like the TV specials I was watching with my golden turkey and I remember the English teacher. She probably didn't find it convincing, and she's like, "Unleash! Unleash, your imagination!" And I started writing things for her that was little stories and so it started in that class.

**Reed:** Tell me about the writing of your first book, *Breath, Eyes, Memory*.
**Danticat:** Well, *Breath, Eyes, Memory* started with another kind of writing that I started doing in high school. I joined a newspaper called *New Youth Connections* in New York City that was written by, it's still published and distributed through high schools, and is written by high school students. When I started writing for them, I got a little bit more authentic in my writing. So I started writing about Haitian Christmas rituals, things that our family did at Christmas time and then started writing about that—wrote about things that were happening in my school and then for my final piece for them they asked me to write about my first day in the United States and I had to go back. There are things that I remember. The lights, of course, but when I was looking back I thought, the most impressive thing to me that day in retrospect was the escalator. This was like this moving carpet. So I wrote about my first day. I wrote about that and other things that I experienced that day and then when I was done I thought, oh, there's something else here and I continued, but I didn't want to write it in my name. So I created a character who was twelve whose name was Sophie and I started writing about her time in the countryside with her grandmother and then her mother sends for her, and so my first book, *Breath, Eyes, Memory* started that way. I started writing about Sophie and wrote about her all through high school, all through college, and graduate school until the book was published when I was twenty-five.

**Reed:** You wrote, or said, I'm not sure which, probably both that, "art is a luxury and a necessity." Can you tell me what you mean by that?
**Danticat:** Well in some communities, art is definitely a luxury, that you need materials for and often if people have to choose between eating and . . . it's not as much a dilemma, but one of the things that is incredibly fascinating to me about Haiti . . . is the way I grew up . . . is how much art was in everyday life and in the life of even the poorest people. So what we call our tap-taps, through the public transportation was just covered in beautiful images with saying and words, and beauty parlor signs were just so colorful and the way art, beauty, was integrated into everyday life and, so, the way everyone had access to that kind of art, made it seem like a necessity. People needed that to

counter the other level of poverty, level of political oppression. It's as if they needed a dose of that to counter all of that in their daily lives.

**Reed:** It reminds me of the old union song the mill workers used to sing called "Bread and Roses." We need bread but we need roses too.
**Danticat:** Exactly, exactly. And when you're poor, people sort of—they underestimate the roses, let's say.

**Reed:** But the roses can get you through the day.
**Danticat:** Absolutely and I think Haitian art and the Haitian arts in general reconfirm that for me every day. This notion that you need both and also that you're not, as a people, completely defined by your need or by your lack or by your want.

**Reed:** In both your fiction and your nonfiction, you really keep Haiti in the conversation. It really is at the center, in a lot of ways, about your writing. Its tragedies and its beauties as well, and I wonder what a fictional story might give a reader that a nonfiction essay might not?
**Danticat:** Well, a fictional story makes the reader intimately connected with the characters in the story. Nonfiction can also do that and I always try to balance both, and I was very glad that I had written some fiction before I wrote my memoir because there are many techniques in fiction that you can use in memoir in terms of pacing. In the first drafts of *Brother, I'm Dying*, I thought I had to put everything that happened in because it happened and then going back to my muscle memory of writing fiction, I realized you still have to tell an engaging story. You still have to have pacing. You have characters, except they're real people, and plot, except that it actually happened. So I think there are places where they meet, and in *Brother, I'm Dying* I wanted to have the reader both become part of my family and also be a distant observer. In order to write this book, I had to go through a lot of official documents and wanted to present them as I would to a family member asking, "What do you think of this? What would you do if this happened to someone in your family?" In nonfiction also that opportunity to draw people close, but you have a limitation that you don't have in fiction in that you're working with events that have already occurred. You don't have the freedom of just going wild with your imagination and adding in stuff, but in nonfiction, you're working a lot with the structure, how to tell the story once you've chosen what story to tell.

**Reed:** Why did you choose to tell that story, *Brother, I'm Dying*?

**Danticat:** I had no choice but to tell that story. I remember the exact moment I decided that I would write this book. After my uncle died, we went to the nearest immigration office to get his briefcase, and we were still trying to figure out how to claim the body from the hospital where he was in and things like that, but the briefcase had his documents and his passport and such things. We were, at that point, not sure whether we were going to send the body back to Haiti or what we were going to do. So we're given my uncle's briefcase and in the briefcase is a transcript of his initial immigration interview in which he is asked things like, "Why are you here?" He said, "My church was ransacked and I lost everything," and things of that nature. It was such a cold exchange and there was a picture of my uncle looking like the proverbial deer in headlights. He looked really like he didn't know what was going on. He was scared and I read the transcript of that interview, which part of which is in the book, and I thought, I have to write this story. It's Kafkaesque. It's surreal and it's my opportunity to bring light to this situation because over the years too I've met so many families that have been in this similar situation. I ended up testifying before Congress and going on *60 Minutes* and doing all these other things and that allows you to meet other people in the same situation. And there were a lot of us whose family members have been detained in a similar situation or died because they were denied their medicine or were deprived of good treatment. And so I also thought I wanted the book to be artful. I didn't want it to be a rant, I didn't want it to be weepy. I wanted it to be artful. I wanted it to have some element of objectivity, which is why I used a lot of documents in it, and I wanted it to be a way of remembering my father and my uncle and what they meant to me and this moment that they left me at the same time that my daughter came into my life.

**Reed:** *Claire of the Sea Light*, when you began writing it—you began writing it before the earthquake and you finished it after—how has the earthquake affected your writing? Has it? I'm assuming that it was just so monumental and you're so connected to Haiti. It must have had an impact.

**Danticat:** The earthquake in 2010, for me, drew a kind of line in terms of what Haiti I was thinking about when I was writing my books, and the Haiti I was always writing about was always my Haiti. It was my interpretation of what I would see when I would go on my visits there to see my family and also my personal history to certain places where I would be or would end up. So that changed, and, of course, because the places change, my uncle's house and church were severely damaged. The house is really no more. I don't go back now to that particular neighborhood. When I go back, I go to other family members, other places, so my footing, my headquarters, if you will, has shifted. So the relation to place changes and the experience that I have changed. My cousin Maxo who was in detention with my uncle died during the earthquake and his children were in the rubble for many days. One of them died but thankfully the others survived and are still in Haiti. So not just the physical ground shifts but also I think a lot of the emotional and psychological connections are rearranged.

**Reed:** As you know, *Brother, I'm Dying* was chosen for The Big Read. What do you hope that readers take away from this book in general and also about Haiti in particular?

**Danticat:** Well, when we talk about immigration, about immigrants these days especially, we talk about people like they're leeches. They come here to take our jobs. All these accusations that we make towards immigrants, young people who are so-called dreamers who come here when they're young and know really no other place, no other country. So I hope my book becomes one of many that presents a face of immigration that people should find familiar because ultimately we are like everybody else. Our parents were dreamers. They were pioneers. They were these people who decided, hey, I want a better life. I'm going to travel to a different country. I'm going to work really hard. I'm going to try to do the best for my children, and so I hope the book gives a face to that to at least one immigrant family, an immigrant family that functions the way a lot of immigrant families function these days in that we are very committed to the country where we are, in this case the United States, but also have very strong ties back home. I hope it offers also a glimpse into a problematic immigration system. One that as we have seen over the past year or so with all these children who are coming, any of these kids could have been me or my brother. People who are afraid for their families, who feel desperate, do desperate things. So I hope the book will allow people to have a context to those stories and also chime in into this immigration debate that we're constantly having because the best way I think for people to understand one another is by sharing their stories, and I hope that by sharing my story I can make it easier for people to understand the story of their own neighbors who might have slightly different stories than we do but still have certain things with us in common. The things that brought my family here and that brings a lot of other families here or the things that many people wish for their loved ones, for their children, a better future, and that's what we came here for and we worked very hard for it like a lot of immigrant families, worked very hard for the opportunities that they have had. So I'm hoping that people will understand that situation a lot better, that they'll get a glimpse of Haiti that is singularly mine, I suppose. I don't want to generalize about Haiti, but I hope the book will also offer some insight into the challenges that many families face not just in Haiti but also when they come here.

**Reed:** Edwidge thank you so much. I really appreciate it.
**Danticat:** Thank you.

**Reed:** It's a wonderful book and it was wonderful talking to you.
**Danticat:** Likewise, thank you.

# Edwidge Danticat Tells the Story behind *Untwine*

## Kreyolicious / 2015

From Kreyolicious.com, July 2015. Reprinted with permission by Kreyolicious.

Edwidge Danticat writes novels the way some moms make dishes. She's always at it, creating literary dishes more delicious than the last. As your girl Kreyolicious revealed recently, *Untwine* is the title of her upcoming YA novel. Quite a poetic title, no? It's about the relationship of twins. Growing up, did you ever look in the mirror and wish that image you saw looking back at you . . . could somehow be duplicated? No? I guess only folks like me thought things like that. In any case, that was the first question I thought of asking Edwidge. [Aren't I presumptuous, calling her by her first name? I'm such a show off. Acting like I get invited to drink *te* at her *lakay* when I questioned her about her next book.] The novel is about loss, and I didn't realize that she had experienced a huge loss a few months prior to the interview. Read on. It'll be like having tea with Edwidge Danticat.

**Kreyolicious:** Growing up, you ever wished you had a twin?
**Danticat:** I have three younger brothers, so growing up I always wished I had a sister. Having a sister would have felt like having a twin. I have a couple of sister friends I think of as my spiritual twins, the way Gisele and Isabell consider themselves each other's physical as well as spiritual twins.

**Kreyolicious:** I think we've discussed before how you always have the most poetic titles for you book. How did you decide on this one?
**Danticat:** My editor, Lisa Sandell from Scholastic, came up with this one. I had a few other titles that just weren't working and she came out and said, "Hey, you use this word a lot in the book. How about we call it *Untwine*?"

When I saw the cover with the word "twin," right in the middle of *Untwine,* I just knew it was right.

**Kreyolicious:** That's so cool. I thought the *Untwine* title was a reference to twins' being joined and disjointed. But wow, this is a way better rationale. You mentioned in a previous interview that this twin story was one you had started and put away before. What made you go back to it?

**Danticat:** Yes, this is a book I was writing at the same time as *Breath, Eyes, Memory.* I started it in graduate school. It was about one teenage girl, no twins. I put it away and concentrated on *Breath, Eyes, Memory.* Then I kept going back to it when I started writing for young people. Lisa—my editor—once wrote me a note asking if I had a book for young adults in me. I picked it up again. Then, my mother became terminally ill with cancer and I was spending a lot of quiet time in hospital rooms and when I got too sad watching my mother sleep, I would work on this book in the dark at her bedside.

**Kreyolicious:** So sorry. . . . Do you see yourself writing another YA book after this one?

**Danticat:** I have a few more ideas I think I'll explore. I have so many teenagers in my life now. I have a teenage niece and nephew and goddaughter and teenage daughters of friends, a set of twins among them. I was really excited about writing specifically for their age range. I have also benefited from their influence by observing and spending time with them and asking them the occasional question about their lives. There is a kind of passion in the teenage readers in my life. They are really invested in the stories the read and are really direct about their likes and dislikes. I'm excited to enter that conversations with them and other teenagers as well as adults who will read this book.

**Kreyolicious:** What would you say to someone who wants to write a novel for that age group?

**Danticat:** Aside from the location of the writing itself, writing *Untwine* has been like writing any other book for me. I'd say don't write down to the reader. Write honestly. Write the best book you know how. Put your all into it like you would any other book. Just because it's for young people doesn't mean you get a pass. I've been reading a lot of young adult books and some are better written than a lot of books that are intended for adults. There are some pretty incredible writers writing for this age group, writers like Jacqueline

Woodson, who is a goddess in my house. So, write the best book you can is always good advice no matter what genre or category you're writing in.

**Kreyolicious:** What's next for you?
**Danticat:** This fall, I also have a picture book coming out. It's called *Mama's Nightingale: A Story of Immigration and Separation.* It's about a little girl whose mother is put in immigration detention. The mother tries to comfort her daughter by sending her cassettes with Haitian folktales on them and the daughter does everything she can to get her mother out.

**Kreyolicious:** Intriguing. It will be so cool to see how you handle such a tough subject. Do you ever stop?
**Danticat:** I know it seems like I am producing a lot, but these things are often years in the making before they come out. Besides, after my mother died, I realized there were so many stories I wanted to tell, for her, for my family. We all have a limited amount of time with the people we love. And it is never the amount of time we want to have. This is, I think, the themes of both *Untwine* and *Mama's Nightingale.* You never know how much time you have. It's very important to treasure that time and make it count.

# Putting Together the Fragments:
# A Conversation with Edwidge Danticat

## Maxine Lavon Montgomery / 2016

Conducted February 2016. Published with permission by Edwidge Danticat.

Long before I had the honor of meeting Edwidge Danticat years ago at a campus lecture where she read from her 2013 novel, *Claire of the Sea Light*, I became familiar with the gifted author through her captivating works of fiction. I taught "A Wall of Fire Rising," one of nine short stories included in *Krik? Krak!*, on a regular basis in my summer course on the short story, and her novels *Breath, Eyes, Memory* and *The Farming of Bones* were mainstays in my graduate course on Contemporary Black Women novelists. What stands out regarding Danticat's work is not only her ability to create a vast assortment of complex imaginary characters whose triumphs and tragedies, successes and failures are inextricably linked with the rich Afro-Caribbean geopolitical landscape out of which the author's works evolve, but also her ability to do so in ways that honor both the resilience of the Haitian population and their timeless cultural traditions. Her rare talent for telling a compelling story that is at once grounded in a specific historical moment and transcends time and place has earned her a lasting place at the forefront of contemporary letters.

The following interview is one that I conducted through an email exchange, which, as it turns out, was the most convenient means of bringing together two busy professionals—one, a university professor and administrator with a hectic schedule; the other, a renowned, award-winning author who had just published two novels that were released only months apart. Danticat kindly agreed to the exchange as I sought insight into a range of issues surrounding her life, art, Diaspora politics, and US–Haitian relations under the Obama administration. She had just published *Mama's Nightingale: A Story of Immigration and Separation* and *Untwine*, two young adult novels that reveal the cross-read nature of her narrative project—the ways in which her fiction speaks on multiple levels to an adult as well as a younger reader-audience.

**Maxine Montgomery:** To what extent, if any, has there been an improvement in US–Haitian relations during the Obama administration?

**Edwidge Danticat:** There has not been much improvement in US–Haitian relations during the Obama administration, I'm sad to say. The Obama administration did not really show much interest in Haiti until the earthquake in 2010. Then Haiti was basically turned over to former President Bill Clinton, who was head of the Interim Haiti Recovery Commission, which was to oversee funds raised for post-earthquake recovery in Haiti. Around that time, President Clinton had his Global Initiative gathering for college students at the University of Miami where I was teaching and I was on a panel with some Haitians and the former president, and all the Haitians on the panel tried to push forward the idea that Haitians can really rebuild their country themselves, if given the opportunity. Given all the power we knew he had, we really tried to get that message across as best as we could. Hillary Clinton as Secretary of State went to Haiti during the last election cycle there and pushed to have Michel Martelly, who came in third place, to be declared the winner, which he was.

**MM:** What changes would you like to see in terms of US policy concerning Haiti, and are you hopeful that at least some of these changes may take place before President Obama leaves office?

**ED:** I would like to see the US let Haiti Live, as we say in Haiti: *Kite nou viv*. When Hillary Clinton was Secretary of State, we learned from leaked e-mails, for example, that the Obama administration lobbied to keep Haiti's minimum wage down because that's what the business sector in Haiti wanted. That's inhumane and cruel. You are basically forcing people to starve so people in the US can buy cheap underwear. It would be great to see US policy in Haiti that favors the good of the majority of the people, but US policy is often aligned with the elites of the world. Then they always seem very surprised when people rise up. No, unfortunately, I don't see any of that changing before President Obama leaves office.

**MM:** You are a compelling voice for Haiti, whether you consider yourself a spokesperson for the nation or not, and, along with individuals such as Junot Diaz and others, your profound insights about a range of issues, including, but not limited to, grass roots activism, immigration policy, eco-logical matters, and humanitarian efforts have helped to bring international attention to the Haitian-Caribbean experience before and especially after the 2010 earthquake. How would you describe the relationship between the political and the artistic in your narrative project?

**ED:** Again, because I am in the community, because I live in a Haitian community, I know there are so many people doing a lot more than I do, whether it is right on the ground in Haiti or in the Haitian Diaspora. There are many people who work very hard and get little credit, people whose voices are louder, bolder, people who advocate for Haiti on a daily basis. But as to what I do, there's really no comparison to the people who work for Haiti every single day without being seen. But for me personally, there is no separation between the work I do as a writer and my personal commit-ment as a citizen. We write about the things we are passionate about and I am passionate about Haiti. I think all politics affect human beings, and as a writer, I am writing about human beings, so the personal is always political and the political is always personal.

**MM:** Is it possible, at least for immigrant artists like yourself who, as you put it in your "manifesto," *Create Dangerously*, "[create] as a revolt against silence, creating when both the creation and the reception, the writing and the reading, are dangerous undertakings, disobedience to a directive" (11), to find a happy medium between the aesthetic and the political?

**ED:** I really don't think of that book as a manifesto. I was trying to explore how people come to their art and how I can be inspired and how others can be inspired by that commitment. I grew up during a dictatorship, so breaking silence of course offered a sense of liberation and each time I write something I realize that many writers, especially during the dictatorship, were not able to write what they wanted to write because their writing might have cost them their lives. Some of them were exiled or had to leave the country. This is happening still in many countries. That being said, I'm not really looking for a happy medium between the political and the aes-thetic. The question implies that one might negate the other and I just don't believe that this is so. I believe they are intertwined. Even a lack of political expression in a text can itself be a political statement.

**MM:** You have spoken often in interviews about your indebtedness to, among other writers, Toni Morrison. Much of your writing, Morrison's writing, and black fictional discourse, in general, relates to the haunting effects of the past and the ways in which traumatic events return in successive generations of diaspora subjects. How has Morrison's writing influenced your work with regard to memory or what Morrison refers to in *Beloved* as "rememory"?

**ED:** I find the way Ms. Morrison engages history very powerful, both in her fiction and in her nonfiction work. I think there is so much about us as a people, a people scattered on many continents, speaking many different languages, that can seem so broken, because there have been efforts to break us, efforts to destroy us and take us apart. I see in her work an effort to mend us and weave our stories together thorough memory or "rememory." Her work inspires me in many ways, but especially in that particular way that she tries to heal us with her words and fill in the gaps where history has removed us or left us out. I was blessed to spend some time with Ms. Morrison when she was in residence at the Louvre in Paris ten years ago and I got to see her engage with all these very timely global ideas, which are even more timely today. What is home? Who gets to decide? These ideas of being a foreigner at home was especially intriguing to me. She has an extraordinary mind and I just feel lucky to live in the same time period as she does.

**MM:** In what ways has the passage of time and the series of natural, social, and economic upheavals in Haiti complicated the process of re-membering the past in the sense of putting back together something that was initially intact?

**ED:** Of course, I am physically removed from Haiti most of the time. I no longer live there or see the places I know every day. So rather than remembering the place as it is or as it was in the past, I have to create a version of it for myself, which is the version that is in my books. I think Haiti is different for each person. Each writer, whether you live there or not, carries a version of the country within, so I am writing the version I carry in me, which resembles the real place sometimes and doesn't at other times. This is especially true in my fiction—I think my remembering, my "rememory" is putting together the fragments that I've lost being away and the fragments I carry with me now.

**MM:** How would you describe the role that your fiction, in particular, plays in enabling the process of healing or recovery on the part of the migratory subject? In other words, how does your writing fill in the gaps associated with a fragmenting, colonizing history in ways that help fictional characters reclaim a past that may be lost or ruptured, but is still very much a part of the present?

**ED:** I try not to give myself such lofty goals. And frankly, I don't think it's the writer's job to really take apart her work and find all of these themes and meanings herself. I can do it with other people's work, but really can't do it with my own. I basically tell stories about people, some of whom are migrants and some of whom are not, some of whom are like me and some of whom are not. Maybe one day I'll get to a point where I am taking the old work apart and analyzing it, but I think if I do it now it will just stop me dead in my tracks and silence me. But I do try, in work like *The Farming of Bones*, which is about a 1937 massacre of Haitian workers in the Dominican Republic, for example, to reclaim some pieces of history and add what we have always been told, basically stuff them in the gaps, that the history books have left out.

**MM:** What emerging authors on the twenty-first century literary scene would you recommend that the public reads? Whose work are you currently reading?

**ED:** There are so many wonderful authors coming up now. I am currently reading two wonderful young Haitian authors—Fabienne Josaphat, who wrote a novel on the Duvalier era called *In the Bawon's Shadow*, and M. J. Fievre, who has a great memoir about her childhood in the 1990s in Haiti that does a great job of depicting that period. Yaa Gyasi, Taiye Selasi, Naomi Jackson, and Angela Fourtnoy are amazing young writers who are really putting out great work right now, as is Roxane Gay, author of *Bad Feminist* and *Untamed State*. I really like Dimitry Leger's *God Loves Haiti*, as well, which is set in the post-earthquake period. Tiphanie Yanique's work is also incredible. There are so many others I'm not remembering, but it's a really exciting time, especially for black woman's fiction, a time that reminds me a bit of when Alice Walker, Toni Morrison, Gloria Naylor, and Terry McMillan were all on the *New York Times* bestsellers list around the same time. Though we've not repeated that in some time and we can always have more, there is some wonderful work out there.

**MM:** Do you envision yourself as being a literary foremother to the next generation of writers, much like Zora Neale Hurston and her "writerly" influence on Alice Walker, Gloria Naylor, Tina McElroy Ansa, and others?

**ED:** I hope others find some inspiration in what I've done, but I am not going to put myself out there in any kind of foremother role. I think that would be presumptions. One of the ways that new generations of artists define themselves is by completely rejecting the old. Consider Baldwin and

Wright, for example. I have encountered a lot of that, where people feel they have to reject my work because people want to merge their work with mine. I hope I'm not sounding too pessimistic, but I expect to see more of that as I get older, much more than the foremother kind of thing, a kind of strong rejection rather than an embrace. I think that's to be expected. At the same time, I am grateful to people who might be inspired by what I've done and I do see those who came before me as foremothers that I've also had the honor of spending time with and in some cases have been privileged enough to call friends.

**MM:** What advice would you offer to emerging creative artists?
**ED:** Be bold. Be brave. Follow your own path. Don't sit around waiting for approval. Don't expect everybody to like you. Do the best you can. Stay the course and don't give up.

**MM:** I am fascinated by your use of "fakelore" in your fictional works. Elaborate on the distinction between folklore and "fakelore" and the intersection between the two mediums in, say, *Claire of the Sea Light*. Is there a sense in which Claire is enmeshed within both realms—the folkloric and the "fakeloric"—as she grapples with the decision of either joining her mother in death or returning to Ville Rose? What about the role of "fakelore" in *Breath, Eyes, Memory*?
**ED:** "Fakelore" is a phrase which I did not invent. I believe the term was coined by American folklorist Richard M. Dorson in the 1950s. To me, fakelore allows me to create my own folklore. I use it because it basically allows me to make up my own stories in the tradition of the stories I grew up hearing. So there is a lot of fakelore in *Breath, Eyes, Memory*, for example. I borrow the rhythm and pace of the old stories and remake them my own. Folklore is pretty much already spoken or written, but we can make fakelore to match the present time and conditions we're living in. So with fakelore, when you hear "Once upon a Time," you never really know what follows. Claire's entire life, her entire existence is a kind of fake lore. In many ways she is a symbolic figure to the folks in the town. The fact that her mother dies in childbirth puts her in a special category of a human being that they tell stories about. So though Claire is a real little girl, she is also a figure of fakelore. I suppose you can say that all fiction is fakelore, at least the kind we make up ourselves.

**MM:** What lessons does the Haitian goddess Erzulie, in her myriad guises, (re)embody for a contemporary reader-audience? Is there a notion that nearly all of the female characters in *Claire of the Sea Light*—from Claire Narcis to Claire Limyè Lanmè to Madame Gaelle—have an investment in that folkloric female figure?

**ED:** Well, I see her as a presence that enters and leaves the lives of the characters in some of my books. I try to tread lightly there, because I want to reflect how she is influential in the lives of my characters without appropriating or exotifying her for the sake of a story, if you know what I mean. When I wrote about her in *Breath, Eyes, Memory*, she was very much attached to the family in the story. I see my characters as being related in some way so she has become a common thread, much like the butterflies in the stories. I wouldn't necessarily say that she is all of the women and girls in my stories. The female characters all have different sources, some of them in actual real people and others in many other figures, both mystical as well as historical. I hope all my characters are multifaceted and this is one of their many connections, certainly, but not the *only* one.

**MM:** How would you describe your contribution to an understanding of the rich body of myth, legend, and lore emanating out of Afro-Caribbean life?

**ED:** I am a storyteller. Stories intrigue me. The ones I tell as well as the ones I hear or read. Again, it's not up to me to decide what my contribution has been. I think it's up to the readers. When we talk about afro-Caribbean life, we are talking about a very broad canvas here. Linguistically, it involves many languages, many different types of encounters with enslavement and colonialism. Haiti is only one part of that, a glorious part, being the first black republic in the Western Hemisphere, but still only one part. And what I have been able to share and write about is a very small part of that glorious history, so I have done a little bit with my work, but there is still a great deal more to be done.

**MM:** Is your aim one involving your attempt to revise that material for a contemporary audience? Are you concerned that your reader-audience may not have a firm grasp of the largely oral body of material out of which your writing evolves?

**ED:** People will sometimes, accusatorily, declare that I, or others in my position, are writing for outsiders. Granted, I'm not writing in my own language so that's a fair criticism. But one never really knows who the audience will be. There is a Haitian proverb that says, "*Pawòl gen pye, pawòl gen zèl.*" Words have wings. Words have feet. But the audience I am often thinking about are people like me and my brothers and their children, people whose stories are a lot like mine. I feel as though people like us need a literature of our own and I am one of many people who are writing from this place and producing work that I wish I had to read when I was a fifteen-year-old immigrant girl in Brooklyn who was looking for some version of herself in book. This also makes me think of what Ms. Morrison says about Tolstoy's not knowing that he was writing for a little girl in Lorain, Ohio. Ultimately, we have no idea who we are writing for.

**MM:** What is the inspiration for *Mama's Nightingale: A Story of Immigration and Separation*?

**ED:** My mother was jailed for a few days when she was pregnant with one of my brothers in the 1970s. She was picked up in a factory immigration raid and was let out of immigration jail only because she was pregnant. Her story, along with contemporary stories of families in similar situations today, is what inspired the story. These days, everywhere you turn, people are talking about immigration, especially presidential candidates. Some want us all out. Some want more walls, more borders. It is often said that the United States is a country of immigrants, so immigration has always been part of the national dialogue. How do we treat men, women, and children who are seeking refuge here? Especially if they are undocumented, what some people call "illegal"? *Mama's Nightingale* addresses these issues by showing how one family deals with the imprisonment of an undocumented mother and the way her being jailed affects her US citizen husband and daughter. Except for the specific details, this is not an uncommon story. There are thousands of "mixed status" immigrant families all over the United States, and in many of those families, the threat of deportation is always looming over one or both parents, just as it does for Saya's mother. I believe this book can help expose and explain this issue to not just children but adults. *Mama's Nightingale* can also bring to light the issue of immigration detention and how it affects families, especially families with small children, whose stories don't always end as happily as Saya's.

**MM:** What factors influenced your decision to write the story for a young adult audience?

**ED:** I have young children now, two daughters, and a lot of young people in my life, so I wanted to start writing for them.

**MM:** *Untwine*, like many of your other works of fiction, is written in English with a sprinkling of Creole. I know that you have spoken often in interviews about your decision to write primarily in English, but can you comment about the relationship between language and identity in your fiction? In what ways does language mirror the complexities of self and place in your narrative project?

**ED:** Language is a tool. I go back to this poem "Bilingual Blues" by Gustavo Pérez Firmat, which Junot Diaz uses as an epigraph for his collection of stories *Drown.* To paraphrase Firmat, he basically says that the fact that I'm speaking to you in English falsifies what I'm saying, but it's basically where I am right now. Some of us came here young and this is our language of creation. We're not the first people to every write in a language other than our mother tongue and we won't be the last. When I write in English as my characters speak Creole, I hear them in Creole and the work is kind of simultaneously translated in my head. I use Creole words because often there is no apt translation that comes close enough.

**MM:** Talk about *Untwine.* What prompted you to write this novel? In what ways does *Untwine* extend the conversation regarding the close interrelationship between sacred and secular, the world of the living and dead, between past, present, and future?

**ED:** This is a book I was writing at the same time as *Breath, Eyes, Memory.* I started it in graduate school. It was about one teenage girl, not twins. I put it away and concentrated on *Breath, Eyes Memory.* Then I kept going back to it when I started writing for young people. Lisa Sandell—my editor—once wrote me a note asking if I had a book for young adults in me. I picked it up again. Then, my mother became terminally ill with cancer and I was spending a lot of quiet time in hospital rooms and when I got too sad watching my mother sleep, I would work on this book in the dark at her bedside.

Watching my mother die taught me a lot about the sacred and the secular, of course. And probably the biggest lesson I learned during that time and writing this book is that every moment is sacred. It sounds corny but it's worth remembering sometime.

**MM:** Toni Morrison is candid about the writing process, mentioning in an interview with Bill Moyers that she begins each text with "a big question." With *Beloved*, that question centers around the limits and excesses of maternal love. Are you similarly disposed in your approach to a work of fiction? In other words, what propels you in the construction of a novel or short story, for that matter? What big question, if any, are you asking, for instance, in *The Dew Breaker, The Farming of Bones,* or *Claire of the Sea Light*?

**ED:** My big question is always "What don't I know? What am I to learn? I see the whole process as heading on a journey with the reader. I am not sure where I'll end up when I begin, but I always know I'll be different than when I started. So each of these books began with a kind of curiosity about a subject or a person, something I tried to follow until I understood it much better.

**MM:** Can you talk about your next project?

**ED:** I am working on a short nonfiction book about how writers write about death. It's called *The Art of Death: Writing the Final Story* and will be published by Graywolf Press in July 2017. It will combine both personal reflections about my experience writing about death in both my novels and nonfiction. It will also examine how other writers have written about death in fiction, nonfiction, and poetry. I will definitely talk about Toni Morrison's *Beloved*, William Faulkner's *As I Lay Dying*, C. S. Lewis's *A Grief Observed*, as well as the Bible. As I mentioned earlier, my mother passed away recently and writing this book has been very therapeutic for me. I was at my mother's bedside as she took her last breath and the whole process of watching her die has made me eager to learn more about how others have coped with and have "written death." Among the topics explored in the book will be writing the process of dying itself—writers writing their own death and the deaths of loved ones—the death of innocence, writing the moment of death itself, then writing grief. Is death a mystery of nature, a function of nature, or the loss of present moment in time, as Marcus Aurelius wrote? These are just a few of the questions I attempt to explore.

**MM:** Thank you very much. I appreciate your willingness to participate in this interview.

**ED:** You are welcome.

# Additional Resources

## Short Stories

"A Haitian-American Christmas: Cremace and Creole Theatre." *New Youth Connections*, 1983.

"A New World Full of Strangers." *New Youth Connections*, 1987.

"Dream of the Butterflies." *Caribbean Writer* 5 (1991): 98–99.

"Graduation." *Caribbean Writer* 5 (1991): 100–103.

"Lost Shadows and Stick Figures." *Caribbean Writer* 6 (1992): 104–6.

"Between the Pool and the Gardenias." *Caribbean Writer* 7 (1993): 66–70.

"Voices in a Dream." *Caribbean Writer* 7 (1993).

"A Rain of Daffodils." *Seventeen* 53.4 (April 1, 1994): 152ff; *Literary Cavalcade* 52.6 (March 2000): 4–9.

"The Missing Peace." *Caribbean Writer* 8 (1994): 104–12; in *Feminism 3: The Third Generation in Fiction*, edited by Irene Zahava. Boulder, CO: Westview, 1996.

"The Revenant." *Granta 54: Best Young American Novelists*, June 20, 1996.

"Water Child." *New Yorker*, September 4, 2000.

"Seven." *New Yorker*, September 24, 2001.

"Nineteen Thirty Seven." *The Oxford Book of Caribbean Short Stories*, 2001.

"The Dew Breaker." In *Gumbo: A Celebration of African American Writers*, edited by Marita Golden and E. Lynn Harris. New York: Harlem Moon, 2002.

"The Indigo Girl." *Sojourners*, 2004.

"Je Voudrais Etre Riche: A Trickster Tale." *Caribbean Writer* 18 (2004).

"The Prize." *Caribbean Writer* 18 (2004).

"Tatiana, Mon Amour." *Callaloo* 27.2 (2004): 439–53.

"Reading Lessons." *New Yorker*, January 10 2005.

"Freda." In *Brown Sugar 4: Secret Desires: A Collection of Erotic Black Fiction*, edited by Carol Taylor. New York: Washington Square Press, 2005.

"Celia." In *A Memory, a Monologue, a Rant, and a Prayer: Writings to Stop Violence Against Women and Girls*, edited by Even Ensler and Mollie Doyle. New York: Villard Books, 2007.

"Ghosts." *New Yorker*, November 17, 2008. 108–13.

"Claire of the Sea Light." In *Haiti Noir*, edited by Edwidge Danticat. Brooklyn: Akashic Books, 2010.

"Hot Air Balloons." *Granta 115: The F Word*, May 19, 2011.

"In the Old Days." In *So Spoke the Earth: The Haiti I Knew, the Haiti I Know, the Haiti I Want to Know*, edited by M. J. Fievre. South Florida: Women Writers of Haitian Descent, 2012. 42–53; *Callaloo* 35.2 (Spring 2012): 355–63.

"Quality Control." *Washington Post*, November 14, 2014.

## Travel Writing

*After the Dance: A Walk through Carnival in Jacmel, Haiti.* New York: Crown, 2002.

## Poems

"Sawfish Soup." *Caribbean Writer* 5 (1991).
"Plunging." *Caribbean Writer* 23 (2009).
"Postscript." *Callaloo* 33.2 (2010): 410.
"Miras." *Callaloo* 33.2 (2010): 409.
"Trimester." *Callaloo* 33.2 (2010): 411.
"Bajou/Dawn." *Afro-Hispanic Review* 32.2 (2013): 149.

## Drama

"Plantains, Please." *Caribbean Writer* 13 (1999).

## Plays

*The Creation of Adam.* Rites and Reasons Theatre, Providence. 1992.
*Dreams Like Me.* Rites and Reasons Theatre, Providence. 1993.
*Children of the Sea.* Roxbury Community College, Roxbury Crossing. 1997.

## Edited Anthologies

*The Beacon Best of 2000: Great Writing by Women and Men of All Colors and Cultures.* Boston: Beacon Press, 2000.
*The Butterfly's Way: Voices from the Haitian Dyaspora in the United States.* New York: Soho Press, 2001.
*Haiti Noir.* Brooklyn: Akashic Books, 2010.
*The Best American Essays 2011.* Boston, MA: Houghton Mifflin Harcourt, 2011.
*Haiti Noir 2: The Classics.* New York: Akashic, 2014.

## Interviews

"Evelyne Trouillot." *BOMB Magazine* 90 (Winter 2004–5): 48–53.
"Junot Diaz, by Edwidge Danticat." *BOMB Magazine* 101 (Fall 2007).
"Edwidge Danticat Interviews Katia Ulysse: 'Rich Stays Here. Poor Stays There. That's the Haiti I've Always Known.'" *Salon,* July 27, 2014.

# Articles

"My Father Once Chased Rainbows." *Essence*, November 1993, 48.

"Let My People Stay." *Essence*, July 1994, 124.

"A Fountain of Peace." In *On the Wings of Peace*, edited by Sheila Hamanaka. New York: Clarion, 1995.

"From the Ocean Floor." In *Rhythm and Revolt: Tales of the Antilles*, edited by Marcela Breton. New York: Plume, 1995.

"We Are Ugly, But We Are Here." *Caribbean Writer* 10 (1996): 137–41; in *Women Writing Resistance: Essays on Latin America and the Caribbean*, edited by Jennifer Browdy de Hernandez. Cambridge, MA: South End, 2005. 23–28.

"Hanging with the Fugees." *Essence* 27.4 (August 1, 1996): 85–86.

Foreword to *Starting with "I": Personal Essays by Teenagers*, edited by Andrea Estepa and Philip Kay. New York: Persea, 1997.

Foreword to *The Magic Orange Tree, and Other Haitian Folktales*, compiled by Diane Wolkstein. New York: Knopf, 1997. vii–viii.

"The Book of the Dead." *New Yorker*, June 14, 1999. 194–99.

Foreword to *A Community of Equals: The Constitutional Protection of New Americans*, edited by Owen M. Fiss, Joshua Cohen, and Joel Rogers. Boston: Beacon, 1999.

Foreword to *Like the Dew That Waters the Grass: Words from Haitian Women*, edited by Marie M. Racine and Kathy Ogle. Washington, DC: EPICA, 1999.

"A Brief Reflection on the Massacre River." *Kreyòl* 5, 2.17 (May 19, 1999).

"Aha!" In *Becoming American: Personal Essay by First Generation Immigrant Women*, edited by Meri Nana-Ama Danquah. New York: Hyperion, 2000.

"Westbury Court." In *The Best American Essays, 2000*, edited by Alan P. Lightman. Boston: Houghton Mifflin, 2000.

Foreword to *Their Eyes Were Watching God*, by Zora Neale Hurston. New York: HarperCollins, 2000.

"Epilogue: Women Like Us." In *Step into a World: A Global Anthology of the New Black Literature*, edited by Kevin Powell. New York: Wiley, 2000.

"My New York." *New York* 33.49 (2000): 96.

"Papi." In *Family: American Writers Remember Their Own*, edited by Sharon Sloan Fiffer and Steve Fiffer. Collingdale, PA: Diane, 2000.

"Bonjour Jean." *Nation* 272.7 (February 19, 2001): 20–22.

Foreword to *Walking on Fire: Haitian Women's Stories of Survival and Resistance*, by Beverly Bell. Ithaca, NY: Cornell UP, 2001.

"Brave New Worlds: The Future in My Arms." *Essence*, May 2001, 169–70.

"I Pass On." *Essence*, May 2001, 160.

Afterword to *In the Flicker of an Eyelid*, by Jacques Stéphen Alexis. Translated by Carrol F. Coates and Edwidge Danticat. Charlottesville: University of Virginia Press, 2002.

Introduction to *Me Dying Trial*, by Patricia Powell. Boston: Beacon, 2003.

"Voices from Hispaniola: A Meridians Roundtable with Edwidge Danticat, Loida Maritza Pérez, Myriam J. A. Chancey, and Nelly Rosario." *Meridians: Feminism, Race, Transnationalism* 5.1 (2004): 68–91.

"No Greater Shame: How Haitian Boat-people Are Treated." In *Haiti, a Slave Revolution: 200 Years after 1804*, edited by Pat Chin et al. New York: International Action Center, 2004.

"On Writing and Significant Others." *Journal of Haitian Studies* 10.2 (Fall 2004): 4–8.

"Roundtable: Writing, History, and Revolution with Dany Laferriere, Louis-Philippe Dalembert, Edwidge Danticat, Evelyne Trouillot and J. Michael Dash as Moderator." *Small Axe* 18 (2005): 189–201.

"Ghosts of the 1915 U.S. Invasion Still Haunt Haiti's People." *Miami Herald*, July 25, 2005.

Preface to *Massacre River*, by René Philoctète. Translated by Linda Coverdale. New York: New Directions, 2005.

Foreword to *We Are All Suspects Now: Untold Stories from Immigrant Communities after 9/11*, by Tram Nguyen. Boston: Beacon, 2005.

Foreword to *Vale of Tears: A Novel from Haiti*, by Paulette Poujol Oriol. Translated by Dolores A. Schafer. Bethesda, MD: Ibex, 2006.

Foreword to *Brown Girl, Brownstones*, by Paule Marshall. New York: Feminist Press at the CUNY, 2006.

"Does It Work?" *Washington Post*, September 24, 2006.

Foreword to *Homelands: Women's Journeys across Race, Place, and Time*, edited by Patricia Justine Tumang and Jenesha de Rivera. Seattle: Seal Press, 2006.

Introduction to *The Kingdom of This World*, by Alejo Carpentier. New York: Knopf, 2006.

Introduction to *Miss Muriel and Other Stories*, by Ann Petry. New York: Kensington, 2008.

Introduction to *Love, Anger, Madness: A Haitian Trilogy*, by Marie Vieux-Chauvet. Translated by Rose-Myriam Réjouis and Val Vinokur. New York: Modern Library, 2009.

"In Flesh and Bone." In *Tent Life: Haiti*, by Wyatt Gallery. Brooklyn, NY: Umbrage Editions, 2010. 8–9.

Foreword to *Aunt Résia and the Spirits and Other Stories*, by Yanick Lahens. Charlottesville: University of Virginia Press, 2010.

Introduction to *Fault Lines: Views across Haiti's Divide*, by Beverly Bell. Ithaca: Cornell, 2013.

Foreword to *The Infamous Rosalie*, by Évelyne Trouillot. Lincoln: University of Nebraska Press, 2013.

"Best Untranslated Writers: Kettly Mars." *Granta 124: Travel*, June, 19, 2013.

"Edwidge Danticat: The Price of Sugar." *Creative Time Reports*, May 5, 2014.

Foreword to *The Other Side of the Sea*, by Louis-Philippe Dalembert. Charlottesville: University of Virginia Press, 2014.

Introduction to *Haiti Uncovered: A Regional Adventure into the Art of Haitian Cuisine*, by Nadege Fleurimond. Signature Book Printing, 2014.

*Caribbeanness as a Global Phenomenon: Junot Díaz, Edwidge Danticat, and Cristina García*, edited by Rebecca Fuchs. Trier: WVT Wissenschaftlicher Verlag Trier, 2014.

*The Good Book: Writers Reflect on Favorite Bible Passages*, edited by Andrew Blauner. Simon and Schuster, 2015.

Foreword to *Poetry of Haitian Independence*, edited by Doris Y. Kadish and Deborah Jenson. New Haven: Yale University, 2015.

Introduction to *Wide Sargasso Sea*, by Jean Rhys. W.W. Norton, 2016.

Introduction to *Go Tell It on the Mountain*, by James Baldwin. Everyman's Library, 2016.

# Films

*Courage and Pain*, 1996. Associate Producer. Dir. Patricia Benoit.
*The Agronomist*, 2003. Associate Producer. Dir. Jonathan Demme.
*The Manchurian Candidate*, 2004. Actress. Dir. Jonathan Demme.
*Writing and the Immigrant Experience*, 2006. Actress. MacNeil / Lehrer Productions.
*Poto Mitan: Haitian Women, Pillars of the Global Community*, 2009. Narrator. Dir. Mark
    Schuller and Renee Bergan.
*Stones in the Sun*, 2012. Actress. Dir. Patricia Benoit.
*Girl Rising*, 2013. Writer. Dir. Richard Robbins.

# Art Books

Demme, Jonathan. *Island on Fire: Passionate Visions of Haiti from the Collection of Jonathan
    Demme*. Nyack, NY: Kaliko, 1997.
Demme, Jonathan. *Odilon Pierre, Artist of Haiti*. NY: Kaliko, 1999.

# Exhibits

Weber, Bruce. *Haiti / Little Haiti*. 2010. Exhibit. Museum of Contemporary Art, North Miami.

# Interviews with Edwidge Danticat

Alexandre, Sandy, and Ravi Y. Howard. "My Turn in the Fire: A Conversation with Edwidge
    Danticat." *Transition: An International Review*, 2002.
————."An Interview with Edwidge Danticat." *Journal of Caribbean Literatures* 4.3 (2007):
    161–74.
Allen, Zita. "A Conversation with Haitian Writer Edwidge Danticat." *New York Amsterdam
    News*, November 19, 2005.
Allfrey, Ellah. "Interview: Edwidge Danticat." *Granta*, January 28, 2011.
Anglesey, Zoe. "The Voice of Storytellers: An Interview with Edwidge Danticat," *Multicultural
    Review* 7.3 (September 1, 1998): 36–39.
"Ask the Author Live: Edwidge Danticat." *New Yorker*, January 22, 2010.
Barsamian, David. "Edwidge Danticat Interview." *Progressive*, October 1, 2003.
Block, Mary, and Jakki Kerubo. "An Interview with Edwidge Danticat." *Washington Square
    Review* 29 (Winter/Spring 2012).
Collins, Michael S. "An Interview with Edwidge Danticat." *Callaloo* 30.2 (2007): 471–73.
Combe, Liv. "Off the Cuff with Edwidge Danticat." *Oberlin Review*, April 20, 2012; "Edwidge
    Danticat." FullStop.com, May 24, 2012.
Dacosta, David B. "Interview." *Convo: Interview Anthology*. Tower Isle, March 14, 2013.
DeSimone, Harrison. "Eight Days, an Interview with Author Edwidge Danticat." *States News
    Service*, March 18, 2011.
"Edwidge Danticat: By the Book." *New York Times*, August 10, 2013.

Fassler, Joe. "All Immigrants Are Artists." *Atlantic*, August 27, 2013.

Freeman, John. "Author Interview: Edwidge Danticat." *St. Petersburg Times* 4 (2004).

Gettleman, Elizabeth. "A Voice in Haiti's Chorus." *Mother Jones*, May–June 2010.

Gilani, Tara. "Women to Watch: Trend Tracker Tara Gilani with Edwidge Danticat." *CBS Miami*, CBS, July 30, 2014.

Golden, Marita. "Edwidge Danticat." In *The Word: Black Writers Talk about the Transformative Power of Reading and Writing: Interviews*, 61–78. New York: Broadway Paperbacks, 2011.

Gonnerman, Jennifer. "2007 National Book Award Nonfiction Finalist Interview with Edwidge Danticat." National Book Award Foundation, Nationalbook.org.

Gross, Rebecca. "Art Works Blog." *Art Talk with Author Edwidge Danticat*. National Endowment for the Arts, October 24, 2014.

Gross, Terry. "Edwidge Danticat, Dealing with Birth and Death." *Fresh Air*, NPR, July 17, 2011.

Healy, Tom. "Haiti beyond the Headlines: Tom Healy Interviews Edwidge Danticat." CreativeTimeReports.Org, March 18, 2013.

Hong, Terry. "Horror, Hope & Redemption: A Talk with Edwidge Danticat about Her Latest Novel, *The Dew Breaker*." *Bloomsbury Review* 24.5 (2004).

Hood, John. "NiteTalk: Edwidge Danticat Gives Us Haiti Noir." *NBC 6 South Florida*, January 21, 2011.

Hoover, Elizabeth. "Edwidge Danticat on the Dangers of Being an Artist." *Sampsonia Way Magazine*, February 1, 2011.

Horn, Jessica, and Edwidge Danticat. "Edwidge Danticat: An Intimate Reader." *Meridians* 1.2 (2001): 19–25.

Jaggi, Maya. "Island Memories." *Guardian*, November 20, 2004.

Josaphat, Fabienne. "Interview: Edwidge Danticat." *Gulf Stream Magazine*, Online No. 5 (2011).

Kat. "Edwidge Danticat: The Interview." Kreyolicious.com. February 14, 2012.

Labaze, Natasha. "Edwidge Danticat Sheds 'Light' on Haiti." *Ebony*, October 22, 2013.

Layne, Prudence, and Lester Goran. "Haiti: History, Voice, Empowerment—An Interview with Edwidge Danticat." *Sargasso, Four Writers: Women Writing the Caribbean* II (2004–5): 3–17.

Lyons, Bonnie. "An Interview with Edwidge Danticat." *Contemporary Literature* 44.2 (2003): 183–98.

Maran, Meredith. "'Be Unafraid': Edwidge Danticat on Fiction and Memoir." *Barnes and Noble Review*, barnesandnoble.com/review, January 25, 2016.

Mirabel, Nancy Raquel. "Dyasporic Appetites and Longings: An Interview with Edwidge Danticat." *Callaloo* 30.1 (Winter 2007): 26–39.

Murphy, Carla. "Junot Díaz and Edwidge Danticat in Conversation." *Colorlines*, August 5, 2014.

Pulitano, Elvira. "An Immigrant Artist at Work: A Conversation with Edwidge Danticat." *Small Axe* 15.3 (2011): 39–61.

Racine-Tossaint, Marlene. "An Interview with Edwidge Danticat." *Voices*, University of California Television, June 1, 2004.

Sert, Aysegul. "A Conversation with Edwidge Danticat." Al Jazeera America, america.aljazeera.com, September 21, 2013.

Shea, Renee H. "Bearing Witness and Beyond: Edwidge Danticat Talks about Her Latest Work." *Journal of Haitian Studies* 7.2 (Fall 2001): 6–20.

——."The Dangerous Job of Edwidge Danticat: An Interview." *Callaloo: Emerging Women Writers: A Special Issue* 19.2 (1996) 382–89.
——. "Interview" [with Edwidge Danticat]. *Belles Lettres* 10.3 (1995): 12.
——. "The Terrible Days Behind Us and the Uncertain Ones Ahead: Edwidge Danticat Talks about *The Dew Breaker*." *Caribbean Writer* 18 (2004).
——. "Traveling Worlds with Edwidge Danticat." *Poets and Writers* 25.1 (January/February 1997): 42–51.
Sutherland, Amy. "Bibliophiles: Edwidge Danticat, Novelist." *Boston Globe*, bostonglobe.com, October 24, 2015.
"Uncomfortable Truths." Interview. *Tweed's Magazine of Literature and Art.*
Wachtel, Eleanor. "A Conversation with Edwidge Danticat," *Brick* 65–66 (2000): 106–19.
——. "Edwidge Danticat Interview." *Writers & Company*, CBC Radio, March 22, 2015.

## Articles and Books about Edwidge Danticat

Alexander, Simone A. James. "M/Othering the Nation: Women's Bodies as Nationalist Trope in Edwidge Danticat's *Breath, Eyes, Memory*." *African American Review* 44.3 (2011): 373–90.
Bellamy, Maria Rice. "More than Hunter or Prey: Duality and Traumatic Memory in Edwidge Danticat's *The Dew Breaker*." *MELUS: The Journal of the Society for the Study of the Multi-Ethnic Literature of the United States* 37.1 (2012): 177–97.
Burchell, Eileen. "As My Mother's Daughter: *Breath, Eyes, Memory* by Edwidge Danticat." In *Women in Literature: Reading through the Lens of Gender*, edited by J. Fisher and E. Silber. Connecticut: Greenwood Press, 2003.
Counihan, Clare. "Desiring Diaspora: 'Testing' the Boundaries of National Identity in Edwidge Danticat's *Breath, Eyes, Memory*." *Small Axe: A Caribbean Journal of Criticism* 37 (2012): 36–52.
Dash, J. Michael. "Danticat and Her Haitian Precursors." *Edwidge Danticat: A Reader's Guide.* Charlottesville: University of Virginia, 2010. 26–38.
Hewitt, Heather. "At the Crossroads: Disability and Trauma in *The Farming of Bones*." *MELUS* 31.3 (2006): 123–45.
Marouan, M. *Witches, Goddesses, and Angry Spirits: The politics of spiritual liberation in African diaspora women's fiction.* Columbus: Ohio State University Press, 2013.
Martin, W. Todd. "'Naming' Sebastian: Celebrating Men in Edwidge Danticat's *The Farming of Bones*." *Atenea* (AteneaPR) 28.1 (2008): 65–74.
Munro, Martin. *Edwidge Danticat: A Reader's Guide.* Charlottesville: University of Virginia Press, 2010.
Nesbitt, Nick. "Diasporic Politics: Danticat's Short Works." In *Edwidge Danticat: A Reader's Guide*, edited by Martin Munro. Charlottesville: University of Virginia, 2010. 73–85.
Rosello, Mireile. "Marassa with a Difference." In *Edwidge Danticat: A Reader's Guide*, edited by Martin Munro. Charlottesville: University of Virginia Press, 2010.
Samway, Patrick, S. J. "A Homeward Journey: Edwidge Danticat's Fictional Landscapes, Mindscapes, Genescapes, and Signscapes in *Breath, Eyes, Memory*." *Journal of Southern Cultures* 57.1 (Winter 2003–4): 75–83.

# Index

child," 144; ED's parents on, 157; Erzulie in, 209; folklore and fakelore in, 208; Maxine Montgomery on, xi, xiv; mother–daughter relationship in, 138–39; Oprah Winfrey and, 162; place in oeuvre, 70; sequel to, 143–44; study of, 97, 203; writing of, 21, 43–44, 195, 211; young adult audience of, 24

*Bridge of San Luis Rey, The* (Wilder), 159

Brooklyn, 68, 187; ED's migration to (*see* migration of ED to United States)

Brooklyn College, 153

Brooklyn Public Library, 91, 166

*Brother, I'm Dying*: Andre Danticat in, 190; creation myths in, 133; gang violence in, 160; Maxo Danticat in, 89; Nathalie Handal on, 117; place in oeuvre, 70; US immigration policy and, 34–35; writing of, 144, 153, 196–97. *See also* Dantica, Joseph

brothers of ED, 5, 53, 158, 185

Brown University, 41

Brutus, Dennis, 60

bullying, 188

burial places, 87–90; of Andre Danticat and Joseph Dantica, 160, 193; in "Claire of the Sea Light," 132; ED's own, 159–60; migrants', 172

Bush, George W., 11

*Butterfly's Way, The*, 7

Cadet, Jean Robert, 142

Calabash (literary festival), 92–93

Camus, Albert: *Caligula*, 86; "Create Dangerously" (essay), 59–60, 73–74, 78–79, 122, 161–62; "Jonas, Or the Artist at Work," 84

*Cane* (Toomer), 159, 167

capital punishment, 11, 47, 74–75

Caribbean identity, 30, 37, 48

Carnival, 68, 124

Castillo, Ana, 14

Castro, Fidel, 14

Catholics, Roman, 58

Celestin, Jude, 118

cemeteries. *See* burial places

Central Intelligence Agency, 18, 98

Centre d'Art, 123

Cerat, Marie Lily, 130

Chancy, Myriam, 142

Chapman, Tracy, 98

characters: developing, 27–28, 43, 139, 163–64; sources of, 48, 153–54, 195

charity, 56

Chassagne, Regine, 57

Chauvet, Marie. *See* Vieux-Chauvet, Marie

Cheney, Dick, 11

chicken, 29

Chideya, Farai, 93, 96

childhood of ED in Haiti, 68–70, 184–87; aspiring to be a storyteller, 40, 194; connection with parents, 69–70, 150, 153, 164, 186–87; early memories, 5, 63; family status and finances, 70, 150, 186–87, 189; hearing stories told, 39, 65, 187; neighborhood, 68; reading and writing, 3–4, 41–42, 65, 194; relationship with uncle Joseph, 184–85; school, 39, 65, 69; shyness, 40; silence, 78–79; theater, 86; wishes for a sister, 200

childhoods of other writers, 111

children: earthquake photography of, 56; in ED's books, 24, 28–29, 31–32; family separation and, 132–33; games, 164; maturity, 25, 28, 29; need for stories, 39; as restavecs, 32; storytelling culture of, 22–23; world ED would create for, 47

children's literature, 23–24, 33

*chimé*, 19

cholera outbreak in 2010, 62, 94, 117

CPSIA information can be obtained
at www.ICGtesting.com
Printed in the USA
BVHW04s2356170518
516593BV00001B/35/P

9 781496 818409